AF842890

on track ...

The Jesus and Mary Chain

every album, every song

Robin Kennedy

SONICBOND

sonicbondpublishing.com

Sonicbond Publishing Limited
www.sonicbondpublishing.co.uk
Email: info@sonicbondpublishing.co.uk

First Published in the United Kingdom 2026
First Published in the United States 2026

British Library Cataloguing in Publication Data:
A Catalogue record for this book is available from the British Library

Copyright Robin Kennedy 2026

ISBN 978-1-78952-562-5

The right of Robin Kennedy to be identified
as the author of this work has been asserted by him
in accordance with the Copyright, Designs and Patents Act 1988.
All rights reserved. No part of this publication may be reproduced, stored in a retrieval system or transmitted in any form or by any means, electronic, mechanical, photocopying, recording or otherwise, without prior permission in writing from Sonicbond Publishing Limited

Typeset in ITC Garamond Std & ITC Avant Garde Gothic
Printed and bound in England

Graphic design and typesetting: Full Moon Media

Follow us on social media:
Twitter: twitter.com/SonicbondP
Instagram: www.instagram.com/sonicbondpublishing_/
Facebook: www.facebook.com/SonicbondPublishing/

Linktree QR code:

This book is dedicated to the memory of Johnny Hannacher (1970-2022), musical mentor and friend.

All that's left behind and all that will be left behind is the music. I think the music stands any test; the Mary Chain's music will still be relevant in 50 years' time, even if it's only to a couple of weirdos in a bedsit. I think our music will be like little seeds that create green shoots, and I think that it will make sense to somebody, somewhere, years from now, and I think that's our legacy. It was never intended to be just show business; it was always intended to be a road map out of your shit situation.
Jim Reid (*Louder Than War*, Issue #8, 2017)

Acknowledgements

Special thanks must first go to Murray Dalglish and Douglas Hart for meeting with me several times over the years and sharing so many stories from the early days of the band.

Sincere thanks to Bernadette Reid for her invaluable assistance, which was truly appreciated.

Additional thanks and respect to the following: Jon Beckett, Scott Blyth, Caroline Brown, Stuart Cassidy, David Cornyn (after all that proofreading, it's time to write your own one!), Grainne Denning, George at GHS Media, Zoe Howe, Kenny Howie, Jamie Johnstone (Radio Darklands and The Fuse), Mikko Kapanen, Alastair Kennedy, Stephen Lambe, Lee Martin (purveyor of 'Psychoanalysis' and a lot of patience), Robin Skilling (the true genius of Orange Overdrive), Dylan D. Turner, Slev and Dez (from The Concrete Garden), Ben Unwin, Iain Veitch, Callum Weir.

Love, as always, to Melanie, Emily and Katherine.

Would you like to write for Sonicbond Publishing?

We are mainly a music publisher, but we also occasionally publish in other genres including film and television. At Sonicbond Publishing we are always on the look-out for authors, particularly for our two main series, On Track and Decades.

Mixing fact with in depth analysis, the On Track series examines the entire recorded work of a particular musical artist or group. All genres are considered from easy listening and jazz to 60s soul to 90s pop, via rock and metal.

The Decades series singles out a particular decade in an artist or group's history and focuses on that decade in more detail than may be allowed in the On Track series.

While professional writing experience would, of course, be an advantage, the most important qualification is to have real enthusiasm and knowledge of your subject. First-time authors are welcomed, but the ability to write well in English is essential.

Sonicbond Publishing has distribution throughout Europe and North America, and all our books are also published in E-book form. Authors will be paid a royalty based on sales of their book. Further details about our books are available from www.sonicbondpublishing.com. To contact us, complete the contact form there or email info@sonicbondpublishing.co.uk

on track ...
The Jesus and Mary Chain

Contents

Introduction

The music of The Jesus and Mary Chain, painstakingly crafted by Scottish brothers William and Jim Reid, spans from their earliest bedroom demo experiments in the early 1980s through to major-label success over the best part of 15 years following their signing to Warner Bros. Records, amidst a blaze of British music press hype and a fair degree of notoriety. Yet it remains surprisingly underappreciated.

A bold opening gambit, one may argue, and yet this most iconic of British bands – too often lazily confined within the broad category of alternative rock and occasionally even dismissed in today's increasingly transient music culture as merely another 1980s retro act – boasts an enviable back catalogue. Across eight major studio albums and numerous standalone singles, the Reids produced music in a variety of distinctive styles while remaining unmistakably Mary Chain in both quality and ambition.

United not only by a sibling bond that has been repeatedly tested over the decades, yet never permanently severed, but also by a deep-rooted love of music formed during childhood, William and Jim Reid saw their lives transformed by the power and promise of punk. As the years passed, an escape route from new-town obsolescence gradually began to emerge.

The purchase of a TASCAM 144 Portastudio in May 1981, alongside additional key equipment including a drum machine the following March, meant that, for both brothers, recording their song ideas became less of a simple artistic outlet and increasingly a means by which musical possibilities could be developed more concretely. William Reid had already been practising diligently on an acoustic guitar shared by the brothers from the late 1970s onwards. He had even ventured into a recording studio situated half an hour from East Kilbride for a six-hour session with friends during late August 1980. For his part, Jim Reid had invested in a Les Paul-copy electric guitar in order to concentrate on his own determined attempts to learn to play. By the time the Portastudio was acquired – albeit an early model prone to frustrating breakdowns that necessitated regular repair – the brothers possessed the basic instruments required to document their songwriting beyond the previously tried-and-tested method of simply recording themselves on a tape recorder (later superseded by a reel-to-reel recorder) while playing early song ideas.

The advantage of being able to use a Portastudio to shape individual song ideas into coherent, tightly structured pieces of music certainly gave both William and Jim the edge over many other aspiring musicians during the early 1980s, and demo tapes were duly dispatched to a range of companies, including Factory, Postcard, 4AD, Mute, Abstract and Rough Trade. Documentation relating to the tapes sent out was conscientiously retained by William Reid, who kept an impressively detailed set of diaries throughout the decade, but no replies were received. Radio stations also became recipients of demo tapes from the brothers, as evidenced by a cassette from May 1983 containing William's 'Sowing Seeds' and Jim's 'Something's Wrong' being sent to the producers of both John Peel and David 'Kid' Jensen. No response from either programme was forthcoming. Radio silence surrounding the as-yet-unnamed group's songwriting remained the established norm, as did a general lack of interest from local promoters regarding the possibility of live appearances. However, it was one such demo cassette, rejected by a Glasgow club promoter before being passed on to a local music enthusiast who might better appreciate the music on the tape's B side (The *Madcap Laughs* by Syd Barrett), that ultimately set in motion a crucial chain of events leading to the band's discovery, live debut and eventual signing.

Disillusionment with the increasingly anodyne direction of the British music scene by the early 1980s – as punk and new wave gave way to safer chart acts – combined with a truly fortuitous turn of events when one of the brothers' demo tapes fell into the right hands. This would ultimately prove pivotal in the career of The Jesus and Mary Chain. Bobby Gillespie, frontman of a similarly nascent musical outfit still taking its own first steps, told the Reids about a friend living in London who perhaps could help, as he ran a small indie label alongside a regular club night for both new and established indie bands. Meanwhile, after the brothers joined forces with Douglas Hart upon realising that attempting to form separate bands had become an increasingly forlorn exercise, the group's eventual name represented a natural progression from Daisy Chain, itself a successor to The Poppy Seeds, under which even earlier demo tapes had circulated. A diary entry from William Reid, dating from October 1983, identifies the first recorded usage of this most distinctive of band names.

There remained the small matter of recruiting a drummer to help The Jesus and Mary Chain establish themselves as a viable live act, and an advert was duly pinned up in an East Kilbride record shop listing influences as 'Sex Pistols, Stooges and Velvet Underground'. The sole respondent was a local teenager named Murray Dalglish, who had been passing by Impulse Records on an idle weekday afternoon with his time at high school now finished. Encouraged by a friend to phone the contact number for further details, Murray successfully auditioned on 13 May and, with that, the Mary Chain were complete. It would then be only a matter of weeks before the band made their live debut following Alan McGee's invitation to perform at The Living Room on Friday 8 June, followed by an equally astonishing repeat performance the following evening.

The rest, as the saying goes, is history. Yet far too often, the music subsequently produced by The Jesus and Mary Chain has been overshadowed by easier and more clichéd retellings of the band's story. A cursory glance online quickly reinforces familiar tropes of riots, feedback and feuds ad nauseam, often with scant reference to the Reids' substantial contribution to modern music. Anyone unfamiliar with the group's fascinating career should look no further than the 2024 publication *Never Understood* for an at-times painfully honest retelling of their story. Told through the perspectives of both brothers, often amusingly at odds with one another, it is surely a narrative they would not have wanted presented any other way.

It is hoped that this detailed study of the complete back catalogue of The Jesus and Mary Chain, the first full-length analysis of the group's recorded work, will help to shine fresh light on the remarkable music written and produced by William Reid and Jim Reid. From the mid-1980s high points of critic favourites *Psychocandy* and *Darklands*, through the lesser-appreciated yet no less impressive *Honey's Dead* and *Munki*, and onwards to the present day with the warmly received *Glasgow Eyes*, few bands of the past 40 years seem more deserving of renewed artistic appreciation.

If anything, a detailed examination of the band's creative trajectory, beginning with their incendiary debut on a then-minor British indie label during the autumn of 1984, has long been overdue. I sincerely hope that you will enjoy working through the sections of this book as much as I have enjoyed researching and writing it. The process has certainly been a lengthy one, but I hope it proves worthwhile for both long-term fans and more casual readers alike.

If you are new to the band, I envy your imminent discovery of a wealth of superb songs that until now may have passed beneath your radar. If, however, you are already familiar with their work, I would like to think this book might allow you to revisit it with fresh appreciation and renewed respect for the songwriting talents of William and Jim Reid. That has certainly been the case for me.

Upside Down (1984)

Personnel:
Jim Reid: vocals
William Reid: guitar
Douglas Hart: bass
Murray Dalglish: drums
Recorded at Alaska Studios, Waterloo, London, between 16 and 18 September 1984
Producers: Reid/Reid
Engineer: Pat Collier
Label: Creation Records

'Upside Down' (3:01)

Purportedly the first full song written by Jim Reid, closely followed by 'Never Understand', and a standout track on the early demo tapes compiled by both brothers, 'Upside Down' – later coupled with 'Vegetable Man' upon its vinyl release during the first week of November 1984 – is fully deserving of its lofty status as one of the most iconic debut singles of all time, regardless of its humble origins on the Creation Records label. At the time of its recording, the track represented as close an approximation on vinyl to the live experience of the band as possible.

Following receipt of another of the band's compilations of demo tracks, further enhanced by a selection of William's own compositions, Alan McGee – while not completely lukewarm in his response – recommended that the band consider a more professional recording of one of the songs for potential inclusion on a forthcoming Creation compilation album of new talent. Although this compilation ultimately never saw the light of day, the Reids did follow the advice given to them and booked a recording session for Friday 11 May at Evenload Studios, situated on the outskirts of East Kilbride, where an ultimately abortive attempt at recording 'Upside Down' took place.

Accompanied by Douglas Hart and a local drummer roped in through powers of persuasion at the eleventh hour, the version that the Mary Chain walked out of the nearby eight-track studio with was sorely lacking in the sound desired by the band. So much so, in fact, that the Reids instead returned to the original late-1983 Portastudio version of the song, opting to overdub additional feedback and an outro of increasingly frenzied shouting in an attempt to compensate for the disappointing Evenload recording. With an accompanying note attached – now part of Mary Chain legend – in which Jim bemoaned how the version attempted in the professional recording environment 'sounded fucking awful, the guitar sound was terrible and the whole thing was very tame, mainly because of the stupid bastard engineer who didn't understand what we were looking for', the enhanced version of the original demo track was subsequently posted to McGee for further consideration. Incidentally, it is this 'second' demo recording of the song that has appeared on subsequent official releases of the track, notably the 2011 *Psychocandy* deluxe reissue and *The Power Of Negative Thinking* 4CD box set from 2008.

As a sidenote, the Evenload recording of 'Upside Down' remains unheard outside of the band's inner circle since the time of its original recording and has not appeared on any retrospective or deluxe reissue programme since. Described by Douglas Hart as 'more Ramones-like' rather than the screeching behemoth of a debut single that would later be recorded in London, the group's first attempt at the song is rumoured to be retained within the subsequently refurbished studio at Riverside Music College in Busby, a ten-minute drive from the centre of East Kilbride. However, such is the precarious nature of the master tapes that any playback would likely render further use impossible through the inevitable shedding of magnetic layers.

It would be mid-September 1984 before 'Upside Down' was revisited by the band, who, despite not featuring the track in any of their half-dozen gigs up to that point, clearly retained a fondness for the song as well as recognition of its strength as a representation of the distinctive sound that The Jesus and Mary Chain were swiftly honing. The band's line-up at that point had been complemented by 16-year-old (closer to 17 by then) local drummer Murray Dalglish. His youthful enthusiasm for the band's music, alongside his ability to keep the beat despite the near-overwhelming feedback from William's lead guitar, marked him out as a key factor in the success of the group's incendiary performances before a select number of alternately stunned or appalled audiences – sometimes both – during the summer of 1984.

Alaska Studios, situated in Alaska Street, Waterloo, was the studio of choice for fledgling Creation artists at the time, not least because of its cheap overnight rates and the flexibility of its owner, Pat Collier, whose approach to the sundry indie bands making regular use of the 24-track studio was largely sympathetic. Collier's own musical background as a former member of punk outfit The Vibrators undoubtedly helped.

The recording of 'Upside Down', together with the accompanying tales surrounding the overnight session of 16 September and into the early hours of the following morning, has taken on a life of its own over the past four decades. These range from the band's ill-advised decision to mix the track on the studio's own Tannoy speakers – sparking serious disappointment upon subsequent playback through more standard hi-fi systems – to the levels of supposed 'production' involvement by those present, namely McGee, Collier and McGee's Creation colleague at the time – and an ever-present figure during the early months of all things Mary Chain – Joe Foster.

Contemporary interviews with both Reids paint a far less hyperbolic account of the recording of 'Upside Down' and certainly do not indicate a particularly hands-on role for either McGee or Foster, both of whom were credited on the original reverse sleeve with production duties on the title track and B-side, respectively. Over 40 years on from the initial overnight recording session at Alaska, what remains free from conjecture is the undoubted power of the version of 'Upside Down' captured for posterity.

Swathed in reverb, and a mere four seconds after the opening drum salvo from Dalglish, the searing feedback that goes on to dominate 'Upside Down' commences and does not subside until the fade-out close to three minutes later. Jim's vocals – an octave apart and relatively restrained compared to his more liberated performances during the Mary Chain's gigs of the time – perfectly complement the Alaska-recorded version of the song, which sounds remarkably different from the original Portastudio demo. It is worth noting that, at the time of this overnight recording session, Jim had only just begun recovering from a throat infection worsened by a lengthy overnight bus journey down to London for a scheduled run of four gigs during mid-September booked by McGee. It is therefore plausible that his comparatively reserved vocal performance may be linked to this precarious condition – never ideal for the lead singer of any band. However, notably, his singing on the B-side 'Vegetable Man' is considerably more impassioned, aptly matching the unhinged nature of the Barrett original, not least during the increasingly manic coda.

Subsequent interviews, and indeed more recent accounts, have all but confirmed that William Reid returned to Alaska for a second mixing session on the evening of 18 September, working alongside Pat Collier in an attempt to boost the power of 'Upside Down', such was the level of disappointment surrounding the original completed mix. However, this was not viewed as a criticism of the engineer involved, in stark contrast to the band's earlier frustrating experience at Evenload. William, now focused solely on remixing the track – and without the distractions or time pressures associated with needing instruments to be recorded again – was free to revisit the five separate feedback tracks and layer them at greater volume and higher frequency throughout the song's runtime.

The resulting final recording was lauded for both its astonishing sonic bravery and its unrepentant core of pop melody, showcasing a staggering level of near-psychotic, seemingly uncontrollable noise, a definite no-no in the all-too-clean FM-friendly pop landscape of the mid-1980s. It would single-handedly launch the Mary Chain's recording career upon its release as the 12th Creation Records single in early November 1984, while simultaneously providing a counterbalance to the group's increasingly controversial and divisive live appearances. Yes, the band could actually play their instruments. Yes, they knew precisely what they were doing. And finally, yes – there was far more still to come.

'Vegetable Man' (3:35) (B-side, 1984)

A key cover version that featured regularly in the band's earliest live sets, and one of several attempted by The Jesus and Mary Chain at the time – alongside 'Ambition' by Subway Sect and 'Barracuda' by The Standells – 'Vegetable Man' was a Syd Barrett-penned track originally intended for release as the late-1967 B-side to the Pink Floyd single 'Scream Thy Last Scream'. The release was ultimately cancelled, and the recordings remained unheard outside of the band for close to a decade, until the bootleg album *Syd Barrett – Unforgotten Hero* began circulating during the mid-1970s, which is likely where Jim and William Reid first encountered the song.

The version recorded at Alaska during the overnight session faithfully retains the original's abrupt key changes while simultaneously providing a significant increase in both volume and intensity, from the crunching drums to the propulsive rhythm guitar and backdrop of alternately shrieking and squealing feedback. Despite the limited studio time afforded to them, the Mary Chain's recording of 'Vegetable Man' boasts a superb double-tracked lead vocal throughout, while even retaining the distinctive shuddering clunk heard at the 2:58 mark, caused by a guitar pedal being accidentally kicked during recording.

The single was reissued in a special 40th anniversary edition in late 2024 on the Third Man Records label for US audiences and via Warner Records for the UK and Europe. One notable omission – other than the removal of the band's original 1984 home contact address – was that of the initial production credits for Joe Foster ('Vegetable Man') and Alan McGee ('Upside Down'), with production instead now attributed solely to Reid/Reid.

Psychocandy (1985)

Personnel:
Jim Reid: vocals, guitar
William Reid: guitar, vocals
Douglas Hart: bass
Bobby Gillespie: drums
Recorded and mixed at Southern Studios, Wood Green, London, between 12 June and 25 September 1985
Producers: The Jesus and Mary Chain
Engineer: John Loder
Label: Blanco y Negro
Charts: UK: 31, NZ: 35, Holland: 47, Australia: 87, Canada: 92, US: 188
Running time: 38:57

There is an old maxim from the recording world that debut albums are often the easiest to make, owing to a surplus of readily available material – more often than not already recorded in demo form – and a band's determination to make the strongest possible impact upon their audience as quickly as possible, capitalising on precious momentum and, indeed, the moment itself.

However, for The Jesus and Mary Chain, the success of this approach first depended upon discovering a suitable recording environment during the opening months of 1985, something that initially proved frustratingly problematic following a wholly disappointing attempt to record their major-label debut single, 'Never Understand'. This took place after signing a one-off 'testing the water' deal with Blanco y Negro Records in the aftermath of the band's provocative performance at the Ambulance Station venue in Southwark on 23 November.

At the behest of Warner Bros. Records, the Mary Chain were initially paired with the young engineer Stephen Street, whose reputation had been rapidly growing through his meticulous work with The Smiths on the Morrissey- and Marr-produced 'Meat Is Murder'. Yet it quickly became apparent that the band and Street were fundamentally at odds regarding both the direction of the session at Island Records' studio in St Peter's Square, Hammersmith ('The Fallout Shelter') and the unique sound the Reids were attempting to pursue.

Both Jim Reid and Douglas Hart have since spoken candidly about the clash in expectations and temperament surrounding the session, so it is little surprise that the collaboration ended prematurely. Jim later admitted during a 2017 *Q* retrospective: 'I think he was freaked out by our lack of professionalism.'

Despite their growing familiarity with Alaska, it was ultimately not considered the preferred location for recording the band's debut album. Indeed, by late spring, the band had moved on to work on basic backing tracks for three songs at Regent Sounds Studios in Denmark Street between 27 and 28 May. These sessions took place prior to the band settling in at what would prove to be the ideal environment for recording *Psychocandy*: Southern Studios in Wood Green, overseen by its owner and engineer, John Loder.

It was Geoff Travis who first suggested Southern Studios, a facility established in 1974 and, by the early 1980s, best known for its association with Crass, functioning almost exclusively as the recording, production and distribution headquarters for the anarcho-punk outfit. An initial meeting was arranged during which Jim and William immediately warmed to Loder, who, in turn, instinctively recognised that his own relaxed and homely working environment (despite its lack of air conditioning and rather dark and dingy atmosphere) was precisely what the band required. Unlike previous studio experiences, Southern offered freedom from unnecessary intrusion, scepticism, or outright hostility from those tasked with assisting the recording process. Loder understood where the band were coming from, what they were trying to achieve and why Southern represented the ideal place for them to attempt it.

Located deep within suburban Wood Green at the unassuming address of 10 Myddleton Road, Southern Studios comprised a converted double garage space in which Loder would set up the 24-channel desk before often retreating to the adjoining house to continue office work, remaining reachable by intercom should the band require further assistance. It proved the perfect arrangement, as both Douglas Hart and Jim Reid later recalled:

> He was the first sympathetic engineer that we worked with. A lot of the time, he would just disappear. Engineering-wise, he was absolutely perfect because he'd let us try to find the sound that was in our heads without saying, 'You can't do that!'
>
> Southern Studios ... was just fabulous because John Loder was there. He was the opposite of those other engineers; he was actually egging us on to go further. His attitude was to set the desk up and then go away. He'd just go to his office and do his work. We needed someone like John. He was essential purely because he let us get on with it. We had the sound in our heads, and he tried to find a way to get that on tape. He did everything he could to help us get that sound.

While critics and fans alike have understandably focused upon the infamous 'noise element' associated with *Psychocandy* – the album itself rather than the beautiful acoustic ballad ultimately omitted from its final running order – it is worth remembering that the record's sonic identity extended far beyond simple volume or distortion. In addition to the remarkable set of 14 songs that constituted the finished album, the sophisticated use of reverb, delay and feedback looping during the Southern sessions remains especially striking.

Alongside the studio's heavily modified 24-track Raindirk Series 3 mixing desk, Southern housed both an AMS RSX-16 digital reverb unit and an EMT 140 plate reverb, each used to particularly inspired effect throughout the sessions. Yet it was perhaps the now-legendary AMS S-DMX digital delay, harmoniser, pitch shifter and sampler that contributed most significantly to the distinctive atmosphere of *Psychocandy*, allowing specially recorded feedback loops – created using William's Gretsch Tennessean fed through a Shin-ei fuzz pedal – to be patched directly into tracks at carefully chosen moments for maximum impact.

With backing tracks largely recorded live within the main building of 10 Myddleton Road – two ordinary rooms merged into a recording space more suited to the band's guitar, bass, drums and vocals set-up – the Mary Chain were then free to retreat into the control room and begin the all-important overdubbing process, the significance of which cannot be overstated in relation to the album eventually released later that year.

Having finally discovered the ideal setting within travelling distance of Hestercombe Avenue in Fulham, the band were now ready to fully immerse themselves in the recording of their debut album, a process occupying much of June 1985 prior to live appearances in Manchester and Nottingham later that month. 'You Trip Me Up' had already been completed at Southern as part of an earlier session.

During this period, the studio's resident engineer, Anton Bukowski, also encountered the band. Invited by John Loder to assist with the forthcoming album recordings, Bukowski declined – a decision seemingly influenced more by the intensity of the group's insular behaviour than by any dislike of the music itself. Given the recent experience with Stephen Street, one can easily imagine another unhappy outcome had yet another outsider been placed in close proximity to the band during such a formative stage of recording.

That many outside the Mary Chain's inner circle remained sceptical about their ability to produce anything beyond a loose compilation of singles and B-sides is perhaps unsurprising, especially given the increasingly belligerent reputation of their live appearances. By this stage, the band had become almost synonymous with confrontational and audience-unfriendly performances. Without access to the carefully assembled Portastudio demos from previous years – nor any real appreciation of the band's determination to create an album capable of outlasting contemporary fashions and short-sighted trends – critics had little else beyond the growing mythology surrounding the group upon which to base their assumptions.

It is therefore unsurprising that *Psychocandy* had such a profound impact upon release in November 1985. One *NME* reviewer, Andy Gill, bordering on disbelief at the album's quality, openly admitted: 'I never expected this…'

That the album even reached the stage of near-universal critical acclaim was itself something of a triumph, particularly following the notably unenthusiastic response from Warners when the completed master tapes were first delivered. Having poured enormous time, care and commitment into the project, Jim and William were dismayed by the label's reaction. The prevailing opinion within the company – with only a few exceptions – was that the Mary

Chain had effectively delivered a collection of demos rather than a finished record, and should now proceed to make the 'proper' album expected of them, ideally alongside a producer chosen to clean up what executives perceived as strong pop songs obscured beneath an abrasive sonic approach.

Fears that *Psychocandy* might become trapped in limbo – with Warners refusing both to release it and to permit its appearance elsewhere – significantly heightened tensions between the band and label. It ultimately required concerted persuasion from the Reids during discussions with Rob Dickins to secure the album's release, alongside suggestions that more chart-friendly material might follow in the future if allowed to first get *Psychocandy* out of their system. Additional reassurances from Geoff Travis that the album would not be removed and remixed by outsiders helped calm fears, though the situation remained precarious until early white-label review copies began circulating within the music press.

When Warners finally promoted the album in the aftermath of its overwhelmingly positive reception, they did so – beyond the now-iconic cover still image selected by the band at the record label's offices on 10 September – with a full-page advertisement in the British music press bearing the slogan 'Suck on This' in typography matching the album title itself. Beneath sat a collection of glowing review excerpts from *NME*, *Sounds*, *Melody Maker*, *Smash Hits* and *The Face*.

And at the bottom of the page, simply:

PSYCHOCANDY. THE ALBUM FROM THE JESUS AND MARY CHAIN.

'Just Like Honey' (3:03)

The album begins with a nod to the past and an immediate introduction to the band's own distinctive 'wall of sound', something many critics would later identify as central to the sonic appeal of *Psychocandy*. From the opening two bars of the instantly recognisable 'Be My Baby' drum pattern onwards – further manipulated through the sampler facility on Southern Studios' in-house AMS unit – the melodic side of The Jesus and Mary Chain is brought emphatically to the fore, immediately dispelling any assumptions that the band were limited to one particular style rooted solely in feedback and confrontation. Instead, 'Just Like Honey' unfolds as a reverb-drenched love song that has remained beloved for over four decades and a permanent fixture of Mary Chain live sets, particularly since its memorable use during the closing moments of *Lost In Translation*.

William has since admitted that the song originally existed in a considerably faster and less delicate form, requiring persuasion from Jim to slow the arrangement down after recognising the strength of the melody when played more softly. It is worth remembering that 'Just Like Honey', like the majority of the material eventually recorded for *Psychocandy*, was initially composed on acoustic guitar. The later demo version released as an additional B-side on the 12" and double 7" editions of the single – dated October 1984 – possesses an almost pastoral quality in the gentle mood it creates.

The song's title and key refrain also underwent several revisions prior to release. First written during early 1984 under the title 'In Her Garden', William subsequently altered this to 'Just Like Alice' – a name later revisited for the opening track on 1989's *Automatic* – though he still remained dissatisfied. Something about the central line simply did not feel right. It would not be until mere minutes before recording the song for a Peel Session in February 1985 that the word 'honey' was finally substituted for 'Alice', despite Jim's reservations that it sounded reminiscent of a Van Morrison lyric from 'Tupelo Honey', the title track of his 1971 album. According to later recollections, a succession of increasingly desperate female first names had already been considered before the breakthrough finally arrived.

Another essential component of the song – and one the band have carefully preserved during live performances ever since their 2007 reformation – is the use of female backing vocals during the closing 'just like honey' refrain, gently counterpointing Jim's lead vocal throughout the final minute. Although the album credits suggest both Karen Parker and Laurence Verfaillie contributed backing vocals together, it is, in fact, only Parker – then Bobby Gillespie's girlfriend – who appears on the final recording, having already debuted the part during the earlier Peel Session.

Laurence and William's girlfriend, Rona, both attempted the vocal at Southern Studios on 19 September, but neither performance satisfied the band, not least because the song's key made the part particularly difficult to sing. However, Karen Parker had visited the studio three months previously during a trip to London, recording a series of softly melodic 'just like honey' refrains. From these, the Mary Chain selected their preferred take, sampling and repeating it throughout the closing section of the track. The final recording, mixed on 20 July, reportedly stunned Dick Green of Creation Records when it was first played to him during a visit to Southern. So markedly different was the song from anything previously associated with the band that Green initially struggled to believe he was listening to a Mary Chain original, let alone a potential hit single. His enthusiasm was quickly shared by Alan McGee, whom Green urged to visit the studio immediately in order to hear the completed track for himself.

The overwhelmingly positive reaction generated by 'Just Like Honey' amongst those within the band's inner circle would later influence the decision to sequence it as the opening track on *Psychocandy*. The rationale was simple: unsuspecting listeners, primed by reputation and media hysteria to expect an immediate onslaught of feedback and hostility, would instead experience the same sense of surprise and disorientation felt by those first hearing the song at Southern Studios.

With a definitive sonic statement established from the outset, the Mary Chain opened their debut album with a love song submerged in reverb and drenched in their own uniquely realised interpretation of the 'Wall of Sound'. While deliberately evoking the girl-group productions of The Crystals and The Ronettes, alongside the cinematic grandeur and emotional intensity associated with George 'Shadow' Morton's work with The Shangri-Las, 'Just Like Honey' nevertheless remains an extraordinary song entirely in its own right. It simultaneously acknowledges a debt to a then largely neglected musical tradition – though certainly not neglected by the Reids or Douglas Hart – while immediately establishing a distinctive sonic identity through painstaking layers of reverb and feedback manipulated to beautiful effect.

'The Living End' (2:16)

Following directly from the romanticism of 'Just Like Honey', the second track on *Psychocandy* presents another love song, though this time filtered through the self-absorbed perspective of the doomed biker anti-hero familiar from classic Shangri-Las narratives such as 'Leader Of The Pack' and 'Out In The Streets'. During a 2017 conversation with Mogwai frontman Stuart Braithwaite, Jim reflected upon the profound influence such records exerted upon the band:

> The Shangri-Las were my favourite of those girl bands. I remember 'Leader Of The Pack' was in a Levi's ad in 1975, and that was the first time I ever heard the song. As a result, I dug up some more stuff of theirs. There's just something magical about that kind of music that stuck with us.

Magical indeed – though the fate awaiting the protagonist of 'The Living End' proves considerably darker. Across what remains the album's second-shortest track, lacerating bursts of feedback accompany the inevitable destruction of its central character. Following an accelerating key change around the 1:45 mark, the biker finds himself 'moving so fast that I can't control the wheels' before the catastrophic aftermath arrives with the grimly memorable image of 'my head is dripping into my leather boots'. There is no romantic escape awaiting the self-obsessed rider; the intoxicating allure of leather jackets, motorcycles and freedom collapses into violent ruin as the song shudders toward its conclusion.

An interesting footnote to the recording concerns the band's early attempts to heighten the dramatic ending of the song through the inclusion of broken-glass sound effects. When 'The Living End' debuted during the February 1985 Peel Session – around the same period, a separate Alaska demo version featuring William on lead vocals was also being attempted – the band requested permission to smash glass in the studio during recording, only to be firmly refused by the understandably cautious producer present. It would be another few months before the band settled on the track's definitive ending.

Following the Denmark Street session of 27-28 May, when multi-tracks were recorded for 'In A Hole', 'Inside Me' and 'The Living End', the definitive version of the song was finalised at Southern Studios in late August. By this point in the recording process, the decision had been made to allow the song to collapse into a chaotic squall of perfectly crafted feedback rather than through literal shards of glass and although the basic structure of the song had been written by William, it was Jim who contributed not only the bass guitar part during the Southern recording, but also many of the clangs, screeches and feedback textures that help give 'The Living End' such impact.

'Taste The Floor' (2:56)

Provided with financial assistance through a share of their father's redundancy payout, William and Jim purchased a first-edition Tascam TEAC 144 during May 1981, a groundbreaking piece of technology first released nearly two years earlier that revolutionised home recording possibilities for aspiring musicians. 'Taste The Floor' emerged as one of the key tracks from the earliest demos recorded by the brothers during 1983 using their shared Portastudio and was also notable for being an original Reid/Reid composition within an otherwise cover-version-dominated early live set.

The primitive demo approach to recording the song – with William plugging directly into the Tascam to capture his guitar parts – was effectively replicated during the later Southern Studios sessions, this time to even greater impact through routing the guitar directly via the mixing desk to generate an enormous, claustrophobic sound that leaves virtually no sonic space unoccupied.

Of the opening triumvirate of *Psychocandy*, it is 'Taste The Floor' that most directly channels the spirit of mid-1960s garage rock, particularly groups such as The Seeds and 13th Floor Elevators. Yet it is the barre-chord-driven approach of the comparatively obscure Canadian garage group The Ugly Ducklings and their single 'Nothin'' that perhaps resonates most strongly within the distinctive opening riff to this particular Mary Chain track.

The song's relentlessly negative lyrical mood – particularly the explicit line 'Just like a big brass drum/and some cunt's always scratching it' – is punctuated by three carefully arranged passages of looped feedback. The first arrives at approximately 1:13 before fading 17 seconds later, the second emerges at the 1:59 mark before gradually disappearing after 20 seconds, while the third and final loop enters at 2:31 and continues through to the song's conclusion.

This approach to manipulating recorded feedback in order to deepen and intensify the music felt entirely unique within the mid-1980s British rock landscape. The Mary Chain's painstakingly hands-on studio methods – patching carefully prepared loops into tracks during playback rather than relying upon more traditional guitar solos – transformed relatively simple chord structures into something punishingly immersive and psychologically overwhelming. For a guitarist who at that point appeared largely uninterested in the conventional technical showmanship of his contemporaries – indeed, some short-sighted critics during the band's early years questioned whether William possessed much interest in guitar technique at all – this now appears, from a distance of over four decades, nothing short of a masterstroke.

'The Hardest Walk' (2:40)

The closest *Psychocandy* comes to pure power-pop, 'The Hardest Walk' opens with Jim briefly singing a cappella – 'I never thought…' – before the track bursts fully into life as a gloriously direct and unapologetically catchy pop song. Despite largely avoiding a conventional verse-chorus structure, the song nonetheless possesses all the hallmarks of expertly arranged guitar pop, complete with an excellent instrumental breakdown that strips proceedings back to Jim's vocal, accompanied only by bass and drums, before the full arrangement returns once more.

William's lead guitar break between the 47-second and one-minute marks is similarly exemplary in its restraint: beautifully straightforward, perfectly pitched and entirely free from unnecessary embellishment. Over the years, William has frequently spoken of his admiration for Bernard Sumner's minimalist lead style in both Joy Division and New Order, groups for whom the Mary Chain openly expressed considerable respect. That influence is especially apparent here, not least during the buzzing two-note lead motif heard throughout the closing 40 seconds of the song.

Despite being among the few tracks on the album not to feature overt feedback passages – with noise instead functioning as harmonic counterpoint to Jim's vocal – 'The Hardest Walk' was nevertheless selected for remixing in late 1986 by producer Stephen Hague for inclusion on the soundtrack to the John Hughes-written and produced film *Some Kind Of Wonderful*. The resulting version, re-recorded by the band from 9-14 November at Advision Studios in Fitzrovia, extended the original by approximately 33 seconds while subtly restructuring the arrangement, most notably through a lengthier instrumental introduction before Jim's vocal entrance.

Reflecting several years later upon the revised soundtrack version, Jim admitted:

> It's a re-recorded version of 'The Hardest Walk' and was mixed without us being present. The truth of the matter is that it's something that I'm quite ashamed of, really, because to me it doesn't really sound like The Jesus and Mary Chain … If we had spent more time on it, we could have got it sounding better. But we were trying to record our LP (*Darklands*) at the time, so we just let it go … It's not the worst thing … It just sounds like one of our demos.

For those curious regarding the song's appearance within the finished film, it can briefly be heard five minutes into proceedings as the protagonist discovers his sister rifling through his record collection.

In *Tenement Kid* (2021), Bobby Gillespie recalls William playing the song's central chord progression at Southern Studios during the *Psychocandy* sessions. Gillespie immediately noted a similarity between the melody and the chorus of 'Honey At The Core', the 1983 single by Scottish indie group Friends Again. Heard in succession, the resemblance is indeed faintly noticeable. Yet whatever passing similarity may exist, 'The Hardest Walk' ultimately transcends any such comparison entirely.

'Cut Dead' (2:47)

Upon the release of *Psychocandy* in November 1985, *Sounds* reviewer Jack Barron famously described the album as an 'immaculate conception of *love* songs', deliberately italicising the word 'love' for emphasis. 'Cut Dead' may well represent the album's purest expression of that idea.

Timed almost perfectly to echo the aching emotional pace of 'Just My Imagination (Running Away With Me)' by The Temptations – itself masterfully produced by Norman Whitfield – 'Cut Dead' unfolds as a devastatingly beautiful ballad. While obvious reference points to The Velvet Underground at their gentlest remain entirely valid – particularly 'Sunday Morning' and 'Femme Fatale' – the song also carries traces of prime The Beach Boys melancholy. More than even 'Just Like Honey', it serves as a gorgeous counterpoint to the harsher white-noise assaults elsewhere on the album.

And yet, despite being perhaps the strongest embodiment of the album's 'candy' side – so tender that even the brief wooden clunk audible around the 20-second mark, reportedly caused by a stray effects pedal being unplugged, fails to disrupt the mood – a distinct lyrical darkness continually cuts against the sweetness of the arrangement: 'beaten black and blue … tearing up my weary head … knock my body to the ground … you cut me dead/nail me down/and kick my head'.

The song also carries the unique distinction of effectively being a Jim Reid solo recording. On a rare occasion when William spent a day away from Southern Studios visiting his girlfriend, Jim recorded virtually the entire track alone. Upon William's return, both brothers elected to keep quiet about the unusual circumstances surrounding the session.

Regardless of its singular recording history – almost entirely unique within the Mary Chain catalogue – 'Cut Dead' remains an exquisitely lovely piece of music. Gentle tambourine rhythms, soft floor toms and a simple two-note bassline underpin Jim's aching vocal performance while delicately strummed acoustic guitars drift through the arrangement with an almost country-like lilt.

And when searching for the perfect concluding description of 'Cut Dead', the final words of Jack Barron's five-star review of *Psychocandy* remain difficult to improve upon:

> The kiss in the fist.

'In A Hole' (3:02)

In an abrupt volte-face, the woozy tenderness generated by 'Cut Dead' is immediately shattered by the opening assault of 'In A Hole', arguably the most extreme track on *Psychocandy*. Yet beneath the initial visceral shock lies something far more substantial than the thrilling live set-opener that the song had already become by 1985. Refined at Southern into a carefully constructed collage of multi-layered guitar tracks, 'In A Hole' evolved from the core arrangement that had featured so prominently in the band's earliest gigs from the summer of 1984 onwards. The version that would go on to feature so memorably on *Psychocandy* was built upon the basic bass, drums and rhythm guitar tracks originally recorded a few months earlier at Regent Sounds Studios in Denmark Street.

Douglas Hart:

> I remember William had all these loops of feedback, like old-fashioned tape loops going round jam jars and that, to build up the layers of guitar. I don't think it really gets enough credit – people go on about the energy and noise, but it's a great pop record, really thought out and carefully arranged.

One of the earliest William-penned Mary Chain compositions and a standout track on the band's 1984 demo compilations, 'In A Hole' operates successfully on two very distinct levels. Primarily, and most immediately, there is the sheer physical assault of the music itself – relentless, unforgiving and driven by the infamous high-frequency 'noise' pushed so aggressively into the mix that it genuinely tests the tolerance of the unprepared listener. Yet beneath this sonic abrasion lies a surprisingly playful and bizarre lyrical sensibility, full of strange imagery that lingers long after the song concludes, not least the memorable couplet: 'How can something crawl within/my rubber holy baked bean tin?' It is perhaps telling that this lyric was selected as one of the extracts printed alongside individual band photographs on the inner sleeve of the album itself, images captured during the group's visit to the Algarve for the 'You Trip Me Up' promotional film shoot.

For many future fans – and indeed for equally bewildered critics unable to comprehend the apparent incompetence being so defiantly presented before them – the band's appearance on *The Old Grey Whistle Test* on 12 February 1985 provided a first genuine glimpse into what The Jesus and Mary Chain represented. The televised performance of 'In A Hole' that evening left viewers and presenters alike visibly stunned by the extraordinary climax of the song. Carefully orchestrated for maximum impact to some, utterly shambolic to others, it remains a television appearance that, more than four decades later, still retains remarkable power.

Initially considered as a possible follow-up single during the spring of 1985 – something hinted at through the etched message 'In A Hole is next' found on the 12" pressing of 'Never Understand' – the song has remained a live favourite throughout the band's career. It is additionally notable for featuring one of the most physically punishing drum patterns on the album, so relentless in execution that the solution adopted at Southern was the use of a looped beat. This mirrored the insistent drum-machine pulse of favourites such as Suicide alongside the lesser-known Doctor Mix and the Remix, whose *Wall Of Noise* mini-album had been enthusiastically introduced to the Reids by Douglas Hart only a few years earlier.

'Taste Of Cindy' (1:42)

The original first side of *Psychocandy* concludes with the album's shortest track, though like so many of the Mary Chain's finest songs, 'Taste Of Cindy' began life as a gentle acoustic composition. Written comparatively late in relation to much of the surrounding material, the song originated with Jim and existed initially in a markedly softer form. The officially released version of the earlier Peel Session recording – ultimately far too strong to remain unheard – later appeared on the 1988 compilation *Barbed Wire Kisses*.

In a 1992 interview with *Guitar Player*, William candidly explained the quality-control approach long employed by the band before committing to the full development of any composition, an artistic philosophy unlikely to have been suspected by many first encountering *Psychocandy*:

> If a song doesn't sound good on acoustic guitar, it gets thrown in the dump. That's the way we've always done it ... People are always surprised by that. It's easy to make noise, but not to write a good song. Playing an electric guitar, you can get fooled; playing chords that you think are powerful just because they're loud, and that what you're singing is somehow a powerful song, when it's really not the case.

Upon completing the original acoustic version of the song, Jim played the then-untitled composition to William and requested assistance with the lyrics. William initially struggled to devise a satisfactory set of verses and chorus ideas to accompany the music, though Jim had fortunately continued working on the song independently and soon produced a lyric that fitted the arrangement perfectly – perhaps unsurprising given that the underlying chord progression and melody had already been composed by him.

Towards the conclusion of a bootleg recording from one of the band's three 1984 performances at The Living Room club – situated above what had formerly been The Roebuck pub on Tottenham Court Road – an audience member can excitedly be heard shouting 'Ramones! Ramones!' in response to the music. Of all the tracks on *Psychocandy*, it is indeed 'Taste Of Cindy' that most clearly recalls Ramones, the hugely influential New York quartet whose 1976 debut album remained a foundational touchstone for countless musicians and whose impact upon William and Jim was instrumental in convincing them that forming a band themselves might actually be possible.

Certainly, the brevity of 'Taste Of Cindy' – timing out at precisely 1:42 – feels distinctly Ramones-esque, their own debut featuring 14 songs across barely 29 minutes. Yet the Mary Chain track is simultaneously far more layered and texturally nuanced than the deliberately stripped-back approach employed by the legendary New Yorkers, with all due respect to their seminal influence. Within its remarkably short running time, several carefully positioned musical elements elevate the song beyond what might otherwise have remained a relatively standard punk-influenced power-pop number.

Most notable amongst these is the sustained single guitar note introduced around the 30-second mark, its keening harmonic tone lingering in the mix for approximately 25 seconds before gradually fading away to reveal a classic Motown-inspired bass-and-drums breakdown. The same note then reappears at approximately 1:12 and remains present for the remainder of the track before once again fading into the distance during the song's closing moments – and with it, the end of side one of *Psychocandy*.

'Never Understand' (2:57)

The earliest Mary Chain home demo recordings featured 'Upside Down' and 'Never Understand' as two clear standouts, remarkably the first songs ever written by Jim. Propelled by the metronomic pulse of the Roland TR-606 Drumatix drum machine, put through its paces by both brothers during their individual home recordings, and underpinned by a simple root-note bassline, Jim's vocal was submerged beneath swathes of fuzz to such an extent that some of the relatively few listeners who heard the demo tape at the time – not least future band member Bobby Gillespie – initially mistook the guitar sound for the white noise of a monophonic synthesiser. Given the Reids' admiration during the early 1980s for groups such as Cabaret Voltaire and Suicide, such a comparison would certainly not have been regarded unfavourably.

Yet regardless of the song's primitive four-track origins, there was never much doubt that the melody and structure of 'Never Understand' stood apart immediately upon first hearing – and indeed every time thereafter. It is therefore still somewhat surprising to consider that both this track and its companion demo highlight 'Upside Down' were only rarely performed live during the band's first 18 months together, not becoming regular fixtures until the group's late-1985 American tour in advance of the US release of *Psychocandy* on the Warners-owned Reprise Records label.

Selected as the follow-up to 'Upside Down' during early 1985, the Mary Chain's ill-fated encounter with Stephen Street ultimately achieved little beyond deepening the band's resentment towards the rigid expectations and professional orthodoxy of traditional recording studios. The group's frustration at what they perceived as Street's attempt to reshape their sound into that of a conventional pub-rock band was expressed in no uncertain terms amongst those within their inner circle.

Little wonder, then, that The Jesus and Mary Chain returned to the familiar surroundings of Alaska Studios for another midnight-to-8 am session on 6-7 January in an effort to salvage the song. Given the collapse of the initial session, this second attempt at 'Never Understand' now carried even greater importance. The resulting Alaska version – timed at 3:25 and later included on both the 2011 expanded reissue of *Psychocandy* and the compilation *The Power Of Negative Thinking* – is unquestionably of considerable merit.

The basic structure of the song remains intact, Jim's vocal performance is already compelling and several key elements later central to the definitive version are now present, including the two-note refrain introduced at approximately 2:16 and sustained through to the conclusion alongside the chaotic screaming outro, with both Jim and William audibly relishing the escalating mayhem.

In the July 1985 issue of *One Two Testing*, William discussed his fascination with the strange unpredictability of feedback, something central to both early recorded versions of 'Never Understand':

> The good thing about feedback is that it's hard to control; it's strange. Sometimes it's actual notes and they wail in and out. Like, there's a bit on 'Never Understand' that goes 'whooo!' … one particular bit with a real note that comes through – it's got a real melancholy quality. Sad. But the sound's always different, as it depends on so many factors. You just can't control feedback live.

However, despite its many strengths, the Alaska recording, mixed by the band during the following overnight session on 7-8 January, suffers somewhat from overly prominent, poorly miked drums, while the feedback, seemingly confined largely to a single track, feels closer in spirit to the abrasive shriek heard during the band's October 1984 Peel Session than the carefully layered sound they ultimately envisioned for the song.

Following additional mixing of the track on 18 January and with the master then cut at CBS four days later, the final released version of 'Never Understand', issued through Blanco y Negro Records during February 1985 and later opening side two of *Psychocandy*, remains the definitive early Mary Chain statement: the perfect fusion of beautiful pop melody and overwhelming noise that the band had long sought to achieve.

Remarkably, with just their second single, the group had succeeded in realising their much-stated ambition of creating a collision between Einstürzende Neubauten and The Shangri-Las – a sound that until then had existed only in their collective imagination. It was an aesthetic that favourites such as Buzzcocks and Ramones had perhaps only hinted at years earlier.

Yet aside from the unexpected (and presumably accidental) resemblance between the song's verses and 'Up On The Roof' by The Drifters, it is arguably the joyous surf-pop melodicism of early The Beach Boys material that 'Never

Understand' most strongly recalls. Another admitted influence was Generation X and, in particular, their 1980 single 'Dancing With Myself', which Jim would later acknowledge as a direct inspiration.

Lyrically, 'Never Understand' functions almost perfectly as an outsider anthem, its protagonist simultaneously damaged and liberated: 'head so heavy and I'm looking thin/but when the sun goes down I'm gonna start again'.

Following the single's release, Jim was repeatedly asked during interviews to explain the song's origins and meaning. Given his later admission – and the encouragement of the band's management at the time – that he frequently invented entertaining stories for journalists, it is perhaps wise to approach his claim that the song concerned an East Kilbride drug casualty with some caution, particularly considering the vividly eccentric portrait he painted of the individual in question:

> He was what people describe as a weirdo, a freak, somebody that they didn't know how to deal with. He was the same age as me, in the same year at school, and he painted his mother and father's garden yellow. And his mother and father's reaction to that was that he was a lunatic, and they threw him out.

The definitive recording of 'Never Understand', underpinned throughout by the same propulsive bassline that had driven the original 1983 Portastudio demo, ultimately runs roughly 30 seconds shorter than the initial Alaska studio version while sounding considerably tighter and more focused. Additional layers of feedback are now integrated with far greater precision, while William's chiming guitar figure enters at approximately 2:04 before gradually disappearing beneath the escalating maelstrom of noise as the song surges towards its unforgettable climax.

Reflecting later upon the track's chaotic conclusion, Jim recalled with obvious delight:

> It ends with everything getting louder and louder, and then we thought, why don't we all just scream and make it sound like a fight or something? It's William doing most of the yelling. He was good at shouting.

An extraordinary pop single regardless of its relatively modest peak position of number 47 in the UK charts, 'Never Understand' captured a band suddenly operating in complete command of their own artistic identity. The accompanying promotional film, directed by Tim Broad for M-Ocean and shot on 7 February in Studio D6 of Metropolitan Wharf, where the production company also maintained an office, reinforces this perfectly. Through knowingly stylised black-and-white close-ups recalling Andy Warhol's famed screen tests of The Velvet Underground during the mid-1960s Factory era, the band establish an image of detached, confrontational cool.

Yet these stark monochrome sequences are periodically disrupted by flashes of colour, grins and smirks from Jim, Douglas and Bobby, subtly undermining the severity of the image and making it clear that the Mary Chain remained fully in control of how they presented themselves. Their presence at the National Film School in Beaconsfield just three days later, when the video was being edited, only serves to underline this point. The resulting mixture of irony, nonchalance and studied cool only made the group appear more exciting. And as the song collapses into itself and the previously restless camera finally settles for the first time since the beginning of the video, William stares blankly ahead, as though the scene unfolding around him has absolutely nothing to do with him at all.

'Inside Me' (3:09)

Early music-press reaction to The Jesus and Mary Chain frequently bordered upon hysteria and, while actively encouraged by management and tolerated to a degree by the band themselves during their formative months, quickly led to comparisons with the Sex Pistols. An introduction to Canadian television programme *The New Music*'s feature on the infamous March 1985 North London Polytechnic performance – a report which spent as much time documenting the ensuing chaos as it did interviewing the group backstage – framed matters in suitably dramatic fashion:

> While most people in the UK would agree that punk is dead, many of them are nevertheless constantly on the lookout for the next Sex Pistols, and the latest band to earn that title is The Jesus and Mary Chain…

Yet in reality, it is with Public Image Ltd – specifically the classic Lydon/Levene/Wobble incarnation and the sonic experimentation of 'First Issue' and, especially, 'Metal Box' – that the Mary Chain's early recordings share the strongest musical kinship. Nowhere on *Psychocandy* is this more apparent than on 'Inside Me'.

During the Southern Studios sessions, the Reids and Douglas Hart encountered both Keith Levene and Jah Wobble, the latter having been invited to contribute to sessions involving Al Jourgensen's Ministry, who were simultaneously developing material for what would become their 1986 album *Twitch* during alternate overnight studio shifts in Wood Green. Wobble later recalled in his autobiography *Memoirs Of A Geezer* (2009): 'The original bass that I had in PiL, the black Fender Precision, was sold by me to The Jesus and Mary Chain. They were delighted to have the bass that had been used on 'Metal Box'.'

Although never formally confirmed by the band, there is every possibility that this very instrument appears on several tracks throughout *Psychocandy*, and perhaps nowhere more convincingly than on 'Inside Me', the closest the Mary Chain came on their debut album to capturing the cavernous dub-informed experimentalism of prime PiL – though crucially without descending into mere imitation.

Opening with a descending four-note bassline before introducing a cyclical buzzing riff reminiscent of the minimalist interplay employed by Peter Hook and Bernard Sumner during the early years of Joy Division and New Order, the track quickly expands into a cavernous sonic landscape of echoing drums and metallic reverbs layered together to deeply disorientating effect. The listener is never entirely certain where sounds are originating from, so carefully arranged are the multiple guitar layers drifting throughout the mix.

A brief moment of respite occurs around the 2:12 mark when the arrangement temporarily collapses to bass and drums beneath Jim's repeated refrain – 'It's living inside me/living inside me' – before further swathes of corrosive feedback are unleashed, culminating in one final unforgiving screech that pushes the track beyond the three-minute mark as it slowly disintegrates.

Recorded in comparatively muted form for the February 1985 Peel Session before its basic multi-tracks were completed during the Denmark Street sessions of 27-28 May, 'Inside Me' originated among the band's earliest home demos. Yet its psychedelic overtones, both musically and lyrically, remain striking. References to expanding consciousness – 'I've seen my head grow/ and I've seen something ... I've seen my head expand' – combined with the song's harsh metallic reverberations, help make it another of the many standout moments on *Psychocandy*.

The track also subtly echoes Jim and Douglas Hart's own earlier lysergic adventures in and around an abandoned paint factory on the outskirts of East Kilbride, where the vast industrial acoustics of the derelict environment and the disorientating sounds produced within it mirrored the altered states they were experiencing themselves. Through its sheer visceral intensity, 'Inside Me' feels perfectly suited to soundtracking precisely such an experience.

'Sowing Seeds' (2:50)

Described by William in the 2024 memoir *Never Understood* with characteristic self-deprecation as the moment when, after 'writing hundreds of terrible songs, the first good one popped out in 1983', this track functions almost as a companion piece to the earlier 'Cut Dead' through its similarly languid melodic melancholy. It also stands amongst the most emotionally delicate tracks on *Psychocandy*.

The painstakingly assembled Portastudio demo composed by William represented the first piece of music with which he felt genuinely satisfied, a judgment shared by Jim and one that immediately suggested the artistic direction the elder Reid envisioned for the band he intended to form. 'Sowing Seeds' was among the very first tracks attempted during the band's initial session in Wood Green on 30 March. By the time work on *Psychocandy* had begun in earnest, the song's considerable potential would be realised to remarkable effect.

Built once more around a variation of the familiar 'Be My Baby' rhythmic pulse – combining sampled guide percussion with live drums – 'Sowing Seeds' deliberately restrains any overt sonic violence for much of its duration. William instead uses the Gretsch to generate a gentle, almost country-like twang until approximately 1:57 into the track, when a perfectly judged distorted lead guitar finally cuts through the arrangement. From that point onwards, additional layers of guitar are gradually introduced through to the song's conclusion.

Perhaps partly due to the relative dexterity required to reproduce its intricate textures convincingly in a live setting, 'Sowing Seeds' was rarely – if ever – performed during the band's early years. More surprising still is its omission from the celebrated November 1985 Peel Session, where the Reids instead prioritised 'You Trip Me Up', 'Some Candy Talking', 'Psychocandy' and 'Cut Dead'.

Fortunately for those attending the 2014-15 *30 Years Of Psychocandy* tour, the song was finally given the live treatment it deserved. Far from creating a lull in the set due to its gentler pace and comparative restraint, 'Sowing Seeds' instead emerged as one of the evening's unexpected highlights.

This is something the present author can personally attest to, having attended the first of the two Glasgow Barrowlands performances on Friday 23 November 2014 – a concert later released in August 2015 under the rather functional title *Barrowlands Live* on the Edsel/Demon label.

'My Little Underground' (2:31)

One of the more underrated tracks on *Psychocandy* – perhaps unfairly overlooked amidst the sheer weight of its companion songs – 'My Little Underground' is a glorious rush of two-and-a-half minutes built almost entirely upon forward momentum from the instant the track lurches into life. Combining irresistible pop melody with persistent buzzsaw guitar textures, it was aptly described by one contemporary reviewer as 'the Scottish Underground.'

Initially written at home in East Kilbride during the early summer of 1984 while recovering from an acid-trip comedown, the track finds Jim singing of withdrawal from the disdain and ridicule of others – 'It's easy to see/that you're laughing at me' – while simultaneously seeking refuge from the outside world within the safety of his own private sanctuary, what contemporary listeners might now aptly describe as a 'safe space'.

Although the Reid brothers have generally remained reluctant throughout their career to dissect the lyrical meaning of their songs too explicitly, it is difficult not to connect 'My Little Underground' with their own lives as young men in East Kilbride and the sense of comfort afforded by the world of music accessible from the shared bedroom in which they spent so much of their time surrounded by a carefully curated record collection. The sensitivity of two brothers who frequently described themselves as shy outsiders –

uncomfortable within an industry seemingly built upon self-promotion and social confidence – can also be detected in the repeated refrain: 'I can't, can't understand it/don't know why, don't know why'.

For all the understandable and perhaps inevitable focus upon the sound of *Psychocandy* following its release, it was only rarely acknowledged that beneath the abrasive surface of skilfully manipulated guitar noise and carefully sculpted reverb lay lyrics that were both heartfelt and deeply melodic. The emotional undercurrent of *Psychocandy* – loneliness, hurt, confusion and sadness – may often be partially submerged beneath the mix, but it is unquestionably present throughout the album. The band themselves even provided clues through the carefully selected lyrical excerpts printed across the inner sleeve artwork.

It is precisely this emotional duality that gives the album so much of its enduring power. Whether experienced during the throes of introverted adolescence or later in life while attempting to navigate personal uncertainty, the notion that one can retreat into the sanctuary of a 'little underground' – whatever form that may take – remains profoundly resonant.

'You Trip Me Up' (2:26)

Released during May 1985 as the Mary Chain's third single – and second for Warner Bros. Records – 'You Trip Me Up' provided perhaps the clearest early distillation of the band's signature aesthetic: the deliberate collision of beautiful pop melody with thrilling sonic abrasion.

Taken in isolation as a standalone 7" release rather than within the broader context of *Psychocandy*, however, the single struggled to find favour amongst British daytime radio DJs. Aside from predictable support from John Peel during late-night broadcasts, mainstream exposure remained frustratingly limited. Unsurprisingly, the single consequently stalled at number 55 in the UK charts – a disappointing outcome following the relative momentum generated by 'Never Understand', which had at least reached number 47 earlier that year.

One of the first Mary Chain songs not to originate from the band's 1983 home demo tapes, 'You Trip Me Up' nonetheless possesses an instantly memorable central melody that, upon closer inspection, carries echoes of both 'Sugar, Sugar' by The Archies and, more significantly, 'My Boy Lollipop' by Millie Small, the irresistibly catchy 1964 hit that reached number two in both the UK and US charts.

By the early 1980s, the newly launched Channel 4 had begun rebroadcasting episodes of the legendary 1960s music programme *Ready Steady Go!,* which the Reid brothers watched avidly. One particular episode featured a 90-second extract of 'My Boy Lollipop' performed during a 1964 appearance, and the track's buoyant melodic energy clearly resonated strongly with William. Slowing the pace considerably, he reworked the jaunty structure into something moodier and more hypnotic before constructing an entirely new middle-eight section around it. Lyrics touching upon mutual frustration and sibling antagonism were later added – sentiments perhaps unsurprising given that both brothers, by their early 20s, were still sharing not only the same East Kilbride house but also the same bedroom.

For perhaps the clearest indication of how 'You Trip Me Up' originally sounded before its transformation within the studio, the acoustic Peel Session recorded on 29 October 1985 – only weeks before the release of *Psychocandy* itself – remains essential listening. While the earlier Peel Session version from almost exactly a year beforehand certainly possesses considerable charm, particularly in the way the vocal melody dominates the mix, it is ultimately the definitive Southern Studios recording that fits most seamlessly into the album itself.

From the ominous opening bass rumble through to the closing ten seconds of cavernous howling feedback, the song unfolds with remarkable precision. Completed relatively early during the band's time at Southern Studios, with the initial recording taking place on 1 April before being mixed two days later and subsequently remixed on 18 April, 'You Trip Me Up' was initially intended solely for inclusion on the debut LP. It would ultimately become one of the album's defining moments, though not without several early recording difficulties. Chief amongst these was the challenge of perfecting the backing track, with Jim required to re-record his lead vocal the following day after both brothers deemed the initial take unsatisfactory.

The Mary Chain once again collaborated with Tim Broad for the accompanying promotional film, which the band hoped would secure regular television exposure alongside the anticipated radio support. This time, rather than remaining confined to the dark interiors of a London warehouse, the group relocated to the bright coastal landscapes of the Algarve from 20-24 April, where, rather typically, persistent rain dominated much of their brief visit.

During intermittent moments of sunshine, however, the band were filmed wandering through the empty backstreets, beaches and cliffs of what was then a comparatively unfashionable tourist destination. Dressed entirely in black, the Mary Chain cut striking figures against the stark Portuguese landscape. On a secluded beach at Carvoeiro, William idly strummed his visually distinctive Kent hybrid semi-acoustic guitar while Jim's own Vox Phantom – purchased from Alan McGee on his 23rd birthday in late December 1984 – was memorably planted upright into the sand like some discarded, surreal ice cream cone.

The resulting promotional video, subsequently edited with direct involvement from the band at Dean Street Studios between 30 April and 2 May, provided some of the most iconic early imagery associated with The Jesus and Mary Chain. It was also during this same trip to Portugal that the non-band collage photography later used throughout the inner sleeve artwork of *Psychocandy* was taken by Mike Laye.

'Something's Wrong' (4:01)

> There's a kind of isolated loneliness that seeps in through everything we do. Even when we left East Kilbride and were living in the big city, London, it's still real, it's still with you. That feeling of where you come from … it stays with you for the rest of your life. I think that will always be with us – writing songs in the bedroom, getting on my mum and my dad's nerves. Those are the years that shaped us.
> **Jim Reid**

The penultimate track on *Psychocandy* is also, by some distance, the album's longest composition, pushing beyond the four-minute mark and arguably coming closest on the debut to the more traditional musical structures of the period. Evolving considerably from the rudimentary outline of its 1983 demo-tape origins – where it appeared under the title 'Another Day' – 'Something's Wrong' moves closer in structure to classic indie rock, for want of a better phrase.

This may partly stem from Jim's later admission that, much like 'Never Understand' had been his attempt to rewrite 'Dancing With Myself', 'Something's Wrong' was similarly inspired by another song, albeit one he has never identified publicly. There are, however, unmistakable traces of early Echo & the Bunnymen within the song's atmosphere and structure, particularly the title track from 'Porcupine' (1983).

Opening with a distinctive sequenced drum pattern whose rolling snare fills provide the rhythmic backbone throughout, 'Something's Wrong' stands among the melodic high points of *Psychocandy,* so much so that its principal guitar motif would later resurface to equally impressive effect just a few years later in 1987's 'Happy When It Rains'.

Yet for all the undeniable beauty of the music itself – where multiple layers of guitar no longer merely double or treble lead lines but elevate them into something genuinely immersive – there remains an unmistakable melancholy running throughout the track that gives it such emotional power. One brief extract from the lyrics – though several others carry equal emotional weight – suffices to illustrate the loneliness and isolation at the song's core: 'Been standing still for much too long/and I realise there's something wrong/I'm feeling strange/I need a change/And I realise that there's something wrong'.

A further melodic layer emerges towards the end of the track through a background synthesizer part heard most clearly from the 3:21 mark onwards. The only keyboard-generated sound to feature anywhere on *Psychocandy*, it was played on an instrument left at Southern Studios by Ministry, whose frontman, Al Jourgensen, had generously permitted the Reids to make use of it should they wish.

Beyond the uncredited synthesizer contribution, the soaring lead guitar break at the 1:42 mark – where Jim's vocal temporarily falls away and the drums reduce to a heartbeat-like pulse – remains another of the album's great musical high points. Indeed, 'Something's Wrong' could easily have served as the perfect closing track to *Psychocandy* were it not for the final song still awaiting the listener.

'It's So Hard' (2:37)

The only track on *Psychocandy* to feature William on lead vocals, 'It's So Hard' is built around a cyclical bass-guitar pattern that persists throughout its two-and-a-half-minute duration and originated as another standout from the band's 1983 demo tapes, where it appeared under the working title 'Tall Walk' – itself a subtle subversion of the familiar idiom suggesting an individual should feel pride and confidence in both themselves and their actions.

On the final *Psychocandy* recording, however – constructed by the Reids alone at Southern Studios with neither Bobby Gillespie nor Douglas Hart present – this sentiment is transformed into something far darker: the difficulty of finding love while remaining true to one's beliefs and artistic identity, resisting the constant temptation to surrender and conform.

The nihilism of the track – its pessimistic lyrics reflecting the struggle to remain true to yourself while retaining the ability 'to walk and not to crawl' – is punctuated throughout by layers of white noise drifting across the mechanical drum-machine backing.

The track concludes with the repeated mantra 'Be in black/be in black' – later extracted and printed on the album's inner sleeve – while howling feedback gradually fades into silence, bringing *Psychocandy* to a fittingly dark conclusion and reinforcing once again the 'psycho' element at the heart of The Jesus and Mary Chain's sound at the true beginning of their recording career.

Contemporary Tracks

There were three additional songs recorded at Southern Studios during the *Psychocandy* sessions that ultimately failed to make the final album release in November 1985. At one stage, the projected running order of the LP would likely have included all three tracks, with lyrical extracts from each printed on the album's inner picture sleeve.

The outtakes would not remain unheard for long, however. Two songs were selected as B-sides for the 'Just Like Honey' single release in October, only weeks before the debut album finally appeared in shops, while the title track itself initially surfaced on 1986's 'Some Candy Talking' before later being included on the comprehensive *Barbed Wire Kisses* compilation in 1988 alongside a range of non-album Mary Chain material spanning from the incendiary 1984 debut single 'Upside Down' through to 1988's standalone release 'Sidewalking'.

'Cracked' (3:46)

Time has not been especially kind to this track, which now resembles less a fully realised Mary Chain composition than a late-hours sonic experiment captured during an increasingly delirious studio session. Most notable is the fact that its rhythmic backbone effectively repurposes that of 'The Living End', with the drums and bass dramatically slowed to a heavy trudge and submerged beneath layers of reverb.

Of particular interest, however, is William's guitar break at the 1:12 mark, introduced through a piercing metallic shriek. The passage feels strangely incongruous – almost as though a glam-rock riff from the early 1970s had briefly wandered into the recording to provide melodic relief before gradually becoming consumed once again by the surrounding chaos as Jim's increasingly unhinged vocal overwhelms the mix.

With repeated shouts of 'fuck!' dominating the final two minutes, this is The Jesus and Mary Chain at their most confrontational and uncompromising. While sonically closer than perhaps any other studio recording to the overwhelming ferocity of the band's live performances during this period, 'Cracked' – much like the notorious 'Jesus Fuck', which caused pressing delays for the 'You Trip Me Up' single release – would likely have struggled to sustain repeated listens on an album already populated by songs that were both structurally stronger and considerably more compelling sonically.

'Head' (3:50)

In sharp contrast to its companion B-side on the double-pack 7" release of 'Just Like Honey', this is a superb track and one that must surely have made its eventual omission from *Psychocandy* an especially difficult decision.

Its subsequent inclusion first on 1988's *Barbed Wire Kisses* compilation and later as the closing track on the first disc of 2010's *Upside Down: The Best Of The Jesus and Mary Chain* strongly suggests that the Reids themselves retained considerable affection for the song long after this formative phase of the band's career had passed.

Driven throughout by a relentless metronomic drum pattern and featuring an impassioned lead vocal from William, 'Head' – originally titled 'Walk Away' during the Southern recording sessions – initially keeps its expected layers of feedback and abrasive guitar textures surprisingly restrained by Mary Chain standards. Menacing rather than overwhelming, the noise remains largely submerged beneath the mix during the early stages of the track.

The principal fuzz-guitar line first emerges at the 30-second mark, carrying the counterpoint melody through much of the song before matters gradually begin to deteriorate during the final chaotic minute. Clanging and shrieking guitars first punctuate the arrangement in brief violent bursts before eventually burying William's closing vocal beneath a disorientating blizzard of white noise.

And as a curious aside, for a band whose supposedly sacrilegious name attracted endless attention – despite there being little genuine intent behind it beyond the gradual word-association progression from Daisy Chain to Mary Chain to The Jesus and Mary Chain – 'Head' contains one of the very few explicit references to religious imagery anywhere in the group's early catalogue, with William singing: 'a man on your cross/cold empty cross'.

A fascinating counterpoint to the sweetness of 'Just Like Honey', 'Head' feels entirely deserving of a place on *Psychocandy* itself. It certainly matches the quality of the album's more overtly 'psycho' moments, though the greater difficulty would surely have been deciding which existing track might reasonably have been sacrificed to accommodate it.

'Psychocandy' (2:54)

First aired during the October 1985 Peel Session in a shortened version lasting little more than two minutes and featuring Jim on lead vocals, the studio recording of *Psychocandy* extends almost a full minute longer – primarily due to its elongated outro section. William handles the majority of the lead vocals until Jim gradually joins him at the two-minute mark before eventually assuming lead duties himself, the song then ending abruptly with the echoed pitch-drop refrain of 'psycho'.

This beautiful ballad – another casualty of the necessary cull required to maintain *Psychocandy* as a 14-track album – finally received a full release during July 1986 as part of the *Some Candy Talking* EP, the release that would ultimately provide the band with their first significant UK chart breakthrough.

The track is notable for its distinctly gentler sonic palette, with far less emphasis placed upon feedback and cavernous reverb than elsewhere across its parent album, instead bearing a closer resemblance to the softer moments scattered throughout *Psychocandy*. Attention should also be drawn to several of the lyrics, which appear to allude rather transparently to romantic and sexual relationships through phrases such as: 'She'll take you down and make you eat her fish/her poisoned fish is on your dish'.

Any momentary distraction caused by the song's suggestive imagery is quickly overshadowed, however, by the beauty of the guitar work and the repeated closing refrain shared between William and Jim. Jim's vocal first enters around the 90-second mark before remaining prominent within the mix as the song steadily builds towards its sudden climax, during which the phrase 'She's my psychocandy' can be heard faintly repeated three times in the background before the recording abruptly cuts to silence.

Perhaps on an earlier sequenced version of their debut album, this is how the Reid brothers had once intended *Psychocandy* itself to conclude, though the song's notably different treatment of guitars, reverb and vocals may ultimately have rendered it too stylistically distinct from the remainder of the LP for inclusion.

The following three tracks are not entirely representative of the Mary Chain's 1985-86 output by the band's own later admission, but were nevertheless issued as B-sides across their first two Blanco y Negro Records releases and therefore merit inclusion here as an addendum to the *Psychocandy* era contemporary recordings.

'Suck' (2:07)

Included as the B-side to both the 7" and 12" releases of 'Never Understand' during early spring 1985 and recorded during the same sessions split between Alaska and Southern Studios, 'Suck' remains an intriguing hybrid of studio experiment and fully formed song.

Its shuddering, reverberating guitar clangs, feedback loops patched in and out of the mix and primitive drum-machine rhythm are suddenly joined midway through by an improbably catchy 'bah-bah-bah' pop chorus introduced with almost absurd ease. That these seemingly incompatible elements mesh together as successfully as they do remains impressive in retrospect.

Yet the song barely has time to fully establish itself before the skeletal drum pattern abruptly halts at the 1:48 mark, with only the dub-referencing delay effect applied to the lead guitar extending the track beyond the two-minute point.

Overlooked for inclusion on 1988's *Barbed Wire Kisses (B-sides And More)* compilation, the band's own enthusiasm for the song appears to have diminished rapidly following its release. Given the sheer volume of considerably stronger material being produced by The Jesus and Mary Chain during the remainder of 1985, such neglect is hardly surprising.

'Suck' was never performed live by the group, further reinforcing the sense that its role remained firmly rooted as a fascinating studio curio rather than a fully realised addition to the band's developing catalogue. It would not reappear officially until the 2008 retrospective box set *The Power Of Negative Thinking*, which gathered together the vast majority of the Mary Chain's B-sides released up to that point in their career.

'Ambition' (3:31)

Another carefully selected Mary Chain cover version regularly played from the band's earliest gigs through to the spring of 1985, 'Ambition' was originally released as a single on Rough Trade Records during 1978 by the Subway Sect fronted by Vic Godard. When asked by Chris Bohn – writing under his Biba Kopf pseudonym – during a mid-February 1985 interview why the band had decided to formally record their own version of the song, Jim responded with typical bluntness:

> We thought 'Ambition' was something that could have been done better.

He arguably had a point. The Mary Chain version – in addition to adding a liberal sprinkling of 'fuck' to the chorus – bears far greater resemblance in spirit and arrangement to the lesser-known Subway Sect album-session recording of the track, still largely unheard at that point during the mid-1980s, than to the more familiar 1978 single version itself. Most notably, the Reids dispense entirely with the prominent organ motif that had originally mirrored the rhythm-guitar line throughout the song.

Rather than functioning merely as a straightforward post-punk tribute, the Mary Chain recording instead emerges as a spirited reinterpretation that reshapes the original into something far more abrasive and confrontational while retaining the melodic backbone that had first attracted the band to the composition.

Omitted from the otherwise impressively comprehensive *Barbed Wire Kisses* compilation, 'Ambition' eventually resurfaced on the first disc of *The Power Of Negative Thinking* before later appearing on the 2011 deluxe edition of *Psychocandy*. It was subsequently included once again several years later on the Record Store Day-exclusive compilation *45s > 84 > 85 <*, released during 2025 and collecting together the band's formative singles and B-sides from the 1984-85 period.

'Boyfriend's Dead' (1:43)

One of the shortest tracks released by the *Psychocandy*-era Mary Chain – alongside the considerably stronger 'Taste Of Cindy' – 'Boyfriend's Dead' was only rarely performed live, with the notable exception of the group's debut New York performances at Danceteria during early April 1985 on their first visit to the United States.

The studio recording, originating from the Mary Chain's first session at Southern on 30 March, begins with a brief fragment of Jim speaking before playback properly commences. This small glitch is difficult to imagine the otherwise meticulous band failing to notice and was therefore almost certainly left in deliberately.

Built around a buzzing lead-guitar motif played against whining feedback textures noticeably less intense than those utilised throughout much of *Psychocandy*, the song is perhaps most memorable for its unusually busy drumming, which sits prominently within the mix and appears to make use of a fuller kit arrangement than the minimal bass-tom-and-snare approach generally preferred by the band during this period.

The live version of 'Boyfriend's Dead' performed during the group's first American shows featured similarly muscular drumming from Bobby Gillespie, and it is arguably within this live environment that the song proved most effective. Surviving bootleg recordings reveal a considerably more forceful and dynamic performance than the comparatively thin studio version later issued as a 12" B-side to 'You Trip Me Up' during May 1985.

Like both 'Suck' and 'Ambition', the track later received archival reissue treatment across subsequent retrospective collections, though 'Boyfriend's Dead' ultimately remains a comparatively minor entry within the extraordinarily rich body of material produced by The Jesus and Mary Chain during the *Psychocandy* era.

Some Candy Talking EP (1986)

Personnel:
Jim Reid: vocals, guitar
William Reid: guitar, vocals
Recorded at Trident Studios, St Anne's Court, London, between 14 and 20 April 1986
Producers: William and Jim Reid
Engineer: Flood, Alan Moulder (both 'Some Candy Talking'), John Loder ('Taste Of Cindy', 'Psychocandy', 'Hit')
Label: Blanco y Negro
Charts: UK: 13, NZ: 37, Ireland: 11
Running time: 9:38

'Some Candy Talking' (3:18)
First making its appearance as part of the legendary acoustic Peel Session recorded on 29 October 1985, 'Some Candy Talking' became the band's first UK top 40 hit single. The version released in July 1986 had been polished considerably from the stripped-back take debuted at Maida Vale, although the basic structure of the song remained close to a rough demo version shared with *NME* readers at the beginning of February as part of a 'Big 4' 7" EP giveaway.

Described in *Never Understood* by Jim as 'the big leftover from the *Psychocandy* era', this skilful merging of two separate songs – sounding at times like an inspired collision between The Shangri-Las and The Velvet Underground – marked a significant advancement for The Jesus and Mary Chain, and not simply in terms of helping establish them as a bona fide charting band following a series of frustrating near misses.

After three Warners singles had each failed to crack the all-important top 40, both William and Jim Reid were increasingly aware of the expectation to follow the overwhelmingly positive response to their debut album – one that had stunned critics and left many scrambling for adequate superlatives – with genuine commercial success. It was all well and good that their Blanco y Negro singles had featured so prominently in the *NME* Singles of the Year 1985 listings, with 'Never Understand' and 'Just Like Honey' taking the top two positions ahead of competition from the likes of Kate Bush, The Smiths, The Pogues and Nick Cave, not to mention that they had been similarly celebrated by John Peel with an identical top-two placing in his own Festive Fifty. However, such acclaim had not translated into the UK pop charts – the true litmus test for a band whose ambitions stretched far beyond the indie circuit. This situation rankled the group and did not go unnoticed at their record company.

'Some Candy Talking' was recorded in a new environment for The Jesus and Mary Chain, who, by this point, were effectively operating as Jim and William working together in the studio. Situated down a Soho alleyway between Dean

Street and Wardour Street, Trident Studios had been the site of numerous iconic recordings by David Bowie, Queen and Lou Reed during the 1970s, while even The Beatles had utilised its then-revolutionary eight-track facilities a few years earlier during sessions for *The Beatles*. At the helm for the recording of 'Some Candy Talking' was Flood, tasked with helping Jim and William capture a sound capable of achieving the desired crossover into radio playlists and the charts. This now seemed imperative to the band's longevity and, if successful, would in turn buy the brothers valuable breathing space before commencing work on the follow-up to *Psychocandy*.

Familiar with Flood's engineering work on recent recordings by Nick Cave and the Bad Seeds, in addition to his previous involvement with New Order's 1981 debut album, the Mary Chain found his youthful enthusiasm – ably assisted by a similarly keen and up-and-coming engineering assistant by the name of Alan Moulder – a welcome contrast to many of their previous studio experiences, with the notable exception of Southern Studios alongside John Loder. However, both Jim and William recognised that repeating the exact sonic formula of their earlier Wood Green-recorded singles could no longer be risked following a run of diminishing commercial returns. Consequently, the recording of the all-important new single was painstakingly completed from the 14th to the 20th April within the unfamiliar surroundings of Trident.

An amusing anecdote from the resulting sessions – one that perhaps also speaks volumes about the pressure the Mary Chain were beginning to feel while recording far from the relative familiarity of Southern – concerned the difficulty of successfully recording the bass guitar part for 'Some Candy Talking'. Discussed with comic incredulity in the May 1992 issue of *Select* magazine and later recounted in their 2024 memoir, Jim and William recalled how band members, Trident staff and even hired session musicians alike proved unable to nail what remains, to this day, a reasonably straightforward bassline. The situation was eventually rescued by Biff Bang Pow bassist – and, at the time, Alan McGee's right-hand man at Creation Records – Dick Green, who quickly mastered the part to the relief of everyone present. Green's timely intervention and subsequent recording credit remained one of the few occasions for several years in which a musician other than Jim or William Reid contributed to a Jesus and Mary Chain studio recording following the collapse of the original *Psychocandy*-era lineup of Jim, William, Douglas and Bobby.

Accompanied by a promo video once again directed by Tim Broad, new recruit John Moore was featured gamely playing along in the background to what was, in reality, a drum-machine track using the standard tom-tom and snare setup favoured by his predecessor. However, the visual presentation for 'Some Candy Talking' deviated somewhat from the previously established 'band looking glum while miming' formula. This was achieved primarily through the incorporation of jump-cut images of both William and Jim walking through an idyllic countryside setting alongside their respective girlfriends, Rona and

Laurence, during the closing moments of the song, with the footage having been filmed the day after the in-studio band performance. The care taken over the promotion of their forthcoming single was further evidenced by the four days spent editing the resulting video from 2-6 July, with the promo completed to the band's satisfaction the following day. Professionally presented and carefully recorded, The Jesus and Mary Chain now appeared poised to take the next significant step in their career and chart success for the new single – supported by Warners once again employing a multiple-format release strategy of 7", 12" and double 7" pack editions – seemed assured.

Initial music-press response was broadly enthusiastic, with relatively few critics dwelling upon the absence of the feedback previously regarded as synonymous with The Jesus and Mary Chain. Such criticism was somewhat short-sighted, considering how different the preceding single, 'Just Like Honey', had already sounded in comparison to the abrasive records that preceded it and indeed much of *Psychocandy* itself. One particularly positive review from the British music papers described 'Some Candy Talking' as 'another addictive love song, its droll opening giving way to a rush of emotion and sparkling melody.'

The band appeared on the cover of *NME* at the beginning of July 1986, where interviewer Mat Snow drew direct attention to selected lyrics from the forthcoming single and its accompanying B-sides, challenging the Mary Chain with the observation that there seemed to be a recurring theme at work, 'the concept, of course, being drugs.' The band immediately rejected the suggestion, with William even arguing that the word 'candy' sounded 'more sexual than drugs'. Nevertheless, it seems likely that this interview marked the point at which controversy surrounding the lyrical content of 'Some Candy Talking' first began to gather momentum.

Further protestations from the band followed, most notably during a news bulletin broadcast on BBC Radio 1 in which both William and Jim vehemently denied any connection whatsoever between their new single and drugs, instead appearing to point the finger at one individual who had interpreted the lyrics otherwise. The bulletin was immediately followed by Gary Davies' Top 40 Chart Show playing the single, which had the distinction of being that week's highest new entry.

With positive reviews secured and initial radio airplay in place, The Jesus and Mary Chain's fourth single entered the UK Singles Chart at number 20 on Sunday 20 July 1986, before climbing to number 13 the following weekend. It appeared as though the band were now perfectly positioned for a long-anticipated appearance on *Top Of The Pops*, effectively rubber-stamping their status as a genuinely popular group with mass appeal, while a top ten placing for 'Some Candy Talking' seemed increasingly inevitable.

However, it was at roughly this point that Radio 1 Breakfast Show DJ Mike Smith, after discussions with producers Chris Lycett and Sue Foster, removed the track from his daily playlist, with others at the BBC soon following suit.

Deprived of the daytime airplay required to sustain its upward trajectory, 'Some Candy Talking' slipped back to number 20 the following week, fell to number 35 the week after that and exited the UK top 50 altogether on Sunday 17 August.

Mike Smith was understandably keen to avoid repeating the notoriety attached to his predecessor's earlier 'ban' of 'Relax' by Frankie Goes to Hollywood, which, despite being removed from BBC radio and television playlists, had spectacularly backfired and instead propelled the Liverpool group towards enormous commercial success, including a five-week stay at number one. The reasoning given for the removal of 'Some Candy Talking' from Radio 1 playlists was that the song supposedly contained references to heroin, with 'candy' allegedly serving as slang for the narcotic.

Swallowing their disappointment while simultaneously sensing an opportunity to capitalise upon the controversy in a manner similar to the way ZTT had skilfully manipulated the Frankie situation, the Mary Chain sought clarification that their top 20 single had indeed been 'banned' by Radio 1. Such confirmation – and particularly use of the specific term 'ban' – was never forthcoming; the track would simply no longer receive daytime airplay and, with that, 'Some Candy Talking' quickly disappeared from the charts.

In retrospect, it is ironic that the same song had already debuted as part of a BBC-funded Peel Session during October 1985, meaning that the corporation itself had effectively financed the recording of music that would become so contentious the following summer. More amusing still, the lyrics – while nowhere near as overtly sexual as those of 'Relax' – contain their own less-than-subtle innuendo within the context of a superb dual-structured track driven by a motorik rhythm reminiscent of prime Velvet Underground and featuring a scathing lead-guitar break that, when performed live, frequently took on the ferocious quality of a visceral Einstürzende Neubauten-style sonic assault, as demonstrated by the band's 2015 Barrowlands rendition.

The first CD issue of *Psychocandy*, released in August 1986, included the recently issued 'Some Candy Talking', sequenced directly after 'Taste Of Cindy', which had previously closed side one of the album so effectively. This inclusion long remained a point of contention among fans protective of the original album's structure, a sentiment ultimately reflected 20 years later when the 2006 remastered reissue restored the original running order by omitting 'Some Candy Talking' altogether. In hindsight, this felt like the correct decision, as the single more appropriately represented the beginning of the *Darklands* era rather than a continuation of what had come before.

'Some Candy Talking' also became the first Mary Chain song to appear on a film soundtrack, featuring as the closing track on side B of *Modern Girls – The Original Motion Picture Soundtrack* (1986). Included alongside artists such as Depeche Mode, Toni Basil and Icehouse, the song plays in full during a scene set within a stylised mid-1980s American goth nightclub.

As a minor point of interest in what ultimately proved to be a box-office flop with only limited US release, 'Some Candy Talking' appears at the 34:08

mark of the film and continues until 37:48. Eagle-eyed fans may notice a discrepancy in runtime, as the track is rather clumsily looped backwards in order to extend its duration and accommodate the scene while the characters discuss their suitably clichéd predicament in keeping with the film's vaguely comedic teen-movie aesthetic. It is difficult to imagine William and Jim Reid being especially pleased with such tinkering. However, since *Modern Girls* never received a meaningful British cinema release and the version included on the US-only soundtrack album remained the correctly timed single mix, the alteration may well have passed unnoticed by the band.

'Taste Of Cindy' (2:00)
A gentle acoustic version of the classic song, this was later issued on the *Barbed Wire Kisses – B-sides And More* (1988) compilation. Placed directly after 'Upside Down' in the running order of side B, its inclusion made for quite the contrast in styles, moving from sonic mayhem to hushed beauty within the space of just a few minutes. Running almost 20 seconds longer than the version that featured on *Psychocandy*, this tranquil take features a particularly impressive vocal from Jim, which helps bring out the sadness within the lyrics, something perhaps partially obscured by the dense noise of the album recording.

'Psychocandy' (2:54)
See previous chapter: 'Psychocandy (1985) – Contemporary Tracks'.

'Hit' (3:29)
Beginning with a slow-paced, primitive drum beat from the soon-to-depart Bobby Gillespie and set against a backdrop of fuzz guitar, Jim's vocals are delivered in a hitherto seldom-used deep register, adding to the ominous atmosphere of this extremely powerful Mary Chain track. At the 2:09 mark, the song's dynamics intensify with swathes of fuzz guitar mixed in, especially notable at 2:50 as the noise grows in intensity alongside Jim's repeated refrain of 'Hey, hey, hey', a melodic fallback the band frequently employed when further lyrics were deemed unnecessary.

Seconds later, the drums come to an abrupt halt, dropping out of the track completely. Jim then issues a blunt instruction for the song to 'Stop' – something that happened rather often during the group's frequently chaotic live performances of the time – and after a final two bars of fuzz guitar from William, 'Hit' duly obeys, ending amidst fading howls of feedback as the cavernous darkness of the track slowly recedes.

Contemporary Tracks

'Walk And Crawl' (2:24)
First included on the 2008 B-sides and rarities box set *The Power Of Negative Thinking*, before later appearing as part of the 'Outtakes' section on the

expansive *Darklands* deluxe CD/DVD reissue in 2011, 'Walk And Crawl' remains an interesting leftover from the full-band *Psychocandy* era, with the key components of reverb and layers of fuzzy noise present and correct alongside an irresistibly poppy lead guitar hook.

William and Jim would subsequently return to the track and develop it further into the later-issued 'Everything's Alright When You're Down'. With notable similarities in both melody and structure, and with the newly written lyrics fitting perfectly over the earlier framework of 'Walk And Crawl', the original song's potential was ultimately realised through what became an arguably stronger track and an excellent B-side in its own right.

Darklands (1987)

Personnel:
Jim Reid: vocals, guitar
William Reid: guitar, vocals
Recorded at Southern Studios, Wood Green and Wessex Studios, North London, between January and July 1987
Producer: William Reid with Bill Price (1, 3, 4, 6, 8, 9), John Loder (5, 7, 10)
Engineer: Tony Harris (2)
Label: Blanco y Negro
Charts: UK: 5, NZ: 20, Holland: 64, Sweden: 38, Switzerland: 23, US: 161
Running time: 35:51

Keen disappointment was felt by the band at the failure of 'Some Candy Talking' to breach the UK top ten and, of course, at the frustrating reason behind its premature exit from the charts. However, the initial success of the single at least confirmed that The Jesus and Mary Chain were a genuine chart prospect and, in its aftermath, provided William and Jim Reid with an opportunity for some much-needed respite after what had been an incredible first two years for the group. It could also be argued that the success of the more restrained single – especially in comparison to the bulk of the tracks on *Psychocandy* from the tail end of the previous year – helped pave the way for audiences to be more receptive to the forthcoming sound of *Darklands*.

Before then, however, there was the small matter of a parting of ways with their manager, Alan McGee – something he later admitted he had been expecting at the time of his dismissal. This took place in mid-August, just as 'Some Candy Talking' left the charts, leaving the Mary Chain without direct representation until the appointment of Chris Morrison in early 1987. Having previously managed Thin Lizzy and Ultravox, and consequently developed considerable industry experience and contacts, Morrison's arrival allowed The Jesus and Mary Chain to concentrate fully on completing the recording of their sophomore effort.

At the recommendation of Rob Dickins at Warner Records, perhaps as a means of gently guiding the band away from the unique sound perfected on their debut album, The Jesus and Mary Chain embarked upon sessions at Wessex Sound Studios in Highbury New Park, North London, working with chief engineer and studio manager Bill Price. His work with punk legends The Clash and Sex Pistols on classic albums recorded at Wessex during the late 1970s was certainly familiar to Jim and William, and his considerable expertise made him a highly suitable collaborator. Price was open to the band's desire to use programmed drums rather than a live drummer on their next batch of songs, and a trial session during the second week of March to test the viability of working together led to the successful production of the single 'April Skies', released to considerable chart success in the same month as its title. Five additional album tracks were produced during the band's time at Wessex, while another key song from *Darklands*, the brooding 'Deep One Perfect Morning', was remixed there after originally being recorded at Livingston Studios with engineer Tony Harris assisting the band.

Despite broadening their experience through recording at a range of renowned London studios since the beginning of the previous year, The Jesus and Mary Chain were still keen to utilise the now-familiar environment of Southern Studios, and three songs from *Darklands* were completed in Wood Green, with John Loder co-producing alongside William Reid.

It was through two BBC sessions – one for Janice Long, recorded on 23 November 1986 and broadcast a few weeks later on 8 December, and the other for John Peel, recorded on 25 November and broadcast on 5 January the following year – that fans gained an early insight into the band's new direction. These sessions effectively broke a self-imposed press silence maintained since 'Some Candy Talking' had left the charts, dispelling rumours circulating in the music press that the band had called it a day – an outcome some critics had even actively encouraged in the wake of *Psychocandy*. After all, how could they possibly improve upon it?

The answer, of course, lay in a further development of the band's sound, placing greater emphasis on the songwriting that had always lain at the heart of The Jesus and Mary Chain, something that, upon reflection, had been overlooked by many reviewers at the time of *Psychocandy*, where critical response seemed equally divided between astonishment at and obsession with the album's overwhelming sonic template. This, the band determined, would not be the case with the material recorded for *Darklands*.

Stripped down to a ten-song album and with an even greater emphasis on melody and emotion than before, *Darklands* was exactly that: moody, atmospheric and, on some tracks, haunting in its stark melancholy. And yet there are also undeniably classic rock songs within its track listing, not least the two hit singles 'April Skies' and 'Happy When It Rains'. Largely free of feedback and driven by focused guitar hooks, the enduring quality of these tracks helped propel the band into mainstream chart success and has stood the test of time ever since.

With feedback now kept to a minimum, *Darklands* offered a more melodic and smoother listening experience, and it was this accessibility that helped The Jesus and Mary Chain find renewed favour with record company pluggers, Radio 1 producers and reviewers alike. It is somewhat ironic that some critics used the Reids' deliberate decision to reduce what had previously been regarded as a barrier to appreciating their songwriting as a reason to find fault with what was, in truth, a masterful step forward in terms of songcraft.

Regardless of such minor gripes from an increasingly fickle music press, *Darklands* has remained a firm fan favourite – from former band members Hart and Gillespie to the legions of Mary Chain devotees – over the four decades since its initial release on 31 August 1987.

'Darklands' (5:27)

The title track of The Jesus and Mary Chain's second album is one of several songs produced by William Reid alongside Bill Price and features the former on lead vocals in a track that immediately establishes an atmosphere of introversion and sadness. The song made its debut towards the close of the previous year as part of a Janice Long Radio 1 session broadcast on 8 December 1986, having been recorded at Maida Vale a few weeks earlier on 23 November alongside two other works-in-progress that would also feature on the eventual *Darklands* album.

This mid-paced track is notable for being one of several nods to past iconic songs over the course of the Mary Chain's second album, and, whether intentional or not, this was certainly picked up on by contemporary reviewers upon original release. In this instance, the vocal delivery during the opening verse bears a striking similarity to David Bowie's '"Heroes"' – also, coincidentally, the title track from his 1977 album – with parts of the phrasing sounding almost note-for-note in places.

Both brothers were very aware early on of the song's potential, and 'Darklands', as the album's title track, consequently received considerable focus from the group. So much so that, following a brief stint at Livingston Studios from 12-14 January, the song was demoed again a fortnight later with Tears for Fears producers Chris Hughes and Ian Stanley at Hughes's home studio in Bath during a four-day session. Things did not go especially to plan for the latter party, however, with the Mary Chain spurning the opportunity to allow the track to be embellished with an overly busy slap bass part supplied by Curt Smith – invited down to the session by the producers – and then, even more galling, a double bass overdub. According to both *Never Understood* and interview sleeve notes for the 2011 deluxe reissue of the album, Hughes and Stanley spent an inordinate amount of time recording these additions overnight, much to the Reids' incredulity. Such embellishments were simply redundant since it was clear to both William and Jim that the deceptively direct simplicity of the track was precisely where its power lay, a quality that became fully apparent once recording of the track resumed at Wessex on 13 April.

The promo video for the single – notably not edited down from its full running time of close to five and a half minutes, a further indication that The Jesus and Mary Chain were unwilling to compromise when it came to their final product – was directed by Peter 'Pinko' Fowler, later to co-create *SNUB TV* but at the time a cameraman regularly filming live gigs and promotional clips for Rough Trade Records artists. Under the band's instruction, Fowler produced a video featuring a combination of William miming to the song in the studio alongside a montage of atmospheric performance footage and abstract imagery, perfectly suited to the mood of the track itself.

An additional version of the song, featuring intermittent string overdubs throughout its runtime, was included on the deluxe release of *Darklands,* but this take (with the strings recorded at Wessex on 23 June) ultimately serves only as a curio for fans since the original simply cannot be improved upon. Setting the tone perfectly for the album, the title track substitutes the *Psychocandy* era emphasis on carefully recorded layers of noise for vocal harmonies and chiming guitars with no less impact. Although its release in late October 1987 as the third and final single from the album failed to achieve major chart success beyond three weeks, hovering around the lower reaches of the UK top 40 – number 33 being its highest placing – there can be little doubt that 'Darklands' set a standard of quality that the remainder of the album would consistently match.

'Deep One Perfect Morning' (2:43)

The second track to make its debut as part of the December 1986 Janice Long Radio 1 session, 'Deep One Perfect Morning' is the first song on *Darklands* to feature Jim on lead vocals, beginning at the very lowest end of his register, and neatly echoes Kris Kristofferson's 'Loving Her Was Easier (Than Anything I'll Ever Do Again)', a song discovered by William Reid by chance late one evening while listening to the radio at home.

Beyond being another example of the band's increasing emphasis on emotional restraint, 'Deep One Perfect Morning' possesses a distinct brooding quality alongside its near 'Mary Chain unplugged' sound, something reinforced by lyrical references to preferring to 'better paint my hate on the walls' and 'picking at the pieces of a world that keeps turning the screws in my mind'. It is also notable for being the only track on the album recorded outside either Wessex Sound Studios or Southern Studios.

The Reids first worked with engineer Tony Harris on this song, along with an early attempt at 'Darklands', at Livingston Studios in North London on 12 January 1987, as they began sessions for a new album, before taking the multi-tracks to Wessex for further development alongside Bill Price. This richly textured, downbeat and mid-paced song is perfectly placed as the second track on *Darklands*, building upon the mood initially established by the title track while further developing the introspective nature of the album. Furthermore, the easy-listening feel of 'Deep One Perfect Morning', sonically speaking, perfectly illustrated The Jesus and Mary Chain's determined effort to push melodies and lyrics to the forefront on their second album.

'Happy When It Rains' (3:34)

One of the three single releases from *Darklands*, this classic The Jesus and Mary Chain track is powered throughout by a Linn LM-1 drum machine, which utilised samples of real drum hits that the Reids were then able to programme into the specific rhythmic patterns required. This would become somewhat problematic in later years in terms of live drummers being able to faithfully reproduce the track's deceptively challenging rhythms. However, regardless of the relative complexity of its machine-driven backing – especially in stark contrast to the opening two songs on the album – it is the soaring main guitar riff and upbeat vocal delivery that so clearly elevate 'Happy When It Rains' and, in turn, *Darklands* as a whole, immediately impressing listeners through the sheer melodic strength of the song's construction.

For a record that unashamedly echoes such legendary artists as The Velvet Underground, The Rolling Stones and The Beach Boys in its refrains – and such is the quality of the Mary Chain's songwriting that these elements only enhance rather than overpower what William and Jim Reid had written – it is notable that the most obvious 'borrow' on the entire *Darklands* album is actually from themselves. The key riff and main chord changes from 'Something's Wrong', the penultimate track on *Psychocandy*, are recycled to powerful effect on 'Happy When It Rains'.

The song deviates from its 1985 counterpart, however, through the manner in which it ties one of the album's most uplifting melodies to a novel variation on the traditional love song, although several of the lyrics also seem to nod back towards the band's early years and, in particular, their meteoric rise from new-town obscurity during 1983 to chart fame – and subsequent infamy – by the middle of 1986: 'And we tried so hard/And we looked so good/And we lived our lives in black...'

This notion is reinforced in the promo video for 'Happy When It Rains', where the band – with John Moore once again on mimed-to-the-drum-machine duties – are accompanied by a stack of portable televisions displaying excerpts from the full range of Mary Chain promo clips released up to that point, from 'Never Understand' through to 'April Skies'. With additional footage projected onto a screen behind close-up shots of Jim and William, the John Maybury-directed promo, filmed on 17 July, a fortnight after the single had been cut at The Townhouse, fittingly captures the nostalgic and self-referential qualities of the track amidst roaming tracking shots, moody close-ups and flickering lights characteristic of the de rigueur 1980s pop-video aesthetic. Following the tradition established by a brief flash image from the 'Just Like Honey' promo providing the cover image for *Psychocandy*, a blurred still from the 'Happy When It Rains' video shoot subsequently supplied the front cover artwork for *Darklands*, complete with a floor-mounted rotating light unit resembling glowing embers scattered around the feet of William and Jim.

Issued at the beginning of August during the lead-up to the album's release later that same month, 'Happy When It Rains' breached the UK top 30 – eventually reaching number 25 – which, considering how irresistibly catchy the song was, should perhaps have been a given. However, following a closing of ranks from BBC producers in the aftermath of the group's one and only performance of 'April Skies', the Mary Chain were once again denied the opportunity to promote their latest single through an appearance on what remained the flagship British chart music programme of the era. Instead, The Jesus and Mary Chain somewhat grudgingly delivered a lacklustre performance – albeit one not especially dissimilar to that accompanying 'April Skies' on *Top Of The Pops* – on the short-lived ITV chart show *The Roxy*. This inevitably managed to ruffle the feathers of another set of producers, however, because a few months later, when it came time for a return to *The Roxy* in order to promote the third and final *Darklands* single, the band were abruptly dropped from the show's schedule and requested to leave the premises immediately following a low-key camera and lighting rehearsal. A spokesperson for the programme, later identified in an *NME* news article from 7 November as producer Alistair Pirrie, complained that:

> They didn't give any performance at all. On a scale of one to ten, they didn't register.

A perfect gateway track into an album containing several slower and more sombre songs, 'Happy When It Rains' is, by contrast, buoyant, melodic and positively uplifting. A demo version of the song, featuring William on lead vocals, formed the basis of the recording sessions from 21-24 April and was initially available only on the 10" EP release of the single. Later appearing on the 2011 deluxe reissue of the sophomore album, this early version remains a fascinating listen, not least because it is a slower take and considerably closer in mood to the more downbeat material elsewhere on *Darklands*. It ultimately took the combination of Bill Price's experience alongside valuable studio time at Wessex for this future Mary Chain classic to evolve into the iconic recording that remains so beloved to this day.

'Down On Me' (2:35)

The shortest track on *Darklands* follows the upbeat pace and atmosphere established immediately beforehand by 'Happy When It Rains' and was the third and final song to receive its premiere during the December 1986 Janice Long Radio 1 session. Marking a further step away from the defined *Psychocandy* era sound of The Jesus and Mary Chain, 'Down On Me' nevertheless leaves one wondering how the track might have sounded had it received the same treatment at Southern Studios during the summer of 1985. Featuring a fantastic early-1960s surf-music-inspired guitar break at the 0:46 mark, the song remains a genuine gem that is often unfairly overlooked simply because of the sheer weight of competition surrounding it on *Darklands*.

Despite the world-weariness of lines such as 'Twenty five years of growing old/it just hangs in front of me' and 'Sometimes in the Summer sunshine/the sky falls down on me' – two key excerpts that reinforce an emotional thread running throughout the album as a whole – in terms of melody and vocal delivery, 'Down On Me' nonetheless remains one of the most upbeat and positive songs on *Darklands*.

The track also contains the sole instance of non-Reid musical input anywhere on the album, namely the ringing power chord that closes the song at the 2:50 mark, reportedly delivered with considerable enthusiasm by the band's original drummer – and by then temporary second guitarist – John Moore, following his direct request to William Reid that he be allowed to contribute something, however small, to a Mary Chain studio recording.

'Nine Million Rainy Days' (4:28)

The second of three songs on the album sung by William Reid, 'Nine Million Rainy Days' closes the first side of the original LP in gloriously dark and brooding fashion, albeit enlivened by familiar backing vocals entering just beyond the halfway point and continuing through to the close. Although some critics found fault with the track's deliberate pace and gloomy torpor – perhaps heightened by its placement immediately after two of the album's most upbeat moments – 'Nine Million Rainy Days' remains a powerful near-ballad of self-obsession, with William's emotionally weary vocal performance standing out in particular.

The song slowly unwinds across its four-and-a-half-minute runtime and, while moody and haunting from beginning to end, nonetheless manages the unique trick of never becoming oppressive or overly depressing. Instead, 'Nine Million Rainy Days', moving at its own languid pace, provides a strangely sympathetic backdrop for the listener – not darkening the mood further but instead offering a curious form of solace.

An undeniably claustrophobic and haunting piece, both William and Jim were fully aware of just how heavy and intense the song sounded while working on it at Southern Studios and consequently opted to lighten the atmosphere ever so slightly through the addition of another distinctive layer: a backing vocal nod to the voodoo-style outro of The Rolling Stones' legendary descent into darkness, 'Sympathy For The Devil'. That virtually every contemporary review of the album identified what had merely been intended as a playful homage to the Stones at their imperious best as a shamefaced lift – despite the Mary Chain backing vocals not being entirely identical – suggests that the joke had perhaps backfired somewhat.

Over the decades since the album's original release, however, it is precisely this clever addition to the track – alongside William's almost country-inflected lead guitar lines drifting through the mix during the closing minutes – that has made 'Nine Million Rainy Days' all the more memorable for fans.

Interestingly, an almost two-minute extract from the song was used prominently in the background of a scene from an episode of the hugely popular US crime series *Miami Vice* entitled 'God's Work'. First broadcast on 6 November 1987 during the programme's fourth season, suddenly hearing the familiar sound of the Mary Chain on primetime American television may well have come as a pleasant surprise for fans idly watching that same evening.

'April Skies' (4:01)

Debuted during a one-off gig at the Kilburn National Ballroom on 15 July 1986, this definitive The Jesus and Mary Chain track originated even earlier that same year, as revealed through an endearing anecdote shared by William Reid during an online interview in 2024. Reid recalled how the song began while he was idly imitating prime 1950s Elvis Presley on acoustic guitar in the kitchen of his Stoke Newington flat. His girlfriend paused to remark on how good his playing sounded and encouraged him to record it before the idea slipped away. From those light-hearted and low-key beginnings emerged the most successful Jesus and Mary Chain single in the UK, a firm fan favourite and one of the defining tracks on *Darklands*.

The first major result of the band's recording sessions with Bill Price at Wessex Sound Studios from 9-15 March, 'April Skies' begins with a heavily rhythmic, almost percussive guitar figure that drives the song from verse to verse alongside Jim's bassline, which keeps almost entirely to root notes while providing unwavering support for the melody. The 1950s-inspired backing guitar – think Chuck Berry or Eddie Cochran – is turbocharged by the production work of Bill Price and William Reid into something closer in spirit to a slower-paced 'God Save The Queen', another legendary Price production from almost a decade earlier. Meanwhile, the 25-second guitar solo entering at the 1:01 mark is absolutely note-perfect: concise, melodic and entirely free of anything unnecessarily flashy that might upset the balance of the song.

A tremendous pop record destined to become an enduring staple of indie club nights and alternative playlists for decades to come, 'April Skies' demonstrated that while The Jesus and Mary Chain had toned down some of the more abrasive elements that made *Psychocandy* such a daunting prospect for casual listeners, they had lost none of their identity in the process. Their reward for doing so was sustained radio airplay for a single that was simply too strong to ignore, aided considerably by a well-supported multi-format release from Warner Records, who had clearly recognised the track's crossover potential.

An immediate top 20 entry upon release, 'April Skies' breached the UK top ten on Sunday 5 May 1987, prompting the producers of *Top Of The Pops* to finally relent and invite the band onto the BBC's flagship chart programme. On the day of recording, however, a self-conscious and visibly uncomfortable group whiled away the long hours between rehearsals and make-up by steadily drinking in an attempt to calm nerves and help ease themselves into an environment they clearly regarded with suspicion. Consequently, when the show aired at peak viewing time on Thursday evening – introduced shortly after 7 pm by the typically overexcited pairing of Steve Wright and Peter Powell – viewers were greeted by the sight of an unmistakably inebriated Mary Chain, with Jim in particular ignoring carefully planned camera cues to the growing irritation of the programme's production staff.

'April Skies' remained in the top ten for a further week after dropping two places, but the band were never invited back for a repeat performance, leaving this sole appearance as a fitting accompaniment to their biggest-ever UK chart hit. Fortunately, there still remained the promotional video to aid sales. Edited to match the extended four-minute album version rather than the shorter 7" edit, director Tim Broad filmed the band on 3 April miming to the track in and around a deserted railway station near Hastings. Complemented by wide-angle shots of the group near a seafront industrial site, the promo differed from previous Mary Chain videos through its relative lack of rapid edits and flash frames, yet still underwent painstaking editing over the course of three days, a week after filming. The result was something far closer to the conventional rock-video aesthetic of the era, perhaps helping to explain why 'April Skies' crossed over into the mainstream so successfully.

Another indication of the single's growing impact came through its inclusion on the hugely popular *HITS 6* compilation during summer 1987, the chief commercial rival to the *Now That's What I Call Music!* franchise. Positioned between Echo & the Bunnymen and Marillion at the close of side B, 'April Skies' stood out sharply from much of the era's disposable chart pop. The accompanying video compilation likewise featured the promo, this time sequenced immediately after fellow Scottish chart stars of the period, Wet Wet Wet – an altogether different proposition in terms of mainstream appeal during 1987. This gradual acceptance into commercial music channels continued through appearances on *Hits 7* ('Darklands') and *Hits 8* ('Sidewalking'), while the Mary Chain would eventually achieve inclusion on a *NOW!* compilation through 'Far Gone And Out' some five years later. The widespread popularity of the track over the past four decades has also led to it being licensed for use in a number of notable television series, including The Walking Dead (Season 9, Episode 7, first broadcast in mid-November 2018) and, most recently, at the conclusion of Episode 1 of the 2026 Netflix crime drama Legends.

Finally, no discussion of 'April Skies' would be complete without acknowledgement of its controversial picture sleeve. The iconic image of a crucified figure leaning backwards while pointing a revolver downward is a blurred still taken from the low-budget 1971 American biker film *The Jesus Trip*. It was Douglas Hart who first spotted the cult movie on VHS – its striking Astra Video cover art impossible to miss – while browsing in a central London video shop in search of a large television set for the club night 'Speed', which he was preparing to run at a Charing Cross Road venue. The tape was subsequently passed around the band, and the crucial moment featuring the image – appearing roughly 72 minutes into the film for particularly devoted Mary Chain obsessives – was painstakingly photographed directly from a television screen by Jim Reid. The same footage later appeared amongst the cut-up visual imagery used during the promo for 'Kill Surf City', the 7" B-side accompanying 'April Skies'.

The still image was eventually brought into Warners by the band, who were reportedly advised against using it by a member of the label's in-house marketing department, concerned that members of the public might find it offensive. Wary of another round of moral panic damaging the success of one of their singles, the Reids briefly considered abandoning the design before being persuaded otherwise by Rob Dickins, who immediately recognised the value of such a provocative and memorable image appearing amongst the ranks of bland pop sleeves in record shops across the country. The fact that the band continued using the image as a stage backdrop as late as their Lollapalooza performances during summer 1992 suggests that they were ultimately right to stick to their guns.

'Fall' (2:26)

One of the darkest tracks on *Darklands*, 'Fall' was first debuted during a John Peel session recorded on 25 November 1986 and subsequently broadcast on Radio 1 on 5 January the following year, before receiving three further repeat airings over the course of the next few months. The Peel version was initially released on a six-track mini-album in 1991 before later appearing as part of the more comprehensive *The Complete John Peel Sessions* collection issued by Strange Fruit Records in 2000.

The second of three *Darklands* songs recorded at Southern Studios during the second week of June, with John Loder assisting with production and engineering duties alongside 'Nine Million Rainy Days' and 'On The Wall', 'Fall' is a downbeat and deeply nihilistic piece. It functions almost as a companion to 'It's So Hard' from *Psychocandy*, sharing both a cyclical structure and an unrelentingly gloomy emotional tone throughout its two-and-a-half-minute runtime.

There is, however, a noticeably busier drum-machine pattern underpinning the song when compared with the 1985 album closer, while the initially rather odd line 'I'm as dead as a Christmas tree' gradually reveals itself to be strangely appropriate within the context of the track's exhausted emotional landscape. Perhaps somewhat overlooked at the time of the album's original release, and despite its undeniably morose atmosphere, 'Fall' remains a highly effective piece that more than earns its place on *Darklands*, not least through the sustained mood it establishes – drawing the listener steadily inward and refusing to let go.

'Cherry Came Too' (3:03)

A reported point of irritation for The Jesus and Mary Chain following the release of *Darklands* was the music press fixation with identifying reference points to the past within the grooves of the album, from the Springsteen-esque title to echoes of The Rolling Stones, The Velvet Underground and – in the case of 'Cherry Came Too' – The Beach Boys. William Reid was keen to address such criticism in a subsequent interview when he pointed out the rather obvious and somewhat inevitable connection:

> I think that there are tons of songs that sound like bits of other songs, but that's basically because ours are all based around classic chords: A–D–B, E–D–A. They're obviously classic. Sonny and Cher's 'I Got You Babe', Phil Spector stuff, The Beach Boys – they're all based around those chords. That's classic pop.

In truth, 'Cherry Came Too', recorded at Wessex alongside 'April Skies' from 9-15 March, is an upbeat and undeniably catchy pop song that further enhances its lightness by incorporating a brief vocal melody strongly reminiscent of 'Do It Again', with Jim singing 'Oh Cherry honey/got me stuck on a rope' almost perfectly in sync with the earlier Beach Boys hit. William then subtly echoes the same melodic phrasing through a lead guitar break that enters at the 1:48 mark. And, as elsewhere on the album, when accusations of musical plagiarism were levelled at the Mary Chain, the very element critics were so eager to identify and condemn as shameless pilfering instead further elevates the quality of the song rather than diminishing it.

That The Jesus and Mary Chain were able to integrate such a clear musical nod to the past so seamlessly into one of the most immediately appealing tracks on *Darklands* should really have been regarded as a strength and indeed offers an insight into something the band were rarely given sufficient credit for at the time: their deep understanding of classic pop construction. Besides, it is hardly as though the Reids were attempting to conceal the reference – after all, it is difficult to imagine a more obvious homage than borrowing directly from a number one hit by one of the biggest bands of the 1960s.

'On The Wall' (5:03)

Introduced by the ticking hi-hat sample of the band's carefully selected drum machine – an inflexible and relentless backing that not only rigidly maintains the pace of the song but also subtly evokes the passing of time itself – the *Darklands* version of 'On The Wall' is a radical reworking of the original 1983 bedroom demo painstakingly constructed by William Reid on Portastudio alongside its companion piece from the same period, 'Up Too High'.

Having reportedly earned an enthusiastic response from Rob Dickins when first played to him at the Warners offices early in the band's tenure with the label, 'On The Wall' somehow failed to make it into the *Psychocandy* recording sessions. Jim later attributed this omission simply to the band forgetting about the song at the time, which, considering the intense focus surrounding the material eventually selected for their debut album, is perhaps understandable. The omission ultimately proved fortuitous because, once revisited and radically reworked in both pace and atmosphere, the track emerged perfectly suited to its eventual placement as the penultimate song on *Darklands*.

With its ticking drum-machine backing and repeated lyrical references to 'the clock on the wall', the song unfolds slowly and deliberately, enveloped in an atmosphere of sadness and weary resignation. Alongside 'Nine Million Rainy Days', which closes the first side of the original LP so powerfully, 'On The Wall' occupies an emotional space largely separate from the remainder of the album, remarkable in just how solemn and deeply moving it manages to sound. Yet, once again, like its companion piece on the opposite side of the original vinyl release, the track somehow avoids dragging the listener fully into the same state of lethargy and emotional exhaustion that William appears to be communicating.

To take a home demo that originally sounded considerably different – not exactly upbeat, perhaps, but certainly faster-paced and driven by busy drum patterns alongside bright, chiming guitar parts – and transform it into such a powerful mood-defining centrepiece of *Darklands* stands as testament to the songwriting and arranging talents of the Mary Chain. 'On The Wall' in its 1987 incarnation is not merely a successful reinterpretation of the earlier demo but arguably the definitive version of the song itself.

'About You' (2:31)

Darklands closes with a tender ballad built around a gently strummed descending chord sequence of A-Amaj7-D and the barest trace of background percussion, where, despite lyrical references to people dying 'in their living rooms' and an all-enveloping 'God almighty gloom', the song ultimately finds solace in the warmth of human companionship as protection against the misery and endless rain of everyday life.

Titled 'In The Rain' when it debuted during a John Peel session broadcast on 5 January 1987, the track was subsequently reworked with John Loder and renamed for inclusion on *Darklands*. The album's consistent emphasis on bringing melody and emotional directness to the foreground reaches perhaps its purest expression here. When legendary 1960s British singer Sandie Shaw and her management were searching for suitable material for her 1988 Rough Trade Records album *Hello Angel*, it was this particular Reid composition that stood out strongly enough to be selected for inclusion. Its original working title, dating back to lyrics written in early June 1985, was reinstated as 'Cool About You' before the song was recorded for the finished LP.

The second Jesus and Mary Chain album may conclude on a weary and rain-soaked note, but 'About You' remains an undeniably affectionate and ultimately hopeful song. It works perfectly as a low-key closing track to *Darklands* – understated perhaps in comparison to several of the album's more immediate highlights, yet no less powerful for the restraint and tenderness with which it quietly brings the record to an end.

Contemporary Tracks

'Kill Surf City' (3:12)

Beginning with a sampled soundtrack excerpt of a motorbike revving into life, 'Kill Surf City' provided casual listeners, diehards and newly converted fans alike – as the B-side to the top ten hit 'April Skies' – with a gleefully destructive reimagining of Jan and Dean's surf-pop classic 'Surf City', a song that had spent two weeks at number one on the *Billboard* Hot 100 during July 1963 while proving a rather more modest number 26 hit in the UK. Given its status as the first surf-music track to top the American charts – and with Brian Wilson as principal songwriter – the song was perhaps ripe for a suitably modern tribute by 1987 or, more fittingly in the case of The Jesus and Mary Chain, a full-scale reinterpretation.

With a fuzz-bass track prominent throughout the mix alongside clattering drum-machine backing, 'Kill Surf City', recorded during the B-side sessions at Southern from 16-19 March, finds the Mary Chain very clearly enjoying themselves in the studio. This is especially apparent as William lists an escalating series of ways in which the mythical Surf City is about to be levelled to the ground. And one suspects there are few examples in the surf-music genre of the immortal line: 'Some evil cunt's gonna get my gun'.

This gleeful act of desecration is delivered with an infectious sense of mischief, the band revelling in the opportunity to unleash blasts of distortion and film samples throughout the song. The replacement of the original lyric 'I love baby/and she loves me' with the pointed inversion 'I hate honey/and she hates me' is another clever subversion of the sunny innocence traditionally associated with surf music and its idealised vision of perpetual good times. By the closing moments of the track, there is even the sense that William is increasingly ad-libbing lines as the song spirals towards collapse, the drum machine eventually grinding to a halt amidst one final eruption of noise.

'Kill Surf City' also enjoys the rare distinction of having an accompanying promotional video directed by Jim Reid himself, one of two 'band-made' films included on the group's 1988 Warner Bros. Records video compilation. Sequenced immediately after 'April Skies', the promo perfectly mirrors the chaotic and joyous mayhem of the song itself through a barrage of rapid-fire editing, flash frames and carefully chosen imagery. Featuring a montage of Super 8 footage shot by Douglas Hart, Jim and William, alongside rooftop footage of William miming to the song in London, the video is further enhanced by the already-notorious 'Jesus Trip' imagery spliced together with excerpts from a National Rifle Association advert, the Stars and Stripes repeatedly punctured by bullet holes. The finished collage is completed by fractured zoom shots of the Mary Chain performing on a beach, filmed during what appears to have been the group's spring 1986 American tour.

'Bo Diddley Is Jesus' (3:17)

Introduced by what initially resembles a fire alarm alongside a playful nod to the opening moments of The Sweet's glam-rock classic 'Blockbuster', the shuffling groove of 'Bo Diddley Is Jesus' – in other words, the unmistakable Bo Diddley beat itself – is given the Mary Chain treatment in a song whose title leaves little ambiguity regarding the band's reverence for the legendary Bo Diddley.

Accompanied by sporadic metallic clangs used as additional percussion alongside the obligatory drum-machine backing, the song is another example of the band funnelling some of their more experimental impulses into the relative freedom afforded by a B-side, again cutting loose at Southern Studios during a three-day mid-March recording session under the encouraging guidance of John Loder. Jim's vocal delivery is perfectly suited to the syncopated Diddley rhythm and William faithfully follows the groove until the 2:35 mark when a blast of white noise tears through the mix, cueing up a 20-second freeform guitar assault before the track crashes back into the central rhythm one final time with renewed force.

While more than an appropriate tribute to one of rock 'n' roll's true originators, it is also interesting to hear the band briefly returning to the closing lyric of 'It's So Hard' from *Psychocandy* when Jim repeats: 'Head to toe and I'm dressed in black'. Employing classic rock 'n' roll outlaw imagery entirely without irony, 'Bo Diddley Is Jesus' remains a hugely enjoyable track.

And as for the mysterious alarm sound that opens the song before returning again two minutes later? According to William, in a 1988 interview with *Guitar Magazine*, the effect originated from what he described as a surf pedal 'designed by a maniac', notable for containing two particularly distinctive settings: one capable of generating overwhelming sheets of white noise and the other producing what he memorably described as 'a sound like a fire alarm. Do it onstage and you get people running out of the fire exit.'

'Who Do You Love' (4:05)

Appearing on the 12" of 'April Skies', the Mary Chain's next cover version, recorded during a three-day session at Southern from 16-19 March specifically to provide B-sides for the forthcoming single, strips away the trademark Bo Diddley beat and instead drags 'Who Do You Love' into a grinding, oppressively slow crawl. While the lyrics of the 1956 original were already steeped in darkness – full of skulls, tombstones, graveyards and chilling screams in the night – much of their menace was partially obscured by the quick pace and swaggering shuffle rhythm of Diddley's version. The same certainly cannot be said for this reinterpretation, where every line is delivered with careful enunciation so that disturbing lyrics such as 'Just twenty-two and I don't mind dying' land with full force.

Driven by Jim's measured vocal delivery alongside fuzz bass and a relentlessly hissing hi-hat drum-machine backing, 'Who Do You Love' radiates menace from beginning to end as the song inches forward at an almost funereal pace. William's lead guitar is deployed sparingly throughout, the band wisely recognising that overloading the arrangement would only weaken the suffocating atmosphere they had created. This is far less a conventional cover version than a complete reinvention of a rock 'n' roll standard.

The Mary Chain themselves argued at the time that there was little point attempting a straightforward version of a song already so definitive unless they radically transformed it, and that is precisely what they achieve here, to astonishing effect. The mixture of self-absorption, nihilistic bravado and unsettling hoodoo imagery woven throughout the lyric almost seems tailor-made for The Jesus and Mary Chain's worldview. Such is the scale of its transformation from the original that the band's 'Who Do You Love' effectively becomes an entirely different and uniquely unsettling record in its own right, standing comfortably amongst the finest cover versions they ever committed to tape.

'Everything's Alright When You're Down' (2:39)

Released as the 7" B-side to 'Happy When It Rains' during August 1987 and amusingly sneaking another expletive onto the flipside of a top 40 hit following William's sweary threat on 'Kill Surf City', 'Everything's Alright When You're Down' is a gloriously melodic and infectious Mary Chain track that illustrates why the band, after a handful of relatively slight early B-sides, became increasingly determined that their supplementary material would match the quality of their A-sides, even if it was perhaps less immediately commercial.

Roaring rhythm guitars propel the track forward from beginning to end while the chorus carries what is surely a deliberate melodic resemblance to The Monkees' 1967 song 'You Just May Be The One', particularly when Jim sings: 'I ... just can't take it/I ... don't you say it'. By the closing moments, Jim is reduced to yelling and howling almost wordlessly – strongly reminiscent of the gloriously unhinged climax of 'Never Understand' – while a counterpoint sweet melody unfolds beneath ringing and screeching guitar lines from William.

The result is one of the standout tracks from the band's entire B-side catalogue and a compelling argument for 'Everything's Alright When You're Down' ranking amongst the very best songs The Jesus and Mary Chain recorded during the *Darklands* era.

'Shake' (2:01)

The Mary Chain play the blues – or at least their own brilliantly deranged approximation of it. And anyone still claiming that the Reid brothers lacked a sense of humour need only listen to 'Shake's final 20 seconds, which collapse into gleeful chaos before ending with the unmistakable sound of either Jim or William's girlfriend laughing at the unfolding antics inside the recording booth.

Initially available only on the 10" EP and limited-edition boxed-set versions of 'Happy When It Rains', the track was co-produced by John Loder, who once again provided the band with the freedom to experiment away from the greater expectations attached to the main album sessions. With more than a hint of improvisation running throughout the recording, 'Shake' is particularly notable for the ease with which William handles the blues-inspired lead guitar passages during the opening minute before the song abruptly degenerates into a ranting mess of groaning feedback, frantic acoustic strumming and escalating absurdity.

At just over two minutes long, 'Shake' is hardly a major artistic statement, yet it remains highly memorable precisely because of how unguarded and spontaneous it sounds. More than anything else, the track offers another reminder that beneath the carefully cultivated cool and confrontational exterior, The Jesus and Mary Chain were often having far more fun than many critics of the period seemed willing to acknowledge.

'Happy Place' (2:21)

Incredibly catchy from its stomping Bay City Rollers-esque opening onwards, 'Happy Place' was debuted as the third and final track during a John Peel session recorded on 25 November 1986 before being broadcast five weeks later on 5 January, followed by a further three repeat airings over the months that followed. William handles lead vocal duties on both the Peel Session and the final studio version of the track, recorded in the basement of Matrix Studios in central London on 4 May, which initially appeared as the 12" B-side of 'Happy When It Rains' in August 1987 before later resurfacing on the following year's *Barbed Wire Kisses* compilation.

The phrase 'escapist pop' suits this particular Mary Chain song perfectly, and the fact that it evokes the immediate appeal of groups such as the Bay City Rollers – the type of music William himself would have encountered during his teens in the mid-1970s – only strengthens its emotional pull. Beneath the bright melodic surface, however, the lyric is concerned with the deeply personal idea of retreating into a mental refuge: a place from the past that can be revisited for comfort, safety and emotional shelter.

In that respect, 'Happy Place' shares thematic similarities with 'My Little Underground' from only a few years earlier. Both songs convey a longing for escape while simultaneously finding solace in memory and private fantasy, with the central metaphor of the 'happy place' functioning less as a literal destination than as an emotional state of security and reassurance. It is surely no coincidence that William frequently admitted in interviews from this period how little enjoyment he derived from the repetitive grind of touring, often remarking that he was happiest either alone in a hotel room or, better still, back in the familiar surroundings of his London flat.

The lyrics also contain a passing reference to Cherry – presumably the same figure from 'Cherry Came Too' – when William pleads for a return to 'the start of it all' before asking her to save, touch and hold him. Yet while there is unmistakable desperation running through these lines, it is ultimately overshadowed by the sadness of the closing admission: 'I live my life for something I can't see', followed immediately by the beautifully wistful final lyric, itself faintly echoing the idyllic escapism of The Beatles' 'Strawberry Fields Forever': 'Let me take you in my Summer dream'.

'F. Hole' (1:07)
A brief fragment of what appears to have been a sonic experiment conducted during a rain-soaked day in Wood Green, 'F. Hole' reportedly originated when John Loder encouraged the band to capture the sound of rainfall outside Southern Studios through the strategic placement of a microphone before layering the resulting field recording with sheets of feedbacking guitar noise – a miniature 'Metal Machine Music', if you will – fading into silence just beyond the one-minute mark.

Originally appearing on the 12" release of 'Happy When It Rains' before later resurfacing at the conclusion of the vinyl edition of *Barbed Wire Kisses* immediately after 'On The Wall' (Portastudio Demo) as an effectively hidden track – omitted from the sleeve listing yet identified on the vinyl label itself – 'F. Hole' remains one of the more curious artefacts within the Mary Chain catalogue. More than anything else, the track prompts speculation regarding what other similarly experimental recordings may have emerged during rare moments of downtime in the studio while the band and Loder indulged their more abstract impulses away from the pressure of album sessions and single releases.

'Surfin' USA' (2:58)
Following the demented destruction of 'Kill Surf City' and the bass-heavy, slow-motion reconstruction of 'Who Do You Love', the Mary Chain next turned their attention towards The Beach Boys' 'Surfin' USA', transforming the Brian Wilson/Chuck Berry hybrid into a jagged and gleefully abrasive romp. While Jim remains broadly faithful to the original lyric throughout, the song is delivered in a conspicuously Americanised vocal accent which, by 1987, had become an oddly persistent point of fascination for sections of the British music press.

Responding to this rather absurd line of questioning during a 1987 interview with *Melody Maker*, Jim pointed out that neither he nor William sang in pronounced Scottish accents simply because it 'wouldn't sound right', further noting that most singers similarly avoided performing in their natural speaking voices. Steering the discussion toward the idea that vocal delivery itself is always, to some extent, performative, Jim jokingly concluded that if such regional authenticity were taken to its logical extreme, then The Jesus and Mary Chain would end up 'singing like The Proclaimers' – ironically, another pair of Scottish brothers named Reid who were themselves becoming increasingly familiar faces within the UK charts during the same period.

Issued as a B-side on the 12" release of 'Darklands' in September 1987 – and also included on the limited-edition 7" gatefold EP – the Mary Chain's version of 'Surfin' USA' carried the subtitle 'April Out-Take', hinting that the song may originally have been attempted during the same sessions that produced 'April Skies'. This does, however, raise an interesting question regarding John Loder's involvement, given that 'April Skies' itself was recorded at Wessex Sound Studios with Bill Price rather than at Southern Studios.

Whatever its precise recording origins, The Jesus and Mary Chain elevate 'Surfin' USA' several levels beyond the original 'Sweet Little Sixteen' rewrite through a combination of fractured production touches, bursts of broken-glass samples and some wonderfully trebly lead-guitar work from William. The track eventually collapses into a closing section featuring the increasingly impassioned voice of an American preacher rising prominently through the mix during the final 30 seconds alongside chaotic freeform guitar noise before the song fades back into the same shattered-glass sample that introduced it, concluding with the oddly fitting line: 'In the mighty name of Jesus, thank God'.

The song later appeared on the following year's *Barbed Wire Kisses* compilation and received a further polish through a slightly extended 'Summer Mix' issued in the United States and Australia during 1988 to coincide with the band's touring commitments. And naturally, the accompanying B-side just had to be 'Kill Surf City'.

'Rider' (2:12)

Appearing across every format of the 'Darklands' single released during October 1987, 'Rider' continued the classic rock 'n' roll biker romanticism previously explored on 'The Living End', another example of the band's well-documented fascination with rebellious Americana and doomed cool. This time, however, rather than centring upon a self-destructive anti-hero meeting an inevitable downfall, 'Rider' presents a more affectionate and straightforward homage to the mythology of 1950s rock 'n' roll culture, complete with references to beaches, motorcycles and a lyric-free chorus carrying an unmistakable doo-wop inflection.

Sung by William – whose voice occasionally strains at the upper reaches of the melody in a manner that actually enhances the vulnerability of the performance – the song initially unfolds at a brisk pace before slowing almost to a complete standstill around the 90-second mark, only to rev back into motion one final time for a slower and more measured closing passage. Structurally simple yet highly effective, 'Rider' succeeds largely because of its warmth and sincerity.

Although charming on record, the song arguably achieved its greatest impact in a live setting where, with Jim assuming lead vocal duties, 'Rider' became a frequent set opener throughout the band's touring between 1988 and 1990 or, at the very least, an early fixture within their performances. In that environment, its rock 'n' roll pulse and romantic imagery proved especially effective at immediately drawing audiences into the world of The Jesus and Mary Chain.

'Here It Comes Again' (2:32)

Released on both the 10" EP and CD single editions of 'Darklands', 'Here It Comes Again' stands as one of the clearest transitional recordings between the *Darklands* and *Automatic* eras, effectively functioning as an early blueprint for the sequenced and rhythm-driven direction the band would pursue far more successfully on their third album.

Particularly notable is the emphasis placed upon sequenced bass patterns, synthesizers and an even more pronounced reliance on programmed drum-machine rhythms. During a mid-1987 interview, Jim Reid somewhat vaguely described the song as a 'dance-synth thing' the band had attempted in the studio before retreating back towards more familiar territory stylistically. His brother, characteristically more direct, simply dismissed the track as 'crap.'

And while it is difficult to deny that 'Here It Comes Again' ranks amongst the weaker recordings released by the Mary Chain during 1987, the song nevertheless remains fascinating precisely because of its willingness to experiment. More than almost any other track from the period, it reveals the growing attraction that contemporary studio technology and sequenced arrangements held for William and Jim Reid, a band just as likely by this stage to cite Suicide or Kraftwerk as influences as they were The Rolling Stones or The Stooges.

If nothing else, 'Here It Comes Again' deserves recognition as an intriguing work in progress – one whose experimental instincts would be refined to striking effect on the superb 'Sidewalking' single the following year.

'Don't Ever Change' (3:35)

Bittersweet, beautiful and infused with a distinctly country-influenced melancholy filtered through the Mary Chain's sensibility, 'Don't Ever Change' is comfortably the stronger of the two *Darklands* outtakes included on the *Barbed Wire Kisses* compilation. With Jim delivering a vocal performance strongly evocative of Johnny Cash, the song unfolds as a tender and understated ballad that must surely have received serious consideration for inclusion on the final running order of *Darklands,* although the version included on *Barbed Wire Kisses* was not recorded at Southern until January 18-19, with a further day's work on the track completed a week later.

Built around acoustic guitars and a softly ticking drum machine rhythm, the arrangement leaves ample room for William's beautifully restrained lead-guitar work, which, notably, resists any temptation toward feedback or excessive distortion. Credit for this cleaner and more spacious sound belongs not only to the band themselves but also to producer Bill Price, whose strengths were openly acknowledged by the Reids during a 1988 interview with *International Musician* magazine:

> Bill's really good at recording a certain type of guitar sound. Not really so much the manic stuff, the feedback stuff, but the kind of Gretsch Country guitar, that's brilliant.

Another particularly memorable aspect of 'Don't Ever Change' is the interplay between Jim and William's vocals. The latter first emerges prominently around the 90-second mark, singing the title refrain before gradually taking over the remainder of the track while Jim recedes into backing harmonies, all beneath a series of inspired guitar flourishes drifting softly through the mix.

It remains unclear precisely how late into the recording process 'Don't Ever Change' survived before ultimately being omitted from *Darklands,* or indeed whether it was ever genuinely close to inclusion at all. Nevertheless, the quality of the song unquestionably warranted release at the earliest possible opportunity, and its eventual appearance on *Barbed Wire Kisses* revealed it to be one of the great hidden gems within the Mary Chain catalogue.

Sidewalking (1988)

Personnel:
Jim Reid: vocals, guitar
William Reid: guitar, vocals
Recorded at Southern Studios, Wood Green, London, between 27 and 31 January 1988
Producers: William and Jim Reid
Engineer: John Loder
Label: Blanco y Negro
Charts: UK: 30, NZ: 23, Ireland: 20

'Sidewalking' (3:34)

A song idea that William Reid brought into the studio to develop further in late January 1988, 'Sidewalking' quickly took shape over the course of just five days at Southern, with recording taking place from the 27th to the 28th before the track was diligently mixed over the final three days of the month. Working in a relaxed environment and under less pressure, given that the track was intended as a non-album recording, the Mary Chain were able to experiment more freely, something Jim later likened to the atmosphere surrounding their earliest studio work:

> It reminds me of the naïve thing that comes across on 'Never Understand' and things like that – a bunch of guys that have just gone into a studio and made a record they didn't really know how to make. There's no reason why it should have that atmosphere, but it seems to have that kinda fun, naïve feeling to it.

The longer the band worked on 'Sidewalking', the more obvious its potential as a single became. Upon playback of the final mix, the Reids realised that the song was simply too strong to be relegated to a compilation release, which had originally been the intention. The fact that its sound represented such a radical departure from the style most fans associated with The Jesus and Mary Chain after the success of *Darklands* only made the prospect of issuing it as a stand-alone single even more appealing. However, the shift in direction was so pronounced that the band were initially worried about how their audience might react, especially so soon after helping propel 'April Skies' into the UK top ten and pushing *Darklands* towards similar chart success. The risk of releasing 'Sidewalking' and alienating listeners through such a dramatic stylistic leap concerned the Reids enough that they even considered issuing it under a different name and possibly with another singer entirely. Ideally, this would have been someone more closely associated with hip-hop who could front the track vocally, thereby distancing it from the group beyond the inevitable Reid/Reid songwriting credits. It took persuasion from Geoff Travis to dissuade the band from pursuing the idea, reminding them just how fantastic the song was and how strongly it deserved to be released as a Mary Chain single. Jim Reid in 1987:

> I'm fed up with all my records. I know everybody's saying it, but I quite like hip-hop. I think somebody can make great music influenced by that music. What I like is the production, the drum machines and all that. You can hear one of those records coming out of huge speakers and it gives you a shiver up the spine.

Increasingly drawn to the fresh and innovative sounds of rap and hip-hop, with their liberal use of rudimentary sampling and heavily amplified drum-machine rhythms, Jim Reid in particular had become vocal in his admiration for the rapidly evolving genre throughout 1987. Name-checking the Def Jam label and artists such as Run-D.M.C., Schoolly D, LL Cool J and Roxanne Shanté in interviews from the period onwards, Jim later revealed that the latter artist's producer, Marley Marl, had even been considered for one-off production duties during the 'Sidewalking' sessions. However, when contacted by Mary Chain manager Chris Morrison and sounded out on the possibility of working with the band, the in-demand producer declined the offer, having apparently never heard of them.

The Reids were already familiar with the genre that was rapidly snowballing in popularity by the mid-to-late 1980s, particularly tracks by Grandmaster Flash and the Furious Five as well as proto-rap pioneers The Last Poets, who featured prominently on the soundtrack to a Mary Chain favourite, Donald Cammell and Nicolas Roeg's late-1960s cult classic *Performance*. Yet the idea of marrying unapologetically upfront hip-hop beats to a song possessing the immediate melodic appeal of prime T. Rex was, at least for the time, almost entirely unexpected from a band who had already been pigeonholed into a particular sound. That narrow perception, rightly or wrongly, was largely dictated by a fixed list of influences which many critics assumed the group had already exhausted on *Darklands*. Further complemented by classic Duane Eddy-style guitar breaks and lyrics evoking the spirit of Eddie Cochran's teenage disaffection – particularly songs such as 'Summertime Blues' and 'Something Else' – The Jesus and Mary Chain succeeded in presenting an original vision that simultaneously acknowledged past greats while suggesting an exciting new future for their own music.

The rhythm backing for 'Sidewalking' came from sampled drums that were looped and carefully integrated into the track. These had been sourced from the 1985 US import compilation album *Def Mix Vol. 1*, released on the Pop Art label and featuring, notably, four of the earliest recordings by Roxanne Shanté at the very beginning of her career. This was especially remarkable given that she was only 14 years old when those tracks were recorded. With the assembled backing slowed down accordingly, the Mary Chain were then able to improvise over the top with guitar riffs and lyrics. Judging by the finished recording – and indeed the speed with which the track was completed – the process appears to have been refreshingly quick and instinctive.

Although typically reluctant to discuss the meaning behind their lyrics, when pressed for some insight into the subject matter of 'Sidewalking' by the fortnightly British pop magazine ***Smash Hits***, Jim Reid conceded that:

> Roughly, it's about a car theft, I suppose. I've never stolen a car in my life … Why not write a song about car thieving; it happens, doesn't it?

Jim remained insistent, however, that the title itself was not intended as slang for car theft, merely something that sounded good and suited the feel of the song. In addition, ridiculous as it may now seem, the band even found themselves having to justify using an obviously American term as both the key lyric and title of the single, something William deftly dismissed by observing that 'Pavement isn't a very rock 'n' roll word.'

'Sidewalking' was released to widespread acclaim in the British music press, with several reviewers considering it the group's finest single since 'Never Understand'. Particular praise was directed towards the grinding bassline that introduces the track, its innovative hip-hop rhythms and the way this inspired reworking of teenage alienation and frustration effectively revitalised the Mary Chain sound while opening up an entirely new creative direction. Even the record sleeve – bright, bold and featuring the band clearly for the first time in a superb Andrew Catlin photograph rather than hidden away in blurry, colour-saturated obscurity – suggested renewed confidence and a bright future. Its subsequent stalling at the comparatively low chart position of number 30 in the UK during early April 1988 still seems a remarkably poor return for such a catchy and contemporary-sounding single.

A strong contender for one of the finest singles in the Mary Chain catalogue, 'Sidewalking' was released across three separate formats – 7", 12" and CD single – and was complemented by two professionally recorded live tracks from a show at Saint Andrew's Hall in Detroit during November the previous year ('Taste Of Cindy' and 'April Skies'). These live tracks were tweaked further at Southern, with the recordings listened back to and elements subtly boosted at key points in the songs from 11-14 January. The full fourteen-song set, recorded on 20 November 1987, was eventually released as part of the Psychocandy deluxe boxed set marking the album's fortieth anniversary, which was issued by Third Man Records in September 2025. The CD version also included two additional takes of the title track. The first, an instrumental subtitled 'Chilled To The Bone', was curiously bass-free, while the extended seven-minute-50-second version of 'Sidewalking' offered listeners an intriguing glimpse into how the original studio experiment may have sounded before the band streamlined it into a concise single. When performed live, the Mary Chain frequently extended the track to a similarly expansive duration, gradually increasing the levels of noise throughout. As recently as the band's 2024 shows supporting their eighth studio album, *Glasgow Eyes*, their approach to performing 'Sidewalking' has remained essentially unchanged and continues to be greeted enthusiastically by audiences worldwide.

The song was revisited during a Peel Session recorded at Maida Vale on 31 May 1988 and first broadcast a fortnight later before being repeated three further times over the course of the year. Meanwhile, the accompanying promo video, directed by John Maybury and filmed on 25 February, remains hugely entertaining in its own right. Beyond the undeniable quality of the song itself – and the fact that Jim is visibly drunk and struggling to remain upright for much of the mimed performance, a battle he eventually loses – the video deliberately exposes the artificial mechanics of the standard late-1980s pop promo. Lights, scaffolding, camera rigs and staging are all left conspicuously visible onscreen, effectively puncturing the illusion of the music-business spectacle the band increasingly distrusted.

Contemporary Tracks

'Just Out Of Reach' (3:06)

The title of a Zombies song featured in Otto Preminger's 1965 film *Bunny Lake Is Missing* – during which the band themselves appear rather incongruously on a television screen performing the track in a London pub scene – 'Just Out Of Reach' inspired the Mary Chain to write their own song sharing the same title, while naturally sounding entirely different. One of the group's earliest home demos, recorded on a Tascam Portastudio during 1983, the track was built around a basic two-note bassline and pounding drum-machine sequence before eventually appearing as the B-side to the 7" release of 'You Trip Me Up' in May 1985, having been recorded during the *Psychocandy* sessions at Southern.

However, this earlier version of 'Just Out Of Reach', recorded at Southern on 11 May, feels comparatively tame by the band's own standards and falls some distance short of the maelstrom of noise the Mary Chain would regularly unleash whenever the song was performed live. It is interesting to note that, just a couple of days after this version of the song was released as the B-side to 'You Trip Me Up', the Mary Chain returned to it to work on a new mix and re-attempt the vocals. This suggests that they remained unsatisfied with 'Just Out Of Reach' as it stood and perhaps even had plans for its inclusion on their forthcoming debut album. Alongside similarly underwhelming early B-sides such as 'Suck' and 'Boyfriend's Dead', this original recording was deemed insufficiently strong for inclusion on *Barbed Wire Kisses*. Yet unlike those other tracks, 'Just Out Of Reach' possessed enough underlying potential that, when presented with the opportunity to revisit it, Jim and William were able to overhaul the song completely. Featuring new guitar overdubs, a far stronger vocal performance from Jim and the complete replacement of Bobby Gillespie's original drum backing with a pounding drum-machine rhythm, the

1988 version expands the track by over a minute and represents a significant improvement upon the original recording.

Alongside the previously discussed 'Kill Surf City', Jim also assembled a homemade promo video for 'Just Out Of Reach'. Again making use of cut-up and unsettling imagery – not overtly violent, but persistently disquieting – the video is filled with scenes that linger in the memory long after the song ends, not least if the viewer initially mistakes a close-up of somebody carving up bacon and eggs for something considerably more sinister. In addition to various frenetic live clips of the band, the video also briefly features Super 8 footage shot in downtown New York during the Mary Chain's first visit to the United States in April 1985, showing William, Jim and Douglas Hart looking, true to reputation, as if they may already be in the middle of an argument.

Further strengthened by the inclusion of the vastly improved 1988 version of 'Just Out Of Reach', *Barbed Wire Kisses* gave The Jesus and Mary Chain a second top ten album within the space of eight months when the compilation reached number eight in the UK Albums Chart upon its release in April 1988. Hugely popular with existing fans who had embraced both *Psychocandy* and *Darklands*, while also attracting more casual listeners thanks in part to the reduced retail price insisted upon by the band themselves, *Barbed Wire Kisses* served as a near-perfect introduction to the world of The Jesus and Mary Chain.

Automatic (1989)

Personnel:
Jim Reid: vocals, guitar, synthesiser, drum programming
William Reid: guitar, vocals, synthesiser, drum programming
Richard Thomas: drums (10)
Recorded at Sam Therapy Studio, West London, between 20 March and 23 May 1989
Mixed at The Church, North London, between 30 May and 12 July 1989
Producers: William and Jim Reid
Engineer: Alan Moulder
Label: Blanco y Negro
Charts: UK: 11, New Zealand: 48, Sweden: 42, Australia: 89, US: 105
Running time: 39:50

After the success of *Darklands* and its accompanying clutch of 7" singles, The Jesus and Mary Chain had reached a point in their relationship with Warners where they had, relatively speaking, proved their value, even if they were never likely to rival the label's genuine global superstars. Energised by the experience of recording 'Sidewalking' with such relative ease – even if the single itself ultimately failed to secure a particularly high chart placing – the band embarked upon sessions for their third album during early spring 1989.

While Southern Studios would continue to be utilised for demo work up until the purchase of the band's own recording base in 1991, the Mary Chain were now searching for a studio where more technologically ambitious recordings could be properly realised, and eventually settled upon the recently opened Sam Therapy, located at 222 Kensal Road on the top floor of Canalot Studios – a collection of rental units situated directly opposite the original location of Paul Samuelson's Southern Studios. The newly built top-floor recording suite, complete with an impressive panoramic view overlooking London, was selected as the ideal base for the band and, following the speedy completion of 'Sidewalking', there was hope that their third album might similarly come together over the course of only a few weeks.

Choosing a producer for the prospective third album, however, proved considerably less straightforward than selecting a recording studio. Following the successful suggestion of outside collaborators that had borne fruit through the band's work with Bill Price on several tracks – including, of course, the top ten single 'April Skies' – the possibility of working with Daniel Lanois was floated. Fresh from the enormous success of co-producing U2's *The Joshua Tree* (1987), which had firmly established the Irish group as one of the defining rock bands of the decade, the prospect of Lanois having a similarly transformative effect on The Jesus and Mary Chain must have seemed tantalising to Warners, and the label were willing to finance the collaboration.

A meeting was duly arranged despite the band's private misgivings regarding Lanois' production pedigree, which, while undeniably impressive in its own right – beyond U2, he had also overseen Peter Gabriel's hugely successful *So* – bore little resemblance to the sound that Jim and William Reid had in mind for the next Mary Chain album. The brothers attempted to explain the more electronic direction they envisaged, complete with sequenced basslines, drum machines and a deliberately synthetic rhythmic feel, but such ideas were seemingly anathema to what Lanois himself proposed. Jim later recalled in interviews that the prospective producer instead appeared to be pitching a far looser scenario where, 'We don't need a studio, maybe we could hire a church, get some spliffs...'

Further 'helpful' suggestions from Warners regarding possible producers met with similarly incompatible results and it quickly became apparent that the Mary Chain's inability to connect creatively with outside candidates, coupled with the difficulty of finding anyone who truly understood their vision for the band's evolving sound, could only lead to one inevitable conclusion. Jim and William would produce the third album themselves, aided by sympathetic engineering support from Alan Moulder, who had previously endeared himself to the band during the *Some Candy Talking* sessions at Trident several years earlier.

In an interview with *Offbeat* magazine at the beginning of 1989, the Mary Chain hinted openly at the musical direction they intended to pursue over the coming year, which, to longtime followers of the band, must have seemed a striking departure from anything they had previously attempted beyond the technological flirtations of 'Sidewalking' and its B-side counterpart 'Here It Comes Again'.

Explaining that the foundations were already firmly in place, William stated that the Mary Chain had...

> ...already got about half the songs and ideas. We're basically trying to figure out how we're going to do this one. Hopefully, we can aspire to do something more rhythmic – and by that, I don't mean disco.

The band's refreshingly open-minded determination to push forward and embrace technology in order to introduce new textures into their music generated a considerable degree of optimism regarding what might be achieved. In addition, basing themselves in a studio specifically designed to accommodate electronic music artists appeared to be the perfect environment for such experimentation.

However, although the original intention had been to complete the album relatively quickly through extensive use of keyboards and rhythm programming, the band soon realised the scale of the challenge they had inadvertently set themselves – not least the ambition of radically reinventing their own sound. William Reid reflected ruefully the following year:

> We weren't going to play any guitars on the album ... it was all going to be electronic, but when we started out, we soon realised how much we were out of our depth.

The recording of *Automatic*, far from becoming the quick and streamlined process initially envisaged, soon developed into a lengthy and often stressful undertaking that stretched across much of the first half of 1989. Yet despite the frustrations and extended hours involved in completing the album, the finished results proved every bit as sonically fresh and musically engaging as anything the Mary Chain had recorded previously. Through persistence, experimentation and a striking degree of creative foresight, Jim and William succeeded in reinventing the band's sound and, in doing so, helped ensure their continued artistic longevity, even if some listeners initially struggled to reconcile the group responsible for *Psychocandy*, 'April Skies' and 'Happy When It Rains' with sequenced basslines, synthesisers, samples and an even more pronounced use of drum machines. Ultimately, the blueprint for *Automatic* had been 'Sidewalking' itself: a perfect fusion of earlier Mary Chain traits with a fresh, contemporary twist that embraced sampling and rhythmic experimentation. Through *Automatic*, the band were moving decisively forward once again.

Automatic failed to match the British chart positions achieved by its predecessor in terms of both album and single sales, stalling just outside the UK top ten at number 11, while the accompanying singles 'Blues From A Gun' (number 32) and 'Head On' (number 57) proved similarly underwhelming commercially. One criticism frequently levelled at the album was that it appeared too enamoured with Americana and it is therefore fitting that the same driving, anthemic songs, which were comparatively overlooked at home, instead made significant inroads across the United States, where the Mary Chain were becoming an increasingly familiar presence on college radio. Heavy MTV rotation for the 'Head On' promo further expanded the band's profile while extensive touring schedules throughout 1989 and into the following decade continued to strengthen their standing in America. However, such relentless touring inevitably extracted a heavy toll upon a band who had never before worked so intensively to promote themselves, all while remaining acutely aware of the opportunities that success in the United States might potentially bring.

America was effectively awakened to The Jesus and Mary Chain through *Automatic* and its associated singles, while the extensive touring that followed helped ensure the band's long-term survival beyond a UK music scene that was becoming increasingly consumed by acid house, dance crossovers and the burgeoning Manchester scene spearheaded by new favourites The Stone Roses and Happy Mondays. The Mary Chain's recent fascination with hip-hop now suddenly seemed somewhat outdated and unfashionable as far as the self-appointed tastemakers of the British music press were concerned, although it remains notable that *Automatic* was only reassessed negatively in retrospect. Whatever accusations might later be made regarding an allegedly dated sound built around sequencers and drum machines, the majority of contemporary reviews upon release were overwhelmingly positive.

During the early autumn of 1989, William Reid reflected ruefully to *Melody Maker* that while the new album...

> ...may sound relaxed … it took seven months to record. It was the hardest work we've ever done in our lives. Everyone tells you it's difficult to make a third album and we discovered it really is.

The enduring reputation of *Automatic* has long since proven that the hard work genuinely paid off.

'Here Comes Alice' (3:52)

The opening track from *Automatic* begins with a classic Mary Chain three-note bassline and accompanying backbeat, with the notable exception that both are now completely machine-driven through a sequenced bassline and drum machine pattern. Previously, Jim would typically play bass guitar in the studio, with Douglas then taking over for live performances, television appearances and promo videos, but 'Here Comes Alice' (subtly altered from its earlier working title, 'Here She Comes') immediately introduces listeners to the more electronic direction that the band had been hinting at in interviews. With vocals from William for the second album opener in a row, the Mary Chain sound confident, upbeat and assured and, in a clear sign of having moved on from the mock outrage fomented in some quarters at the supposed drug references of 'Some Candy Talking', there is little disguising the intent of lyrics such as 'You got the shakes/and it's gonna get worse', 'She's got the hit that takes you into space' and 'make a deal for that taste'.

Instantly accessible from the first listen onwards, behind the scenes, the track had received considerable attention while recording at Sam Therapy, with four days' dedicated work over two separate recording sessions between March and April devoted exclusively to the album opener. Regardless of its lengthy gestation – and it is notable that an entire day (11 May) was then spent recording William's vocals – 'Here Comes Alice' introduces *Automatic* with undeniable swagger, a nonchalant shrug in the direction of critics and an invitation for the initiated to get with the new programme, sort their own fix out (in whatever form that may take) and relax into the swing of things. The gloriously phrased 'cool black Pepsi Coke' appears as the first iconic American reference on the album, with several more to follow.

'Here Comes Alice' was recorded for a late November Peel Session a few months after the release of *Automatic* and then broadcast in mid-December 1989 before being repeated a month later, on 17 January, in a rather stripped-back acoustic version. On this occasion, William seemed to struggle slightly with the key of the song while simultaneously playing guitar. At under three minutes, this notably shorter version of 'Here Comes Alice', as with several previous Mary Chain tracks presented in this format, allows the underlying melodic quality to take centre stage while also hinting at the song's earliest form prior to being fleshed out and further developed in the studio.

'Coast To Coast' (4:13)

A skilful updating of the timeless cars-and-girls theme so prevalent in late-1950s rock 'n' roll, 'Coast To Coast' is a literally driving song: propulsive, fast-paced and sounding almost as if it was deliberately mixed for blasting loudly while cruising down an idealised sun-drenched American highway rather than sitting in an inner-city London gridlock. It could even be considered a streamlined Mary Chain update of The Rolling Stones' own version of 'Route 66', with the chrome-plated polish of the sound elevated several notches further by William's characteristically bold guitar work.

By the time The Jesus and Mary Chain were engaged in the *Automatic* sessions, they had become increasingly adept at weaving electrifying bursts of noise into their music, with loops and samples now even more carefully finessed and strategically placed at precisely the right moment. An abrupt eruption of detonating reverb and feedback during the instrumental break from the 1:43 mark also reminds listeners of the band at their most abrasive just a few years previously. With the song essentially complete by the 3:30 point, 'Coast To Coast' slowly disappears into the distance during its final 40 seconds, fading away on automatic while the key riff repeats and the machine-driven backing pounds relentlessly onwards.

First issued on the 2008 B-sides and rarities compilation *The Power Of Negative Thinking* before appearing a few years later on the 2011 deluxe edition of *Automatic*, an early take of 'Coast To Coast', identified as having been recorded at Southern Studios during January 1988 and featuring William on lead vocals, differs significantly from the completed version lyrically, with very little carried over to the final album recording. Structurally and melodically, however, virtually everything associated with the finished 1989 version is already in place, including the distinctive guitar solos that would later be enhanced further through the addition of keyboards. This track, alongside 'Her Way Of Praying', was the first to be worked on by the band, and the early sessions took place at Mayfair Recording Studios in Primrose Hill between 6 and 10 March, with Alan Moulder assisting. The vocals were completed on 15 May, once the Mary Chain were fully settled into recording at Sam Therapy, while final mixing took place at The Church almost a month later, on both 1 and 11 June.

'Coast To Coast' was also included as part of a four-song Peel Session recorded on 31 May 1988 and broadcast on 13 June before being repeated three more times over the following months. This version is shorter than the album recording by just under a minute and features vocals mixed slightly higher alongside more prominent guitar solo breaks. Another notable point of interest is that the 'Route 66'-influenced namechecking of Texas, Missouri, Detroit and St. Louis present in the Peel Session rendition was omitted from the final version of the track. Perhaps such an inclusion was ultimately considered just a little too obvious for a band who had become increasingly irritated by influence-spotting reviews following the release of *Darklands*.

'Blues From A Gun' (4:44)

A superb blend of elements drawn from the Mary Chain's own recent work alongside several of William's longstanding pop obsessions – mid-1960s Dylan and peak-period T. Rex being the most obvious – 'Blues From A Gun' was selected as the lead-off single from *Automatic* in September 1989. First recorded at Sam Therapy during a two-day session on 27-28 March before being revisited on 16 May, the track was released across four separate formats despite initial resistance from Warners, who felt that a lighter-sounding song, preferably 'Halfway To Crazy', would provide a more suitable comeback single for the band eighteen months on from 'Sidewalking'.

The Reids ultimately prevailed, convinced that 'Blues From A Gun' was the ideal statement to announce that The Jesus and Mary Chain were back and, while the single's chart placing proved even more disappointing than the lowly number 30 achieved by 'Sidewalking', both releases shared the same irresistible arrogance, momentum and contemporary feel.

If 'Sidewalking' had been viewed as a homage to some of Marc Bolan's greatest pop moments – a comparison only really valid in spirit rather than direct sound – then 'Blues From A Gun' comes far closer sonically to the chart-topping incarnation of T. Rex itself. The iconic riff from '20th Century Boy' clearly lingers in the background as an influence, if not quite note-for-note, while the track is further strengthened through carefully layered keyboard overdubs.

Lyrically, there is something effortlessly cool about the way William opens alternate verses with 'I don't care/about the state of my hair' and 'I don't mind/about the state of my mind', while echoes of Dylan's 'Subterranean Homesick Blues' surface through lines such as 'Too young kid/you're gonna get hit'. Yet 'Blues From A Gun' remains a wonderfully crafted and contemporary-sounding track entirely in its own right, one that even allows space for a superb extended coda. At the 3:07 mark, Jim's vocals enter the mix as William temporarily drops out before returning around 30 seconds later to repeat the final line, 'Well I guess that's why I've always got the blues', the brothers then singing together repeatedly until the drum machine abruptly halts and, after a few final guitar strums, the track comes to an end.

As expected of virtually every major-label act by the close of the 1980s, The Jesus and Mary Chain also had an accompanying promo video shot on 8 September for 'Blues From A Gun', this time collaborating with young director Dani Jacobs. Working at Manchester's legendary Hacienda nightclub as a video jockey, Jacobs had been creating projected visuals and lighting effects for the club alongside filming in and around the venue itself. Moving into independent music films, it is one of Jacobs' earliest efforts – the promo for A Guy Called Gerald's acid-house landmark 'Voodoo Ray' – that 'Blues From A Gun' most closely resembles, particularly through its use of a clockwork Bolex 16mm camera, briefly glimpsed in Jim's hands during the video, alongside lo-tech hand-drawn animation inserts throughout the song's runtime, all given a distinctly Mary Chain twist.

Individual lyrics, dollar signs and the soon-to-be ubiquitous star outline associated with the album's promotion and tour merchandise flash across the screen at regular intervals in a manner reminiscent of British experimental filmmaker Jeff Keen, whose work specialised in frenetic visual collages and abstract animated assaults. The pace of the cut-up imagery in the promo for 'Blues From A Gun' is so relentless that several viewings are required before many of its clever details fully register, whether it be William's 'Route 66' T-shirt, Jim filming Douglas shaking his dreadlocked head or stand-in drummer Richard Thomas attacking the stripped-back *Psychocandy*-era two-drum setup with such force that the snare collapses just as the song concludes. Fans may perhaps prefer to overlook the rather incongruous inclusion of a pair of go-go dancers, who seem entirely out of place even within such an intentionally artificial setting.

Regardless of its final chart placing – rarely a reliable indicator of musical quality by the close of the 1980s – 'Blues From A Gun' has long since secured its place amongst the Mary Chain's strongest moments and, like its companion single from the album, 'Head On', has remained a regular highlight of live sets ever since the *Automatic* tour.

'Between Planets' (3:27)

A very catchy and upbeat pop song recorded over the course of three individual sessions at Sam Therapy two months apart before being mixed during two days in early June, 'Between Planets' boasts a killer chorus. If there were ever any lingering doubts that the neurotic tension of the Mary Chain's earlier era had dissipated, then the sound of The Jesus and Mary Chain in such a relaxed and confident mood was ample proof that those days were gone – or, at the very least, temporarily set aside. Wonderfully scuzzy and noisy pop music, 'Between Planets' features superb vocals from Jim while the lyrics seem more attuned than usual to the universal state of teenage angst and the frustration of being driven to distraction by a certain someone, not least through the pleading repetition of the closing lines: 'Baby/you drive me crazy/don't come around here no more'.

Complemented by a note-perfect solo, the song once again demonstrates the Mary Chain wisely favouring an economical guitar break when many of their late-1980s peers may instead have opted for something far more histrionic and painfully obvious.

A fantastic live version of 'Between Planets', more than 30 years on from its original appearance as the fourth track on *Automatic*, can be found on the 2022 release *Sunset 666 – Live At The Hollywood Palladium*. Recorded on 15 December 2018, the performance showcases the touring incarnation of the Mary Chain at that point in time – including powerhouse drummer Brian Young – in blistering form.

'UV Ray' (4:04)

Along with 'Take It', which appears later on the album, 'UV Ray' (given the working title 'SPI' when recorded at Sam Therapy between 14 and 18 April) stands among the most uncompromising and experimental material that the Mary Chain attempted on *Automatic*. It is interesting to note that these were the very tracks Jim identified as 'our version of dance music – two years ago, I wouldn't have seen or known that' during a late-September 1989 interview with the *NME* while promoting the album's release.

While there were critics who regarded *Automatic* as the point in the band's trajectory where The Jesus and Mary Chain took their foot off the pedal artistically – the principal complaint being that the album had been mixed too deliberately for, and commercially aimed towards, American radio airplay – 'UV Ray' alone serves as a complete rebuttal. Lyrics referencing 'Broken down Jesus with the taste for trash', 'TV poison' and 'tear-stained nightmares in the cold light of day' hardly suggest a bid for heavy rotation and that is before the thoroughly uncompromising sound of the track is even considered.

The innovative combination of screeching guitars and chittering, insistent drum-machine patterns – accelerated beyond the often measured pace of hip-hop beats – effectively sketches out a blueprint for the next stage in the band's progression, while the squall of feedback that closes the song would not have sounded remotely out of place on *Honey's Dead* either.

A fair criticism of 'UV Ray' might be that it is not quite as immediately engaging as some of the stronger songs on *Automatic*, yet it still sounds fresh, innovative and remains a fascinating amalgamation of contemporary studio technology, the rapidly evolving dance music scene that the Mary Chain had clearly become receptive to and, of course, classic guitar noise, albeit held somewhat in check until the outro. Perhaps an underrated track, but certainly one worthy of reappraisal.

'Her Way Of Praying' (3:46)

The second half of *Automatic* opens with a cranked-up rhythm guitar intro that immediately recalls the beginning of 'April Skies', which, coincidentally enough, had also occupied the opening slot on side two of *Darklands*. Unlike its 1987 counterpart, however, 'Her Way Of Praying' sounds far more aggressive, with Jim's lead vocals (recorded from 8-9 May at Sam Therapy) – particularly in the way he drawls 'It's her way of talking to Jesus Christ' – delivered to gloriously sneering effect. Layers of guitar tracks also gradually thicken the central riff, lending the song a distinctly T. Rex-inspired glam-rock swagger not unlike that heard earlier on 'Blues From A Gun'. The track was mixed over two days at The Church from 6 to 7 June, while a further remix session took place on 5 July, with the band painstakingly working on the song in order to maximise its impact.

There is also an unapologetically sleazy undercurrent to the lyrics, which perhaps explains why, when a promo video was filmed for the track during early 1990, it was shot amidst the rain-slicked neon of Times Square and 8th Avenue in New York. The touring lineup of the band – now augmented by Ben Lurie on rhythm guitar and Richie Harris on drums – stand expressionless in black leather jackets while a dark-haired model, similarly attired and wielding a Bolex camera, prowls around them filming the lurid surroundings. Another promising young music-video director, Dale Peterson, worked with the Mary Chain as cinematographer on this rarely seen promo, although, ultimately, the track was never formally released and only a relatively small number of promotional CD singles intended for American radio play were produced.

'Head On' (4:11)

Beyond the band's extensive coast-to-coast touring schedule across the United States during 1989 and into 1990 – alongside the inevitable succession of promotional duties involving record company representatives and local radio stations between gigs – it was this soaring track that truly helped *Automatic* take off in America and throughout Europe. This boost in fortunes for the band occurred largely to the exclusion of the UK, where The Jesus and Mary Chain were increasingly suffering ever-diminishing returns for their efforts.

'Head On', in the mould of 'April Skies' before it, is a brilliant song and ranks amongst the finest tracks the band ever recorded, which, given the extraordinarily high standard maintained throughout their career, is saying something indeed. The track is classic Jesus and Mary Chain guitar pop – or, more generically, alternative rock – an inspired fusion of a 1950s-style central riff played between verses, buzzing distorted guitars, a sugar-coated vocal melody and propulsive drum-machine backing. The synth bassline meshes perfectly with the beat, pounding out strict root-note eighths that simultaneously drive and underpin the entire song. It is interesting to note that, over a week before the track was worked on at Sam Therapy, Richard Thomas had recorded live drums during a session on 21 April. However, by the time the band resumed work on the track on 18 May, the drums for 'Head On' had been replaced by the machine patterns that listeners have associated with the song ever since.

It would be fair to claim that 'Head On' almost provides a checklist for the perfect Mary Chain track, with all the essential ingredients firmly in place: lyrics referencing death, the stars and the sky alongside a suitably twisted yet exhilarating desire for self-degradation in 'the dirty part of town'; a memorable guitar solo that elevates the euphoric thrill of the song even further; a breakdown at the three-minute mark followed by a gradual build-up and finally an almost call-and-response outro of 'hey yay ay ays' and 'yeah yeah yeah', seemingly tailor-made for audience participation. While it would perhaps be cynical to suggest that this final section was consciously constructed with live performance in mind, whatever the motivation, it works perfectly, and, although 'Head On' could easily have hit its mark in under three minutes, the fact that the band were sufficiently confident in the strength of the song to extend it beyond four speaks volumes.

The promo video for 'Head On', filmed on 29 October, gained significant traction on MTV, leading to a brief period of everyday offstage recognition for Jim as the group toured America, while the song's heavy rotation on alternative radio playlists helped propel the single to number two on the *Billboard* Modern Rock chart. This ranking compiled the most-played tracks on college radio stations broadcasting primarily to younger audiences who were increasingly embracing British alternative acts such as New Order, The Cure and Depeche Mode, and now, joining them, The Jesus and Mary Chain.

Through being such an effortlessly great song, 'Head On' proved ripe for reinterpretation in the form of cover versions ranging from the sublime – Pixies – to the faintly ridiculous – David Hasselhoff – with the latter sounding almost like a bargain-bin Billy Idol impersonation. In contrast, the Black Francis-led Pixies opted for a breakneck reinvention of the song, precisely the sort of radical reinterpretation that the Mary Chain themselves generally favoured when approaching cover versions. Having reluctantly agreed to an accompanying promo video for their considerably shorter take on 'Head On', the resulting single soon gained popularity through regular MTV airplay. Indeed, such was the success of the Pixies version – which received MTV's 'Breakthrough Video' award in 1991 and reached number six on the *Billboard* Alternative Airplay chart – that when The Jesus and Mary Chain returned to America during the summer of 1992 for the ill-fated *Lollapalooza* tour, many younger audience members unfamiliar with the band mistakenly assumed that it was the Mary Chain covering Pixies rather than the reverse.

The success of 'Head On' outside the UK can largely be attributed to the regular radio and television exposure denied to the band in their home country, meaning that the Mary Chain were forced to seek alternative methods through which to boost the chart prospects of the second single lifted from *Automatic*. Yet even with the release spread across seven separate formats – including the unusual strategy of issuing four different 7" singles over four consecutive weeks to sustain chart momentum – 'Head On' barely scraped into the UK top 60 at number 57 before progressing no further. This failure was made all the more galling given the success of the promo video elsewhere, particularly in the United States and mainland Europe, where the band even relented to promoting the single on the short-lived chart show *Hit Studio International*, broadcast on the fledgling SKY satellite channel and hosted by Paula Yates and, ironically enough, Radio 1 DJ Bruno Brookes. However, such was the level of disinterest in maintaining even the pretence of miming to the song that both Jim and William simply drank cans of Budweiser throughout the performance, while, with half a minute still remaining, Jim abandoned the charade altogether by wandering around the set, grabbing at his bandmates' guitars before eventually exiting stage right entirely. It perhaps comes as little surprise that the band chose not to include this particular promotional 'performance' on the DVD accompanying the 2011 deluxe edition of *Automatic*, regardless of its undeniable entertainment value decades later.

'Take It' (4:34)

During the band's interview with James Brown for the *NME* in late September 1989, the journalist drew specific attention to the visual quality of the music on *Automatic*, observing how 'the images and sounds flicker by very quickly' and it is on 'Take It' that the Mary Chain become their most confrontational and experimental. On an album featuring undeniable pop thrills such as 'Head On' and 'Blues From A Gun', this remains perhaps the most impressive track of all, not least because of the band's bold use of an abstract collage of samples in such an innovative manner on a mainstream alternative rock album.

The song first appeared during a Peel Session recorded at Maida Vale on 31 May 1988 and broadcast on 13 June before being repeated three more times later that year. Interestingly, this early version omits the sample collage outro that would become such a defining component of the *Automatic* recording, suggesting that William and Jim only opted to incorporate the barrage of cut-up sounds during the track's recording at Sam Therapy between 23 and 24 March, before an all-day mixing session took place on 31 May.

Both versions retain the overdriven fuzz bassline – the closest that bass on any *Automatic* track came to resembling a genuinely live instrument – and it is this element, alongside a particularly busy beatbox rhythm (Jim had, after all, identified both 'Take It' and 'UV Ray' as the Mary Chain's own version of dance music), that provides the foundation for the song. 'Take It' is punctuated throughout by blasts of reverberating distortion and features a scorching lead guitar passage erupting at the 1:21 mark before returning just over a minute later in even more extreme form. The song then abruptly cuts away at the three-minute point, more or less exactly where the earlier Peel Session work-in-progress version had concluded.

The painstakingly assembled sample collage created by Jim and William crashes in from the 3:02 mark onwards and functions as the aural equivalent of somebody frantically flicking through television channels with a remote control. British audiences in the late 1980s, still operating with relatively limited viewing choices compared to their American counterparts, would likely have found this barrage of clips especially disorientating and it is indeed American television that provides the primary source material. Following the arrival of a video recorder in the Reid household during the autumn of 1982, Jim and William began assembling their own cut-up compilations of advertisements and programme excerpts, and while it seems unlikely that one of these homemade tapes was directly used for the final 90 seconds of 'Take It', spiritually the approach feels identical.

The samples dart rapidly from clip to clip alongside industrial guitar noise from William and the ever-present drum machine, although only one source remains immediately recognisable: an extract from *Midnight Cowboy* (1969) in which Jon Voight's title character is asked 'Do you love me Joe?' by Crazy Annie during one of the film's fragmented flashback dream sequences. *Midnight Cowboy* was a particular favourite of the band, not least because John Schlesinger's film excelled in its depiction of Times Square sleaze, degradation and urban poverty during the late 1960s.

By 1990, when the Mary Chain were regularly incorporating 'Take It' into live sets, the sample collage from the *Automatic* version had been replaced with a similarly timed extract from William Burroughs' legendary 1960s cut-up work 'The Last Words Of Hassan Sabbah', including the particularly striking line at the one-minute mark:

> I bear no sick words/junk words/love words/forgive words/from Jesus.

Accompanying live performances of 'Take It' was a projected visual collage featuring rapid-fire excerpts from bootleg copies of *Scorpio Rising* (1963) and *A Clockwork Orange* (1971), alongside a barrage of cut-up symbols and images of classic Americana. This writer can personally attest to the impact of suddenly glimpsing the sinister face of Alex DeLarge looming over the audience during the Glasgow date of the extremely well-attended spring 1992 *Rollercoaster* tour. For those unfortunate enough never to have witnessed the Mary Chain live during this period, the deluxe edition of *Automatic* includes footage from the BBC indie music programme *SNUB TV*, filmed during the autumn 1989 British leg of the *Automatic* tour, where both the Burroughs extract and projected collage can be seen accompanying the band's performance of 'Take It'.

'Halfway To Crazy' (3:41)

Unmistakably the Mary Chain at their most accessible on *Automatic*, this highly melodic track offers a neat tip of the hat to Lou Reed's 'Vicious' – a standout from his iconic 1972 Bowie-produced *Transformer* album – while remaining both upbeat and strangely uplifting. Beneath the appealingly poppy chord changes and instantly memorable top-line melodies, however, 'Halfway To Crazy' dwells firmly in darker territory lyrically, with references to falling apart, suicide and homicide intensified further by the repeated closing refrain of the outro: 'I'm going crazy…'. A brief guitar solo enters at the 1:36 mark, which would not have sounded out of place on the more upbeat moments of *Darklands* and bears a particularly strong resemblance in feel – if not exact notation – to the lead break from 'Happy When It Rains'.

The track received two days' dedicated work on 12-13 April before returning to Sam Therapy for another full day's recording exactly a month later. It was then considered close to completion following the recording of the vocals on 22 May, before finally being mixed on 11 June at the mid-point of the Mary Chain's time at The Church.

An inversion of many tracks on *Psychocandy*, where walls of formidable noise often concealed vulnerable or emotionally raw lyrics, the penultimate song on *Automatic* instead packages its grim lyrical content inside one of the Mary Chain's most immediately appealing melodies. Yet given the increasingly uneasy relationship between the band and British radio producers by this stage – regardless of how deceptively bright the song initially sounded before the lyrics fully registered – William and Jim were probably correct in insisting that Warners look elsewhere on the album for a single release. A few years later, however, any lingering concern over the sensitivities of radio pluggers, producers and presenters would be very much far gone and out.

'Gimme Hell' (3:18)

Significantly strengthened by the presence of live drums from Richie Thomas – who would remain with the band for the following 18 months – *Automatic* powers towards its conclusion on original vinyl pressings with the swaggering drawl of 'Gimme Hell', a title neatly echoing the classic *Raw Power*-era Stooges track 'Gimme Danger'. It also carries the distinction of being the first Jesus and Mary Chain song to feature explicit language printed in the accompanying lyric sheet.

With a handful of recycled lyrical motifs from the preceding 'Halfway To Crazy' and a distinct air of menace sustained throughout, 'Gimme Hell' serves as an exceptionally strong album closer. The combination of Jim's suitably tortured lead vocal and the distinctly 'Sympathy For The Devil'-styled dual backing vocals during the final minute works perfectly. The song gradually builds towards a howling crescendo before culminating, via a deft lyrical liberation from a Lee and Nancy track ('Got It Together'), in one final invocation of quintessential Americana: 'I've been good/and I've been mean/ and I've been looking for a Coke machine'.

The Mary Chain's fascination with such iconic cultural imagery was expanded upon by William Reid during a September 1989 *NME* interview with James Brown, when he explained that, much like the Coca-Cola bottle or Coke machine:

> The American flag is a completely trashy image ... but it's one of the least disposable and one of the most powerful images in the world.

A scorching live version of 'Gimme Hell' from the band's autumn 1989 British tour was broadcast alongside 'Take It' on *SNUB TV* and later included on the DVD accompanying the 2011 deluxe edition of *Automatic*.

'Drop' (1:55)

One of the more obvious value-for-money tactics of the late 1980s concerned the inclusion of bonus tracks exclusive to cassette and CD formats. Cynics might equally argue that this simply encouraged devoted fans to purchase multiple copies of the same album and *Automatic* remains one of the few examples in the Mary Chain catalogue – alongside *Barbed Wire Kisses* – where such a strategy was fully embraced.

The first of two short bonus tracks appended to selected versions of the album, 'Drop' – recorded and mixed at The Church between 7 and 9 July towards the end of the Mary Chain's work on *Automatic* – is a delicate William Reid acoustic ballad, gently paced and accompanied by subtle synth strings alongside a softly mixed drum-machine metronome that keeps time without distracting from the vocals and guitar. The lyrics are superbly matched to the lead melody and contain several quietly effective observations on frustrated love and emotional disconnection.

A slightly alternative version of 'Drop' appeared as one of the B-sides to 'Head On' under the subtitle 'Acoustic Remix'. Running for exactly the same duration, this take merely omits the synth overdubs and is otherwise virtually identical to the album version. William was not quite finished with the song, however, as 'Drop' was revisited during the *Stoned & Dethroned* sessions, recorded over a two-day session on 30-31 May, before later being included as a B-side to that album's lead single, 'Sometimes Always'. Ironically, despite appearing somewhat out of place as a bonus track on *Automatic*, 'Drop' arguably fits more naturally within the atmosphere of the Mary Chain's later 'acoustic but not quite' album, and the subtle country-inflected lead guitar on the 1994 recording is particularly lovely.

During November 1989, the band made a rare British television appearance on the late-night Channel 4 series *Halfway To Paradise*, a surreal cabaret programme hosted by the late actor Iain McColl in character as 'Mr Sinclair' and featuring a rotating cast of musical guests with a distinctly Scottish flavour. After claiming to have received a letter from 'a Mr Reid of East Kilbride' insisting that his sons would be perfect for the programme, Sinclair jokes that they would first need to abandon the name 'Jesus and The Toilet Chains' – where he apparently drew the line – and 'start to smile a bit' before earning their big break. Introduced instead as 'a young band from East Kilbride who are going to be huge on the cabaret circuit … Happy Go Lucky', the Mary Chain proceed to deliver a lovely live rendition of 'Drop' with Jim taking over lead vocal duties.

Interestingly, only the Reid brothers and Ben Lurie are shown in close-up throughout the performance, playing acoustic and electric guitars, respectively. Hart and Thomas were nevertheless present for the recording, given that live bass and drums are clearly audible throughout, despite the pair barely featuring onscreen. Regardless, the appearance demonstrated once again that The Jesus and Mary Chain possessed a genuine sense of humour and, under the right circumstances, were perfectly capable of embracing exposure to new audiences.

'Sunray' (1:35)
On first impression, 'Sunray' appears to be a straightforward 90-second experiment in caustic distortion and relentless drum-machine rhythms. Listen a little more closely, however – particularly from around the 35-second mark onwards – and traces of the melodic structure from 'Coast To Coast' begin to emerge beneath the otherwise near note-less guitar noise.

The track concludes with a swirling rotor-blade synthesizer effect while sheets of unforgiving white noise and feedback – recalling the band's earliest recordings at Southern Studios – explode across the mix.

Ending both cassette and CD editions of *Automatic*, 'Sunray' functions as a reminder, arriving so soon after the fragile beauty of 'Drop', that The Jesus and Mary Chain were capable of operating comfortably across radically different sonic terrains and that this brief instrumental perhaps hinted most strongly at the harsher direction they might pursue as the 1990s approached.

Contemporary Tracks

'Shimmer' (2:49)
One of the B-sides to 'Blues From A Gun' and a song laden with religious imagery from beginning to end, 'Shimmer' contains references to paradise, rivers, a forbidden tree, Heaven's gates and the devil's silver eyes within the space of just under three minutes. The track possesses a languid, hazy and – yes – shimmering quality, with William's vocals complemented by beautifully understated lead guitar parts as the song invites the listener to bask in this prime example of late-night Mary Chain blues. The track's musings on pleasure and pain unfold alongside the slow accompaniment of a simple metronomic drum-machine backing. A leisurely and sonically opulent B-side, 'Shimmer' is extremely well produced and another example of a genuinely high-quality song hidden away as a bonus track, ultimately deserving of far greater attention.

'Penetration' (2:50)
During an early 1987 interview, when the Mary Chain were hard at work recording tracks for *Darklands*, Jim Reid was already envisaging a future album where the band would focus on synthesizers and drum machines almost exclusively, with Alan Vega and Martin Rev serving as key inspirations:

> A lot of people are going to look at Suicide as the godfathers of the next punk rock movement. Synthesizers are the future, and it's not out of the question that our next LP will be a synthesizer LP.

'Penetration', the second of five separate B-sides to 'Blues From A Gun', certainly sounds like Suicide – although it is the heavily sequenced 1988 incarnation of the group heard on their *A Way Of Life* comeback album, rather than the spooky minimalist electronics of the duo's revolutionary debut from a decade earlier, that this Mary Chain track most closely resembles.

Introduced with an uncharacteristically enthusiastic (for The Jesus and Mary Chain at least) cry of 'Come on!', the track skirts close to the sound of the largely ridiculed – and by 1989 utterly irrelevant – wannabe sci-fi rockabilly outfit Sigue Sigue Sputnik, as well as pop trio Westworld, who had enjoyed brief chart fame during 1987 with their single 'Sonic Boom Boy'. Sequencers, stabbing synth bursts and loops of percussive distorted guitar noise – alongside the obligatory drum machine – provide the backing to a set of sleazy, salacious lyrics delivered with gusto by Jim, channelling his own amusing take on the hi-NRG histrionics of Divine (a not-so-guilty secret Reid favourite) to the extent that the track almost tips over into unintentional parody. A basic horn keyboard riff enters the mix at the 1:50 mark and repeats until the final ten seconds of the song, when, bizarrely, a lead guitar suddenly appears that uncannily seems to be picking out notes from the intro to 'Last Train To Clarksville' by The Monkees.

'Penetration' was briefly featured in Gregg Araki's black-comedy indie film *The Doom Generation*, released in 1995 and gaining a degree of infamy due to its queasy combination of sex and overt violence. The Mary Chain track is heard around the 37-minute mark and runs for approximately 40 seconds in the background of the scene. It was also included on the accompanying soundtrack album, released via Def American in the same year, and the song's inclusion in *The Doom Generation* perhaps explains why the label also opted to resurrect the then six-year-old track for the US-only compilation *The Jesus and Mary Chain Hate Rock 'N' Roll* during 1995.

'Break Me Down' (2:33)

Another acoustic beauty from the Mary Chain, 'Break Me Down' would have been a surefire album highlight had *Automatic* not developed in the way that it ultimately did sonically, leaving little room for such an abrupt mood shift. The song would also have fitted snugly onto *Darklands*. Included on *The Sound Of Speed* – the band's second compilation of B-sides and rarities from 1993 – for the benefit of those who had missed out on the multiple-format release of 'Blues From A Gun', this is another jewel in the crown of The Jesus and Mary Chain and a fine example of their talent for crafting country-influenced tunes.

Incorporating double-tracked lead vocals from Jim and a measured use of sparkling guitars, the song almost feels too brief, as another verse or two would have been more than welcome. What *is* present, however, is glorious, and 'Break Me Down' served as further evidence that the Mary Chain were more than capable of turning their talents towards an acoustic-based album. It would take the purchase of their own recording studio in South London – alongside another four years of touring and recording – before the release of *Stoned & Dethroned* finally brought such a tantalising prospect to fruition.

'Subway' (2:08)

Notable for its chugging guitar rhythm – achieved primarily through palm-muting the strings near the bridge of the instrument – 'Subway' contains a glorious pure-pop moment early on when the track suddenly drops down to just the drum-machine beat for a few fleeting seconds before cueing in Jim's vocal hook of 'I gotta get get you', swiftly followed by William's lead break. The key change that follows is slightly jarring at first, but the return of the rhythm guitar backing quickly stabilises the track and 'Subway' takes off once more before abruptly cutting out just beyond the two-minute mark.

While stronger than several other B-side selections recorded during the *Automatic* sessions, 'Subway' was another Mary Chain track omitted from *The Sound Of Speed,* and it was not until the 2008 four-disc box set *The Power Of Negative Thinking* that the song finally reappeared.

'In The Black' (2:57)

The Mary Chain effectively pay tribute to themselves on this B-side to 'Head On', a track perhaps best described as 'Just Out Of Reach' fused with elements of 'The Living End'. In fact, try singing the lyrics to the latter over 'In The Black' and they fit with remarkable ease. Perfectly comfortable recycling aspects of their own previously recorded material, similarities even emerge towards the end of the track with the 1983 demo tape song 'Send Me Away', the sole early Mary Chain home recording that was never carried forward and properly revisited by the band – perhaps unsurprising given the experimental nature of the piece itself.

Mid-paced and rather staid in content, 'In The Black' ultimately suffers from arriving during a period when the band were steadily breaking new ground with each subsequent album release. Overly indebted to previous Mary Chain songs in both style and substance, it remains one of the lesser-appreciated 'bonus tracks' attached to later reissues. Its absence from the otherwise comprehensive *The Sound Of Speed* compilation is probably a fairly strong indication of how the band themselves regarded the track only a few years after recording it.

'I'm Glad I Never' (1:33)

Band favourite Lee Hazlewood, whose 1968 album *Love And Other Crimes* was selected by Jim in a 1994 *Q* magazine feature on some of his favourite records, is covered here with distinction by the Reids, the original's country-rock style adhered to closely in a notable departure from the Mary Chain's usual preference for radically reinterpreted cover versions. By paying tribute to the 90-second opening track from Hazlewood's cult 1971 album *Requiem For An Almost Lady* – a collection that featured frequently bizarre spoken-word introductions from Hazlewood himself on each of its ten tracks – The Jesus and Mary Chain revealed the depth of their enduring affection for the singer-songwriter.

This admiration eventually led Jim and William to approach the maverick and somewhat enigmatic musician about guesting on a future Mary Chain recording, widely believed to have been 'Sometimes Always', although despite an initial agreement, the collaboration sadly never came to pass.

'Terminal Beach' (2:27)

Sharing its title with the 1964 collection of science-fiction short stories by J.G. Ballard, this track opens with the obligatory sequenced bass and relentless drum-machine backing that featured on so many songs recorded during the *Automatic* sessions. 'Terminal Beach' also introduces early on a pop melody strikingly similar to that heard during the opening lines of 'Never Understand'. So far, so promising – but the track soon begins to fizzle out and, in truth, even sounds slightly bland by the time it reaches the closing section.

Cut from the same sonic cloth as the likes of 'Head On' and 'Coast To Coast', 'Terminal Beach' unfortunately lacks the quality of either of those two album highlights and instead gives the impression of being one of the band's earliest demo sketches for *Automatic*, later revisited and recorded primarily for use as a B-side.

'Deviant Slice' (3:05)

Perilously close at times to sounding like Sigue Sigue Sputnik circa their Giorgio Moroder-produced 1986 debut album due to its heavily sequenced synth-bass track, 'Deviant Slice' is ultimately redeemed by the bedrock of a propulsive, whirling helicopter rotor-blade synthesizer sound – also heard on 'Sunray' – and a caustic feedback-drenched guitar backdrop that appears intermittently throughout the song's three-minute runtime.

Like 'Terminal Beach', 'Sunray' and – to a lesser extent – 'Penetration', this Mary Chain B-side arguably represents another instance of style edging ahead of substance. Unlike two of those aforementioned tracks, however, 'Deviant Slice' at least secured a place on the *Sound Of Speed* compilation album.

'My Girl' (3:05)

First unveiled as an unexpected treat during the BBC Peel Session recorded at the end of May 1988 alongside 'Sidewalking', 'Coast To Coast' and 'Take It', this delicate rendition of 'My Girl' (completed on 1 June) is distinctive for its sparse arrangement of voice and guitar alone, with only the faintest trace of reverb adding further texture to the performance. The vocals are notably double-tracked in the chorus, accompanied by whispered backing repetitions of 'my girl' falling off the beat in further tribute to the original Temptations song.

This cover clearly remained a favourite of both William and Jim, eventually appearing as a B-side on the 3" mini-CD release of 'Blues From A Gun' before later being included on *The Sound Of Speed* (1993), where it functions as a gentle acoustic interlude within the track listing prior to the considerably louder and less restrained cover versions of 'Tower Of Song' and 'Little Red Rooster'. The recording would subsequently reappear on *The Complete John Peel Sessions* (2000), the then-career-spanning *The Power Of Negative Thinking* (2008) and most recently on the extensive deluxe reissue edition of *Automatic* released during 2011.

Rollercoaster EP (1990)

Personnel:
Jim Reid: vocals, guitar
William Reid: guitar, vocals
Recorded at Sam Therapy, Studio, West London, between 28 and 31 May 1990
Producers: William and Jim Reid
Engineer: Flood (tracks 1-3), William Reid (4)
Label: Blanco y Negro
Charts: UK: 46, Australia: 110, Ireland: 25
Running time: 15:05

Released at the end of August 1990, this stand-alone Mary Chain EP featured three non-album tracks alongside a Leonard Cohen cover version, all four songs previously unavailable on any LP. The recording sessions took place at Sam Therapy during the final four days of May, with the 31st devoted to recording the vocals for each of the songs. The tracks were then subsequently mixed at Swanyard Studios in Islington from 1 to 3 June. The only exception to this schedule was the recording of 'Tower Of Song', which was completed by William at home on his own 12-track Akai studio. The title track was accompanied by a promo video assembled by Jim Reid from footage sourced from the 'Her Way Of Praying' shoot, omitting earlier clips of William playing guitar and the young female model mock-filming the band with a handheld Bolex camera. The resulting promo for 'Rollercoaster' instead features further Times Square footage of the 1990 touring lineup of The Jesus and Mary Chain in and around the neon wonderland of pre-clean-up New York City.

Despite the quality of the material included, the EP stalled at a disappointing number 46 in the UK charts on 8 September 1990, dropping five places the following week before disappearing from the top 100 entirely by the third week of the month. All four tracks were included across every format released, and both 'Lowlife' and 'Tower Of Song' subsequently made the cut for the 1993 compilation *The Sound Of Speed*. The complete set of EP tracks was later reunited on the 2008 *The Power Of Negative Thinking* box set and again on the 2011 deluxe edition of *Honey's Dead*, where they were sequenced immediately after the parent album.

'Rollercoaster' (3:50)

The first of three Mary Chain tracks engineered by Flood and produced by Jim and William Reid during late spring 1990, the version of 'Rollercoaster' that appears on the EP differs noticeably from the re-recorded take included on *Honey's Dead* two years later and is arguably the stronger of the two. There is also a marked shift away from the colder, more synthetic textures of *Automatic*, with a less mechanical-sounding drum machine backing and the welcome return of live bass guitar, played by Jim, replacing the sequenced approach previously favoured by the band.

William's lead vocal is especially strong throughout, although it would be remiss not to acknowledge that the verse melody bears more than a passing resemblance to The Byrds' hit version of 'Mr. Tambourine Man'. When this was raised in a mid-August 1990 *Melody Maker* interview, an exasperated William replied that 'there's only so many fucking chord changes in the world. I don't deny it, I won't even try justifying it.' It was a typically blunt response but also an illuminating one, particularly for a band whose music had always worn its influences openly and proudly.

'Silverblade' (2:56)

Sharing its title with a short-lived DC Comics fantasy character whose limited series ran between 1987 and 1988, 'Silverblade' was first recorded as part of a three-track Peel Session on 26 November 1989 and broadcast the following month. The oft-criticised and characteristically busy drum machine backing remains present, but 'Silverblade' is melodically stronger than several of its *Automatic*-era contemporaries and builds towards a tremendous finale when huge clouds of feedback, previously rumbling away beneath the mix, are suddenly thrust to the forefront from the 2:15 mark onwards.

The resulting racket is exhilarating and perfectly suited to lyrics concerned with pain, disruption and – a recurring Mary Chain theme – personal confusion. The Peel Session version runs slightly longer than the EP recording but is otherwise very similar, including the use of live bass guitar, played by Douglas Hart during the BBC session, although the extended outro is faded out more gradually.

'Lowlife' (3:25)

Beginning with a sample of William Burroughs delivering an extract from the fragmented monologue of his legendary cut-up poem 'The Last Words Of Hassan Sabbah', the third Reid/Reid composition on the *Rollercoaster* EP then bursts into life with impressive force. Particularly notable, beyond the quality of the song itself, is the prominent use of fuzz bass and tremolo-drenched lead guitar, both of which would become key sonic ingredients during the recording of major tracks for the next Mary Chain album just a year later.

Another especially effective moment arrives during the middle-eight breakdown at the 1:20 mark, where the song lurches into a stop-start rhythmic pattern before snapping back into its central groove 20 seconds later. 'Lowlife' shares its title with New Order's third album as well as a scathing Public Image Ltd. track from John Lydon's post-Pistols debut, coincidentally highlighted in a *Vox* magazine feature published a month after the release of the EP on some of the Mary Chain's favourite records. While this track may not have sounded as radically confrontational as its PiL namesake did to punk audiences in the late 1970s, it nevertheless demonstrated that The Jesus and Mary Chain were continuing to push their own music forward as the new decade began.

'Tower Of Song' (4:50)

The doo-wop stroll of Leonard Cohen's 1988 original was ripe for reinterpretation, and, having purchased the CD while on tour, it was Jim who became especially enamoured with 'Tower Of Song', one of the standout moments from the synthesiser-heavy *I'm Your Man* album. After an increasingly drunken backstage run-through and a decision to reduce the song to a cyclical chord pattern with just enough room for lead guitar breaks – thereby dispensing with the original's middle-eight entirely – the Mary Chain took to the stage of New York's Ritz on the evening of April Fool's Day 1990 and debuted their own distinctive version towards the end of the set.

In a December 2010 interview with *Artrocker*, Jim recalled that once the band had rehearsed the song a few times in the dressing room, they 'went and belted it out on stage and we actually did it alright, but I had to stand there with the lyrics on a piece of paper.'

The recorded version of 'Tower Of Song', engineered by William Reid and completed in his own home studio, remains respectful to the source material up to a point but largely dispenses with the wry elegance of Cohen's original as the Mary Chain instead power relentlessly through the song's near five-minute runtime. Jim's vocals are superb, William's slide guitar breaks faultless and, by the end of the track, 'Tower Of Song' effectively belongs to The Jesus and Mary Chain: not merely covered but wholly reclaimed through a characteristically inspired reinterpretation.

Contemporary Tracks

'Guitarman' (3:41)

Given their long-standing affection for late-1960s Elvis – particularly the legendary *'68 Comeback Special* and the *From Elvis In Memphis* album that followed a year later – it is easy to imagine that The Jesus and Mary Chain were pleased to contribute a cover version to *The Last Temptation Of Elvis*, an NME-curated charity compilation with profits donated to the Nordoff-Robbins Music Therapy Centre in London.

With participating artists asked to reinterpret songs from Presley's films, the Mary Chain selected 'Guitarman', originally featured on the otherwise largely forgettable *Clambake* soundtrack, although notably absent from the film itself. Recorded on 15 August 1989 at The Church studio in North London, where the band had recently spent several weeks mixing *Automatic*, the session also amusingly resulted in Jim and William providing backing vocals for Erasure, who happened to be recording upstairs at the same time. Alan Moulder engineered the session with Dick Meaney assisting, both of whom would continue to play important roles in subsequent Mary Chain recordings.

The completed version of 'Guitarman' is an exuberant romp through a song originally written and recorded by Jerry Reed in 1967 before being adopted by Elvis. Jim's vocal performance is excellent throughout, and there is a palpable sense of enjoyment in his delivery, particularly during the exaggerated Elvis-style ad-libs. William's guitar work is equally strong, ranging from percussive riffing to an impressive approximation of Reed's famed acoustic solo at the 1:25 mark, introduced with Jim's enthusiastic cry of 'Show him, son!'

The song concludes with a squeal of feedback immediately following an amusing sample of 'He was a degenerate's degenerate', sourced not from an Elvis film but from the 1966 Paul Newman detective caper *Harper*. The sample appears during a prank phone call scene between Newman's titular private investigator and his estranged wife, played by Janet Leigh, who gleefully takes the opportunity to ridicule his character flaws. It is a typically obscure and mischievous choice of reference point from the Mary Chain.

One of the most enjoyable cover versions the band ever recorded, 'Guitarman' later resurfaced as a B-side on the 'Reverence' single in February 1992 before appearing on *The Sound Of Speed*, *The Power Of Negative Thinking* and the B-sides bonus disc accompanying the deluxe edition of *Honey's Dead*.

'Reverberation (Doubt)' (3:47)

Despite choosing the same song as Warner labelmates ZZ Top, The Jesus and Mary Chain still contributed a track to a 1990 tribute album dedicated to Roky Erickson, frontman of legendary Texas psychedelic pioneers The 13th Floor Elevators. The two cover versions ultimately bookended the album, with ZZ Top opening proceedings and the Mary Chain closing them.

The compilation itself was assembled both to raise funds for Erickson and to help introduce his music to a wider audience. William and Jim's version of 'Reverberation (Doubt)' is a remarkably faithful interpretation, reverent rather than radically transformative and notably restrained compared to the sonic demolition previously inflicted upon covers such as 'Surfin' USA' and 'Who Do You Love'. While the original version from *The Psychedelic Sounds Of The 13th Floor Elevators* (1966) ran for under three minutes, the Mary Chain stretched their own take by an additional 60 seconds without sacrificing any momentum or intensity.

This respectful and highly effective cover would later reappear as a B-side on the 'Almost Gold' single in June 1992 before subsequently being included on *The Sound Of Speed*.

Honey's Dead (1992)

Personnel:
Jim Reid: vocals, guitar
William Reid: vocals, guitar
Steve Monti: drums and percussion (2, 3, 4, 5, 6, 9, 10, 11)
Recorded at The Drugstore, South London, between July and October 1991
Producers: William and Jim Reid
Engineer: Alan Moulder (all tracks except 9, engineered by Flood)
Label: Blanco y Negro
Charts: UK: 14, New Zealand: 21, Sweden: 41, Australia: 44, US: 158
Running time: 42:39

Other than a solitary gig commitment during January 1991, for most of the year, The Jesus and Mary Chain were – as far as the UK music press was concerned – effectively off the radar. The reality, of course, was very different, and those familiar with the band and their previous 'disappearances' during 1986 and 1988 would have known that William and Jim Reid were inevitably preoccupied with writing and recording new material. The key difference this time was that the latter process was now taking place in the band's own recording studio in the Elephant and Castle area of South London – 9A Amelia Street in Southwark had become the new premises for 'The Drugstore'.

After the lengthy recording process at Sam Therapy, followed by additional mixing work for *Automatic* at The Church, both secured at favourable rates for the band, the Mary Chain had begun looking seriously at alternative options. When Warners presented the recording budget for their next album, Jim and William realised that there was a unique opportunity to invest the funds in a studio of their own. The attraction of no longer needing to record with one eye fixed on the clock, while having the freedom to experiment creatively in surroundings that genuinely felt comfortable, had been something they had discussed for some time.

William Reid had already been recording band demos at home for several years and, with the aid of an Atari ST computer, had even begun experimenting with rudimentary dance music tracks. As Jim commented in a September 1990 interview with *Sounds*, when it came to releasing these recordings, even under a pseudonym, 'he hasn't got the confidence to do anything about it.' Plans for the Mary Chain to establish their own recording base had initially developed from ideas to expand a smaller basement studio setup using recording equipment previously owned by former Ultravox member Billy Currie, purchased with the assistance of manager Chris Morrison, who had earlier managed Currie and his bandmates during their commercial peak in the early to mid-1980s. In theory, the investment would allow the Mary Chain to develop songs beyond the limitations of Portastudio demos. However, advice from musician friends and engineers encouraged the band to think on a larger scale, leading them to consider several possible premises before eventually securing the best option and, despite initial resistance from Warners regarding the intended use of the recording budget, making it their own. On 21 June 1991, having signed the lease for the building the previous day, The Jesus and Mary Chain collected the keys and took over the premises where Terminal 24 had operated as a commercial recording studio for more than five years.

The Mary Chain finally had the freedom to dictate their own pace within a bespoke studio environment, working on music at leisure and refining the results in sophisticated surroundings free from the oppressive nature of time constraints. The new approach quickly paid dividends, with 'Sundown', 'Tumbledown' and 'Sugar Ray' all being worked on in quick succession during mid-July; William Reid later described the *Honey's Dead* recording sessions in an extensive interview with *The Guitar Magazine* in June 1992 as: 'Just me, Jim and Alan Moulder all through the summer making music and having a bloody good laugh.

Later in the same interview, William also praised the live room at the newly established Drugstore, describing it as the best he had ever worked in and acknowledging how instrumental it had been in shaping the sound of *Honey's Dead*. Photographs of the touring Mary Chain lineup rehearsing in this very room appeared in the April 1992 issue of *Select* magazine alongside a major interview with Jim and William ahead of the British leg of the *Rollercoaster* tour, where the band would be supported by a rotating cast including Dinosaur Jr., Blur and My Bloody Valentine. Meanwhile, fellow favourites Curve and Spiritualized joined the lineup for the North American leg of the *Rollercoaster* tour later that autumn.

The music scene that The Jesus and Mary Chain returned to during spring 1992 had shifted considerably since they had last immersed themselves in it during mid-1990. With the *Rollercoaster* EP managing only a disappointing top 50 chart placing alongside growing indifference from sections of the UK music press who appeared to have decided that time was up for their former favourites – a *Melody Maker* cover feature from 18 August 1990 had even carried the ominous headline 'J&MC R.I.P.?' – the Reids increasingly felt as if they had their backs against the wall. The distinct impression was that many critics had decided the Mary Chain had already had their moment and were now outstaying their welcome. This was especially frustrating given the disproportionate influence wielded by a relatively small number of London-centric music journalists during the 1980s and early 1990s, figures capable of helping to elevate or derail both emerging and established acts.

It was therefore unsurprising that William and Jim increasingly looked beyond Britain, focusing particularly on touring America while the UK music scene became consumed by the rapidly changing landscape of dance music, the rise of Madchester spearheaded by The Stone Roses and Happy Mondays – both bands openly admired by the Mary Chain – and, most significantly, the explosion of American grunge into the mainstream following the extraordinary success of Nirvana during late 1991.

Yet it was among the so-called shoegazing bands – a term coined by the British music press and not intended particularly kindly – that The Jesus and Mary Chain could most clearly recognise the impact of their own music, particularly the influence of *Psychocandy* and the group's broader noise-pop aesthetic. The list of bands shaped directly by the feedback-heavy, effects-driven guitar sounds pioneered by the Reids was extensive, and Creation Records in particular had become home to many of them. Among this new generation, it was arguably My Bloody Valentine, led by Kevin Shields, with whom Jim and William felt the greatest artistic kinship, making their inclusion on the *Rollercoaster* tour feel entirely appropriate.

Despite receiving the strongest and most uniformly positive reviews since the ecstatic response to *Psychocandy* more than six years earlier, *Honey's Dead* nevertheless reached only number 14 in the UK album charts. There must have been some disappointment at the album spending just a single week inside the top 20, continuing the gradual commercial decline that had followed *Automatic*. Regardless, The Jesus and Mary Chain soon embarked upon the British leg of the *Rollercoaster* tour, which at least provided relief from endlessly revisiting the same mid-sized venues around the country that had become overly familiar during the previous four years.

The inspiration for a touring package featuring multiple like-minded artists had come from Perry Farrell of Jane's Addiction, who, inspired by the example of the Reading Festival, helped establish the travelling alternative music carnival that became Lollapalooza. The Mary Chain had originally been approached to appear at the inaugural 1991 festival but declined due primarily to commitments surrounding the recording of their new album. The following year, however, they accepted an invitation to join the second Lollapalooza tour alongside Soundgarden, Pearl Jam, Red Hot Chili Peppers, Ministry, Lush and Ice Cube. Unfortunately, the experience proved disastrous. Forced to perform low on the bill in broad daylight before largely indifferent crowds, Jim and William quickly realised they were contractually trapped within a two-month tour that neither enjoyed nor could escape from, an ordeal that ultimately had a seriously damaging effect on both brothers.

Their fourth studio album, *Honey's Dead*, remains one of the defining achievements of The Jesus and Mary Chain's career: an exhilarating and consistently powerful collection of songs that successfully introduced the band to a new generation of alternative music fans while reaffirming their importance to longtime followers. Numerous younger groups clearly owed a significant debt to the Mary Chain and the welcome chart success of February's incendiary lead single 'Reverence' served as a timely reminder that William and Jim Reid still held the upper hand.

'Reverence' (3:40)

A scalding, soaring and coruscating album opener, 'Reverence' was also chosen by the band as their comeback single and, on paper at least, represented the most defiantly uncommercial – and therefore commercially unlikely – choice imaginable. William and Jim, convinced that they would once again be largely ignored by radio and television regardless of which track was selected, instead opted for the song that best represented the next evolution in the Mary Chain sound, and to hell with the consequences. The resulting reward of a UK top ten hit – the second-highest chart placing of their career – came as a very pleasant surprise for both band and label alike.

When The Jesus and Mary Chain returned to the charts during the early weeks of February 1992, they entered a musical climate where indie rock-dance crossover had become an increasingly calculated move for bands seeking broader commercial appeal. 'Reverence' certainly featured a looped breakbeat sample that gave the track a lurching, almost baggy groove, although its rhythmic pulse was nowhere near as dancefloor-friendly as many of its chart contemporaries. Yet any similarities with the wave of sample-heavy, drum-machine-driven indie crossover acts ended there. Remarkably, it was still just about possible to dance to 'Reverence', albeit rather awkwardly, as the audience of late-night Channel 4 programme *The Word* demonstrated when the Mary Chain chose to unveil their comeback single live on the programme's Valentine's Day special, filmed on 14 February.

Love, however, was decidedly absent from proceedings that evening as the new touring lineup of the band seethed their way through the track. Douglas Hart and Martin Thomas had both departed – for careers in video direction and Renegade Soundwave, respectively – and were replaced by bassist Barry Blackler and drummer Matthew Parkin, formerly of The Starlings. The performance, included on the 2011 deluxe edition of *Honey's Dead*, remains worthy of repeated viewing, not least for Jim's magnificently icy delivery only feet away from selected representatives of exuberant early-1990s youth culture.

Whether in its original album form or the derisorily titled and even more abrasive extended 'Radio Mix', 'Reverence' sounded utterly unparalleled in early 1992 and remains astonishingly confrontational even now. Few songs as hostile, radical and unapologetically noisy have ever reached the UK top ten. Lyrics such as 'I wanna die just like JFK/I wanna die on a sunny day' would already have guaranteed controversy, but following them with 'I wanna die just like Jesus Christ/I wanna die on a bed of spikes' ensured that daytime radio predictably recoiled from the track's gleefully blasphemous provocations. Some things, evidently, never change.

Both the album version and the expanded 'Radio Mix' (remixed at The Drugstore on 16 December 1991) foreground the song's debt to the descending chord structure of The Stooges' immortal 'I Wanna Be Your Dog', particularly during the section accompanying Jim's declaration that 'I wouldn't sell my soul/but I'd hang for this'. Buried amidst the hissing layers of guitar and distortion, the Mary Chain's fondness for obscure sampled sounds also resurfaces at the 1:50 mark. William later admitted in a June 1992 interview with *The Guitar Magazine*:

Above: A promotional photo of the Reid brothers taken during a visit to Portugal in spring 1985 for the 'You Trip Me Up' video shoot. (*Mike Laye*)

Left: Pictured here is the initial release of 'Upside Down', subsequently reissued by Creation with several colour sleeve variants following its November 1984 debut. (*Creation*)

Right: A brief moment from the promo video for 'Just Like Honey' supplied the iconic cover image for the band's debut album, *Psychocandy*. (*Blanco y Negro*)

Right: 'Some Candy Talking' provided The Jesus and Mary Chain with their first top 20 success in July 1986 before controversy halted its progress. (*Blanco y Negro*)

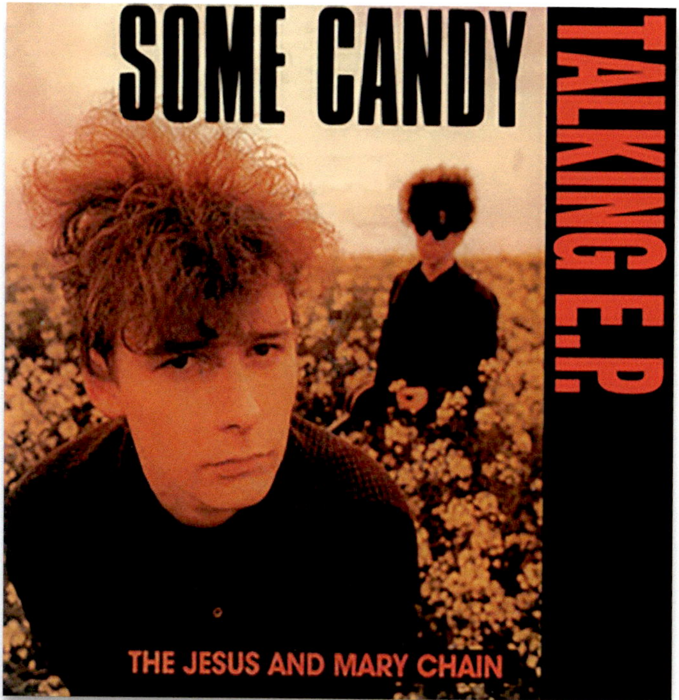

Left: The band's highest-charting album, *Darklands*, alongside its accompanying singles, represented an early commercial high point for the Mary Chain. (*Blanco y Negro*)

Above: Marking the occasion of their debut recording session, the band are pictured outside Evenload Studios, East Kilbride, in May 1984. (*William Reid*)

Below: Onstage during their first-ever gig at The Living Room on Friday 8 June 1984. William Reid is out of shot. (*Stuart Cassidy*)

Top: A Blanco y Negro promotional photograph captures William, Jim and Douglas in early 1984 inside a disused East Kilbride factory. (*Stuart Cassidy*)

Above: The quintessential Jesus and Mary Chain lineup with Bobby Gillespie, as featured in a promotional photograph issued by Blanco y Negro in 1985. (*Author's collection*)

Left: The inlay of an advance cassette sent to journalists for review in autumn 1985. Note the absence of an album title. (*Author's collection*)

Right: The band's biggest UK singles-chart hit featured a striking cover image photographed by Jim Reid directly from his television screen: a scene from cult film *The Jesus Trip*. (*Author's collection*)

This page: A selection of Jesus and Mary Chain postcards from the mid to late 1980s. (*Author's collection*)

Left: 'Chilled to the bone and five miles to home…': The 1988 standalone single 'Sidewalking' saw the group utilise hip-hop rhythms to memorable effect. (*Blanco y Negro*)

Right: *Automatic* made significant inroads with new audiences in America thanks to its radio-friendly singles, 'Blues From A Gun' and 'Head On'. (*Blanco y Negro*)

Right: The standalone *Rollercoaster* EP marked an interim period for the Mary Chain at the start of the 1990s. (*Blanco y Negro*)

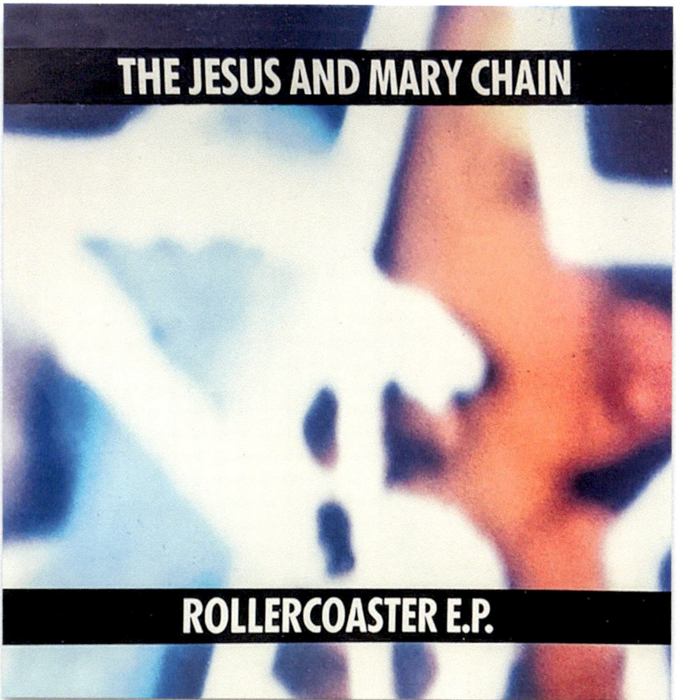

Left: Recorded during summer 1991, *Honey's Dead* was the first album to emerge from the group's newly acquired South London recording studio, The Drugstore. (*Blanco y Negro*)

Left: A critical success upon its 1992 release, *Honey's Dead* lost out to contemporaries Primal Scream for the Mercury Music Prize. (*Author's collection*)

Above: Local East Kilbride graffiti close to the Reids' former family home, reflecting the band's enduring legacy. (*Murray Dalglish*)

This page: A selection of Jesus and Mary Chain concert tickets from 1985 to 1998, with prices doubling over the course of 13 years. (*Guy Kuperman*)

Left: *Sound Of Speed* was the second Mary Chain EP in three years to feature a uniquely deconstructed cover version. (*Blanco y Negro*)

Right: With notable contributions from guest vocalists Hope Sandoval and Shane MacGowan, the 'almost acoustic' album, *Stoned & Dethroned*, marked a further development in the group's sound. (*Blanco y Negro*)

Right: Featuring arguably their most uncompromising music since the mid-1980s, 'I Hate Rock 'N' Roll' found the Mary Chain back to their divisive best. (*Blanco y Negro*)

Left: Despite its troubled gestation, *Munki* remains a firm band and fan favourite. It was the last Jesus and Mary Chain album for almost two decades. (*Creation/Sub Pop*)

This page: The return to Creation Records in the late 1990s provided a last hurrah for the established trio of William, Jim and Ben Lurie. (*Author's collection*)

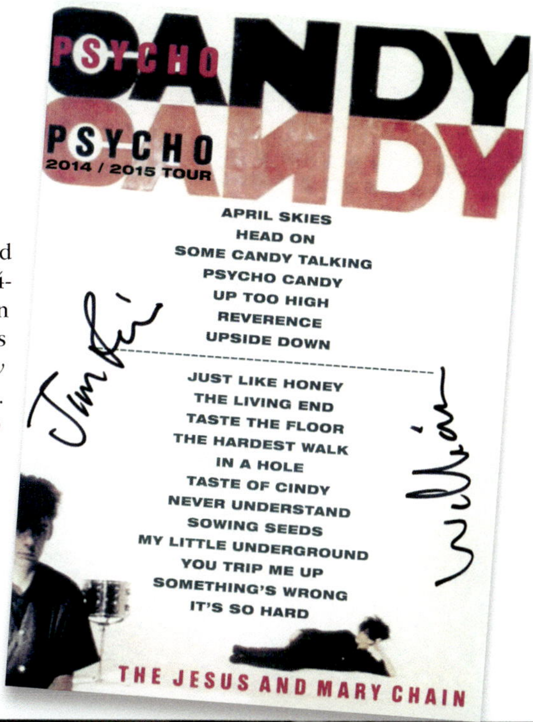

Right: The band toured extensively during 2014-15, opening shows with an intriguing selection of songs before performing *Psychocandy* from beginning to end. (*Author's collection*)

Above: The Mary Chain rewarded fans in 2017 with *Damage And Joy*, older and wiser (perhaps), but with their creative talents as strong as ever. (*Author's collection*)

Left: Continuing a long tradition of distinctive cover art, *Damage And Joy* didn't disappoint either aesthetically or musically. (*Artificial Plastic*)

Right: Marking their 40th anniversary, *Glasgow Eyes* found The Jesus and Mary Chain returning to their roots on several tracks across an electronically driven album. (*Fuzz Club*)

> I have DATs full of little sounds and things that I have absolutely no idea where they came from, pirate radio, an old record from somewhere. There's one on 'Reverence', the single, and I don't know who it's by.

At its core, 'Reverence' is a vicious and malevolent Mary Chain record, one that somehow fuses dance rhythms with near-industrial levels of guitar violence into a genuine chart hit. Ironically, considering the latter element and William's inspired levels of guitar abuse throughout the recording, the Al Jourgensen remix actually softens some of the harsher aspects of the song, presumably not what the Ministry frontman's involvement might initially have suggested. This version, absent from the deluxe reissue of *Honey's Dead* but later included on *The Power Of Negative Thinking*, remains an interesting curio rather than a definitive reinterpretation.

Ultimately, it is the Mary Chain's own extended 'Radio Mix' that remains the definitive version of 'Reverence', the arrangement most closely mirrored in the countless live performances that followed. Yet William Reid's near-acoustic, blues-inflected reinterpretation of the track during his Lazycame solo shows around the turn of the millennium is equally fascinating and hints at an entirely different path the song might once have taken during early sessions at The Drugstore.

The 2011 deluxe edition of *Honey's Dead* also includes the promo video for 'Reverence', another excellent Jim Reid-directed effort assembled after Warners refused to finance a proper promotional shoot for a single they assumed would receive little mainstream exposure. That Jim managed to create such an effective visual accompaniment on what was reportedly a grudgingly conceded budget of little more than a thousand pounds is greatly to his credit. Through rapid edits, flash frames and relentless visual overload, the resulting video perfectly mirrors the sensory assault of the music itself. Unsurprisingly, it received minimal exposure beyond a handful of sympathetic outlets and was naturally deemed unsuitable for broadcast by the BBC, with a *Top Of The Pops* spokesperson claiming the lyrics were 'unsuitable for broadcast at 7 pm when children are likely to be watching'. Regardless, the promo remains the perfect visual companion to one of the most uncompromising – and finest – tracks The Jesus and Mary Chain ever recorded.

'Teenage Lust' (3:06)

Sharing its title with a superb piece of power-pop by Detroit insurgents the MC5, 'Teenage Lust' is arguably the clearest example on *Honey's Dead* of the Mary Chain's instinctive songwriting philosophy, succinctly summarised by William Reid: 'If it doesn't sound good on acoustic guitar, it gets thrown in the dump.'

The song grinds immediately into view atop a descending chord structure, propelled by an overdriven bassline and the muscular drumming of Steve Monti, who, while still a member of Curve, contributed to the majority of the album's tracks. Recommended to the band by Alan Moulder, Monti completed his performances relatively quickly thanks to both his own formidable abilities and the relaxed atmosphere cultivated by the Reids during sessions at The Drugstore. 'Teenage Lust' received three days each devoted to its recording (29-31 July) and mixing (18-20 September), a level of care and attention that is clearly reflected in the finished result.

The track's salacious subject matter – lurid enough that Jim appeared visibly uncomfortable discussing it when prompted by Radio 1 DJ Mark Goodier during promotional interviews – is intensified through waves of wah-wah guitar that rise and collapse around the song's central riff. Barely controlled squeals of feedback increasingly invade the mix as the song drives toward its climax, all while that filthy bassline continues grinding away beneath the surface.

Memorably described by Stuart Maconie in the *NME* as 'a wonderfully half-lit moral abyss of a song' and more bluntly by biographer Zoe Howe as 'a sleazy portrait of virginity lost', 'Teenage Lust' certainly raised eyebrows upon release and has lost little of its unsettling power since. An intoxicating collision of sex, danger and distortion, the track remains deeply compelling even when stripped back to its acoustic foundations on the alternate version later issued as the principal B-side to 'Almost Gold'. Beneath all the feedback and noise, the song's relentless melodic drive remains completely intact.

Two George Drakoulias remixes of 'Teenage Lust' appeared on a limited promotional CD issued during the North American leg of the *Rollercoaster* tour in late 1992, although neither version particularly flatters the original recording. Both are dominated by extremely dated hip-hop loops and suffer badly from the baffling reduction of William's guitars – rarely a wise move when remixing a Mary Chain track. The 'Desdemoana Mix' additionally features an ill-judged pornographic sample that moves from mildly amusing to deeply irritating almost immediately and now sounds painfully juvenile. One suspects the band themselves had little affection for either remix, despite the former appearing on the 2011 deluxe edition of *Honey's Dead*. The longer 'Pimpin Ain't Easy Mix' fares little better beyond the occasional scratchy wah-wah guitar figure that shadows the melody line. Its absence from every subsequent Mary Chain reissue since 1992 feels entirely justified.

Several filmed performances of 'Teenage Lust' survive. One appearance on late-night ITV music programme *The Beat* during 1993 featured the post-*Honey's Dead* touring lineup miming to the backing track while Jim sang live, his vocals sounding notably muffled – perhaps explaining why the footage was omitted from the deluxe reissue. Far stronger is the live performance captured for MTV's *120 Minutes*, included on the 2011 edition, where Jim, William and Ben deliver the track live against what appears to be a stripped-back backing tape. The accompanying Ian Owles-directed promo video, meanwhile, remains one of the sleaziest visual pieces in the band's history. Set within a strip-club environment featuring fluorescent revolver-shaped water pistols, semi-nude dancers and queasy-looking band members – Jim appearing especially worse for wear – the resulting video is intentionally grimy and disorientating. One can only imagine what was left on the cutting-room floor. Its atmosphere of deliberate decadence would later find an unlikely companion in Ben Unwin's equally unsettling video for 'Cracking Up' six years later.

'Far Gone And Out' (2:51)

The oldest Mary Chain track to feature on *Honey's Dead* was first debuted during a Peel Session alongside 'Silverblade' and 'Here Comes Alice' on 12 December 1989, before being repeated five weeks later. This early version of 'Far Gone And Out', featuring William on lead vocals, already had its key melody in place and is undeniably catchy, well-structured and upbeat. In an even earlier incarnation, the song had been far more indebted to the Velvet Underground in style, something that, by the time of recording it properly for inclusion on *Honey's Dead*, following a three-day stint exclusively focused on working up the track at Berwick Street Studios from 22-24 May, William and Jim were perhaps understandably keen to avoid. The introduction of a new bassline provided by Jim transformed 'Far Gone And Out' from a rather polite, almost country-pop song into a much stronger piece of music altogether, skilfully blending pop hooks with drummer Steve Monti's percussion talents.

The song was further developed at The Drugstore in mid-August during a two-day session, with vocal tracks recorded individually on 2 September, before then being mixed to the standards deemed acceptable by the band from 23-24 October. Once complete, 'Far Gone And Out' stood very much at the vanguard of the Mary Chain 2.0 renaissance during the early 1990s and remains a brilliant pop song, with guitars alternating between crunching barre chords and intricate arpeggiated picking at exactly the right moments alongside a set of wonderfully fitting lyrics: 'I'm taking my thoughts to a railway station/put 'em on a train just to see what's coming back ... it's coming like a heart attack'.

The construction of the track is made even more impressive through its inspired use of a Schoolly D percussion sample loop appearing at the 1:40 point, slightly sped up from its origins on 'Saturday Night' (1986) by the Philadelphia rap pioneer. The early work of Schoolly D was particularly notable for its powerful drum-machine backing tracks, which had found favour with both Jim and William. Steve Monti then rejoins the song at the 1:45 mark, with the pace-keeping loop gradually fading from the mix as both live drums and sampled rhythms are sequenced seamlessly together.

In the aftermath of the welcome chart success of 'Reverence' in mid-February, when advance sales of the single immediately placed The Jesus and Mary Chain in the UK top ten, 'Far Gone And Out' was swiftly released as a follow-up barely a month later. While not enjoying the same level of chart success, its placement at number 23 at least suggested that the band were no longer being regarded as permanent absentees from the mainstream British charts. The Mary Chain's newly restored credentials were further reinforced by the inclusion of 'Far Gone And Out' on the seemingly ever-present UK chart compilation series *Now That's What I Call Music*, with the track appearing on *NOW 21* alongside typically mixed company, albeit with notable fellow outsiders in the form of The Cure and The KLF.

'Far Gone And Out' also received remix treatment, thankfully to a far better standard than some of its *Honey's Dead* counterparts, with the 'Arc Weld' version proving particularly impressive in its radical departure from the original through being slower paced and feedback heavy. Despite stripping away much of the bass and electro-acoustic guitar work, George Drakoulias' take on the song functions surprisingly well, and the Neil Young live album reference in the title of the mix is especially apt. Originally included on the Def American CD single release of 'Far Gone And Out' – itself sold rather fancifully as a 'Collector's Edition Holographic Disc' – the commendable five-minute mix was rightly included on the 2011 deluxe reissue of *Honey's Dead*.

'Far Gone And Out' also has the unique distinction of having had two separate promo videos filmed for the single. One, directed by Samuel Bayer, arrived at a point when he was riding high on the success of his work on Nirvana's 'Smells Like Teen Spirit' and had been enthusiastically recommended by Warners. The monochrome result, edging dangerously close to a storyline-based video with a protagonist gradually becoming drunker inside an industrial nightclub where The Jesus and Mary Chain just happen to be performing, served as evidence of what can happen when a band hands creative control to an outsider, regardless of that individual's credentials. Bayer's promo, filmed on 10 June and aimed specifically at American audiences, is notably absent from the DVD bonus disc of the deluxe edition of Honey's Dead, unlike the superior Miles Aldridge-directed video for the same track. Aldridge's version feels much more aligned to the Mary Chain aesthetic of the early 1990s, complete with psychedelic colour dissolves, jump-cut negative profile shots of the band miming in an empty warehouse, roaming camera angles and repeated broken-glass effects across the screen.

With doors creaking open once again for the band following the unexpected success of 'Reverence', The Jesus and Mary Chain accepted an invitation to perform on BBC2 arts programme *The Late Show* during March 1992. Of the two tracks recorded, 'Far Gone And Out' was selected for inclusion on the bonus DVD disc of *Honey's Dead*. Unfortunately, the performance pales somewhat beside the accompanying rendition of 'Catchfire' and is hampered initially by the low mix of Jim's vocals, an issue thankfully corrected shortly afterwards, while the Schoolly D sample is also much louder here than on the recorded version. Regardless, the clip remains more than worthy of inclusion, capturing the band live just days before the release of *Honey's Dead* and the commencement of the UK leg of the *Rollercoaster* tour.

'Almost Gold' (3:19)

Amongst the listed credits in the sleeve notes was the useful detail of how many songs each brother sang on the album, and it is on 'Almost Gold', a shimmering semi-ballad, that William's lead vocals are first heard.

The gleaming quality of the song is reflected in the album artwork itself, which features a detail from a beautiful Pre-Raphaelite oil painting by Arthur Hughes, completed between 1851 and 1852, portraying Hamlet's dejected lover Ophelia prior to her suicide. Some fans may have assumed the golden hues and delicate, forlorn face were intended to represent the Honey of *Honey's Dead*, while more pointed critics sighed at what they perceived as the band returning once again to the imagery of 1985. However, the album title itself was intended to suggest that the previous incarnation of The Jesus and Mary Chain was well and truly gone and that Jim and William were consciously moving beyond their past. The Greg Jakobek sleeve design for the single release of 'Almost Gold' may initially appear rather plain, but stare a little closer beyond the bold lettering of the band name and song title and there is the distinct impression of a gold-tinted, blurred image of underwater reeds – the very same amongst which poor doomed Ophelia drowned herself. It is an inspired detail entirely befitting the song itself.

'Almost Gold' evokes a glimmering, hazy atmosphere of gentle sadness at the passing of time, an almost autumnal reflection upon a loving relationship now faded into memory, and it is therefore no surprise that this is one of the tracks on *Honey's Dead* where the noise element so often associated with The Jesus and Mary Chain – and indeed a defining feature of much of the album itself – is toned down considerably. Great care was taken with the song, as evidenced by four consecutive days from 23-26 July being devoted to developing the music before another full day in August was spent completing the track, which was then mixed separately on 25 September. Lovely pitched guitar tones, at times reminiscent of the harmonic figure running throughout Buffalo Springfield's 'For What It's Worth', accompany the clean major-to-minor chord changes in 'Almost Gold', while the unexpected progression used for both the chorus and outro is genuinely beautiful, arguably elevating the song to emotional heights not reached since *Darklands*.

A moment of respite and introspection before the album redoubles its noise-pop assault, 'Almost Gold' was selected as the third and final single from *Honey's Dead*. Released in the UK on 22 June 1992, it unfortunately stalled just outside the top 40 at number 41. This disappointing placing came despite the best efforts of Warners, who employed an extensive multi-format release strategy with the single available on 7", 12", standard CD and even gold-tinted CD editions. There was also a 10" version featuring the opening three tracks from a *Rollercoaster* tour set recorded earlier that year at Sheffield Arena. A radio-broadcast edit of the show, trimmed to eight songs from the full setlist, later appeared on the 2003 *BBC Live In Concert* CD and is more readily accessible via the 2011 *Honey's Dead* reissue.

Due to the single's lack of chart success, the promo video for 'Almost Gold', filmed on 9 June and marking the Mary Chain's second collaboration with Samuel Bayer, was not widely seen upon its original release during the late summer of 1992. Its inclusion on the DVD bonus disc of the deluxe edition of *Honey's Dead* is therefore particularly welcome, allowing fans to revisit what is a refreshingly understated, gold-hued promo in which William and his preferred guitar of the period, a sunburst Gibson 330 (with the Varitone rotary switch visibly engaged, for those interested in such details), receive a generous amount of screen time. Eagle-eyed viewers may also spot Mark 'Wiff' Smith – later drummer on the Mary Chain's *Ruby Trax* contribution – appearing in the background on drums. It was from this very promo shoot that the front and inner sleeve photographs of Jim and William used for the 1993 compilation *The Sound Of Speed* were sourced.

'Sugar Ray' (4:41)

Following the tranquil detour of the previous track, the juddering sound of percussive distortion – not unlike helicopter blades cutting through the air – ushers in 'Sugar Ray', complete with a recycled and accelerated 'Sidewalking' bassline. Punctuated by a shrill looped sound akin to a siren wailing somewhere deep in the background, the verses leave little to the imagination as Jim delivers a series of lewd enquiries with equal measures of malice and relish: 'Did you feel my lips?/Did they slide and slip?/Did you feel my head/shaking through your wrist?'

Painstakingly assembled over seven separate days from mid-July to early August, 'Sugar Ray' is another *Honey's Dead* track in which sex appears with unapologetic candour. Ironically, it also recalls several of the less sonically polished moments from *Automatic*, and not merely because that earlier album contained the similarly titled 'UV Ray' and 'Sunray'. The sweet refrain of 'All I want is you', which cues William's ultra-fuzzed lead guitar break at the 2:06 mark, may echo some of the solos from the 1989 album, but the percussion arrangement on 'Sugar Ray' – built around two separate Steve Monti loops running simultaneously – far surpasses the drum-machine backing that had dominated all but one track on *Automatic*.

A 27-second instrumental extract from the track, incorporating elements of the introduction, the distinctive siren effect and a brief snippet of the main guitar solo, was used in a 1994 American television advertising campaign for Budweiser Ice Draft Beer, with the sound of 'Sugar Ray' accompanying footage of a laser cutting through a block of ice to reveal the branded bottle beneath. The novel experience of hearing a fragment of prime Mary Chain on heavy television rotation was unfortunately limited to American audiences, as the advert never aired elsewhere. It nevertheless proved a far more satisfying commercial outcome for the band than the previous year, when Reebok used a near-identical 15-second section from the opening of 'Reverence' without permission in a series of adverts for their 'Planet Reebok' campaign.

Played live regularly from the UK leg of the *Rollercoaster* tour onwards, a particularly powerful rendition of 'Sugar Ray' from an April 1995 performance at Bristol's Trinity Centre later appeared as the penultimate track on the 2003 *BBC Live In Concert* release and is more easily located today on the second bonus disc of the comprehensive 2011 deluxe reissue of *Stoned & Dethroned*.

'Tumbledown' (4:10)

The first side of *Honey's Dead* concludes with the fuzzed-out pop of 'Tumbledown', a tune that by this stage in their career the Mary Chain seemed capable of carving out with relative ease, although the four days spent meticulously recording the track's individual elements between 11 and 16 July might suggest otherwise. Jim's casual delivery of the lines 'Don't expect to get inside me … Slip right to me/slide right through me' during the bridge section is all the more remarkable given that the track was assembled over several sessions, complemented by an additional two days devoted to final tweaks and mixing, and speaks volumes about how effortless it had become for the band to write and record songs of this quality. The addition of real drums – played by the exceptionally talented Steve Monti – contributes even greater power and urgency to the track, particularly during the final 40 seconds of 'Tumbledown' when additional guitar layers are introduced against a scathing metallic backdrop before it is left to Monti's pounding rhythm contribution to bring the song to a close.

A regularly namechecked influence during the early days of The Jesus and Mary Chain, when Jim and William Reid were explaining their desire to fuse thrilling noise with irresistible pop melodies, was the experimental German outfit Einstürzende Neubauten, formed in West Berlin during 1980 and led by Blixa Bargeld. One of the pioneers of what would later become known as industrial music, Einstürzende Neubauten specialised in an uncompromising blend of rough-edged punk structures and abrasive noise, much of it created using homemade machinery, rudimentary electronics and found objects salvaged from scrapyards and factories.

The band's debut album, *Kollaps* (1981), was clearly a record with which the Mary Chain were familiar and a looped sample from its opening track, 'Tanz Debil', is used to memorable effect on 'Tumbledown'. Heard during a thrilling breakdown at the 1:26 mark, the sample runs for approximately 17 seconds before the song resumes at full pace. Asked during a live phone-in appearance on *KDOC Request Video* – two days after the American release of *Honey's Dead* – about the significance of the sample to the band's evolving sound, Jim's response to the seemingly sincere enquiry from 'Klaus from Fountain Valley' appeared far more sarcastic than serious:

> That particular sample that you're talking about, that's about the best two and a half minutes of the whole industrial music scene … but it's there for the stealing, and we stole it.

The Mary Chain's appearance on the live phone-in show remains a highly entertaining watch, with a notably relaxed Jim and William complaining about the set décor around them while enjoying the various 'lunatics' phoning in ('We're here to talk to American psychopaths'), but the dismissive comment regarding the 'Tanz Debil' sample was almost certainly made in jest. This seems especially likely given that the extract itself was simultaneously being used as part of the intro tape on the *Rollercoaster* tour, accompanied by an extended section from William Burroughs' 'Last Words Of Hassan Sabbah' cut-up poem immediately before the Mary Chain took to the stage and launched into the next song on *Honey's Dead*.

'Catchfire' (4:47)
Cued in by a descending bassline with a pronounced groove set against a shuddering backdrop of tremolo distortion, 'Catchfire' erupts in a blizzard of noise and barely relents for the majority of what is arguably the most impressive track on *Honey's Dead* and one of the finest songs in The Jesus and Mary Chain's entire catalogue.

Featuring the very same Schoolly D 'Saturday Night' loop that had earlier been put to such effective use on 'Far Gone And Out', 'Catchfire' captures William Reid at perhaps the absolute peak of his imaginative powers as a guitarist. His extraordinary solo in the middle of the track is a tour de force of ingenuity, achieved technically through the core mechanism of a Boss tremolo pedal being housed inside a wah-wah enclosure, allowing greater manipulation of the sound during live performance. Reportedly, both William and Jim had to work closely together inside the live room at The Drugstore – one holding the guitar while the other manually manipulated the pedal – in order to capture what Stuart Maconie, in his *NME* review of *Honey's Dead*, described entirely approvingly as 'an unhinged guitar solo'.

An early version of the song was completed at Berwick Street Studios, deep in the heart of Soho, from 20-21 May 1991, before being further developed two months later at The Drugstore, then revisited for additional work on both 9 and 13 August. Clearly, considerable effort was put into the recording of arguably the album's high point, where the grinding momentum of the album version was achieved through a combination of Jim's live bass playing, sampled loops and drum machine rhythms, but it was in concert that 'Catchfire' truly came alive. An outstanding performance of the track was recorded live for BBC2 on 18 March alongside 'Far Gone And Out', although it was not broadcast until a few days after its poppier counterpart had aired. Here, and indeed throughout the *Rollercoaster* tour that followed, William reproduced the extraordinary range of guitar sounds largely through nimble footwork around his effects pedal board, and his handling of the solo during the *Late Show* performance of 'Catchfire' is an astonishing sight. It remains a genuine shame that this particular rendition was omitted from the DVD bonus disc of the *Honey's Dead* reissue, although a superb live take from Sheffield

Arena – initially featured on the 10" release of 'Almost Gold' before appearing on the 2003 *BBC Live In Concert* CD – is more easily accessible via the 2011 deluxe edition of the album.

'Good For My Soul' (3:05)

Sharing vocal duties on an album almost equally for the first time, Jim's next contribution to *Honey's Dead*, recorded across three days between 1 and 5 August before being mixed at The Drugstore on the last day of September, is another gorgeous and rather haunting love song. The seamless manner in which 'Good For My Soul' integrates into the wider flow of the album serves as clear evidence that The Jesus and Mary Chain had, by this stage, fully mastered the dynamics of studio recording on an album which, upon release, rivalled *Psychocandy* itself as a renewed statement of intent.

Beginning with a gentle pulsing synth motif reminiscent of some of Jason Pierce's contributions to the final Spacemen 3 recordings and accompanied by a wash of distorted, delayed guitar buried deep in the background, the beauty of 'Good For My Soul' lies largely in its structural simplicity. A synthetic, shuffling backbeat – this being another Monti-less track – is replaced at the 1:08 mark by a more forceful looped rhythm that remains in place for the remainder of the song while Jim repeats the beautiful refrain: 'She can take the world on another journey into her soul'.

Whether 'Good For My Soul' originated from little more than a pair of drum loops and a riff assembled in the studio or evolved gradually from the bare bones of a two-chord acoustic guitar strum at home, the end result is a truly beautiful piece of music, meditative and melodic from beginning to end. The looped rhythm that drives the song towards its conclusion is accompanied by the sound of the Mary Chain's Gibson 330 being played through William's home practice amplifier – a humble Fender Sidekick that he had owned for years and kept in his flat. It was used specifically on *Honey's Dead* to help create the tight, punchy guitar tone heard as 'Good For My Soul' drifts away on that same glorious two-chord progression.

'Rollercoaster' (3:46)

Beefed up considerably from its original incarnation on the 1990 *Rollercoaster* EP, this revised version (worked on exclusively at The Drugstore from 7-8 October 1991) replaces the earlier drum-machine backing with driving live percussion while also adding an extra guitar layer that, unfortunately, contributes relatively little to the arrangement. At times, it even renders the overall sound somewhat muddier than necessary, with the distinctive jangling guitar outro no longer nearly as clear or effective as it had been on the original recording. Another notable difference is the reduced echo effect applied to William's lead vocals, further raising the possibility that this revisited version of 'Rollercoaster' may have been added relatively late in the sequencing process when finalising the running order of *Honey's Dead*.

'I Can't Get Enough' (2:56)

Honey's Dead marked a massive return to form for the group, containing some of the strongest music that The Jesus and Mary Chain had recorded up to that point, and 'I Can't Get Enough' – noisy and brash yet still retaining clear melodic undertones – is another prime example of how the band were able to maintain such remarkable purity and simplicity within their songwriting.

Recorded from 14-16 August and then mixed during an all-day session less than two months later, 'I Can't Get Enough' launches immediately into William's lead vocal over a strummed rhythm guitar backing, not unlike the similarly upbeat propulsion of 'Far Gone And Out'. The arrangement dispenses almost entirely with unnecessary embellishments beyond a percussive loop that appears briefly at both the 1:09 and 2:23 marks, the latter carrying the song through to its conclusion. The combination of Jim and William's dual backing vocal harmonies during the chorus is especially effective and there is a genuine sense throughout the track that recording it must have been enormous fun, such is the positivity and immediacy radiating from the finished performance.

'Sundown' (4:59)

Sharing its title with half of a particularly cinematic Nancy Sinatra and Lee Hazlewood collaboration from 1968, the final full-length song on *Honey's Dead*, despite ironically being the first to be recorded in earnest at The Drugstore, begins in a deceptively gentle and reflective mood, slowly unfolding at a measured pace with delicate electro-acoustic guitar accompanying William's delivery of lines that include the memorable admission: 'The planet's more fucked up than I'll ever be.'

The aching soul of the track – as bare and confessional as anything the Mary Chain recorded throughout their entire career – steadily builds towards the 3:11 mark when a scorching white-noise coda finally erupts, accompanied by the repeated and ultimately optimistic refrain of 'shine on'. From this point onwards, the song gradually dissolves into increasing dissonance and discord, multiple guitar layers colliding together across the remaining two minutes of runtime.

The heavily distorted and grungy guitar textures that dominate the climax of 'Sundown' were created through a combination of a Boss Distortion pedal and a uniquely sounding semi-acoustic Höfner guitar that Jim had purchased years earlier while on tour – a regular pastime within the band as a means of alleviating boredom on the road – but which had never previously found a place on a Mary Chain recording until finally reaching its perfect moment here. The eventual use of the instrument during the devastating finale of 'Sundown' more than justified the original investment.

'Frequency' (1:21)

And after the devastating climax of 'Sundown', The Jesus and Mary Chain conclude *Honey's Dead* in suitably idiosyncratic fashion, undercutting the preceding intensity with a deliberately low-key reprise of the album opener, tinged with bathos. Recorded over a two-day session from 19-20 August with the somewhat self-explanatory working title of 'Outro', William assumes lead vocal duties as the song quickly mutates into a tribute to The Modern Lovers' legendary 'Roadrunner', complete with the repeated refrain of 'radio on', before 'Frequency' then dissolves into a welter of shuddering distortion without ever quite threatening to outstay its welcome.

Contemporary Tracks

'Heat' (3:02)

During an extensive and illuminating interview conducted at The Drugstore for *The Guitar Magazine* in late spring 1992, William Reid described the process of recording B-sides as follows:

> Either a right pain in the arse or they're totally brilliant. At the moment, we're on a roll, so it's all going very well indeed ... It's a free rein, a chance to do anything you want. I love it.

It is precisely this spirit of liberation and enthusiasm that helped generate some superb B-sides during the *Honey's Dead* era, and 'Heat', built around a descending chord sequence from E major to A major with clear echoes of the progression used on 'Teenage Lust', is such a strong track that it would not have sounded remotely out of place on the finished album itself.

With Jim delivering the vocals in hushed tones, the lyrics are almost entirely overwhelmed shortly after the one-minute mark by a tremendous extended tremolo guitar solo – every bit as blistering as its counterpart on 'Catchfire' – which continues uninterrupted until the end of the song, steadily increasing in ferocity before finally collapsing into silence. Perhaps it was the core sonic similarity between 'Heat' and 'Catchfire' that ultimately led to the track being omitted from the final running order of *Honey's Dead*.

Originally recorded on 4 December 1991, 'Heat' was another Mary Chain recording that unexpectedly found favour with American advertisers, with a thirty-five-second extract featuring Jim's vocal later used in a television campaign for Coors beer under the tagline 'Epic Refreshment'. The song was originally issued as the principal B-side across the 7", 12" and CD single formats of 'Reverence', with engineering duties – as with the majority of the era's accompanying B-sides – handled by Dick Meaney, continuing the relationship established during the *Automatic* mixing sessions at The Church alongside Alan Moulder.

'Why'd You Want Me?' (3:13)

Released as the flip side to 'Far Gone And Out' and featuring William on plaintive lead vocals, 'Why'd You Want Me?' is almost archetypal Mary Chain in terms of its lyrical concerns. The blues, drink, drugs, sin and the night all make their customary appearance, but the twist lies within the very title of the song itself because, despite all the acknowledged failings and vices of the protagonist at its centre, he is still forgiven, accepted and ultimately wanted.

With redemption at its emotional core and an endearing simplicity – particularly in its use of a sparse bassline and restrained percussion backing – 'Why'd You Want Me?' possesses a lovely melody and marks a welcome return to the country-rock inflections, tinged with a little Dylan influence, that The Jesus and Mary Chain could apply to their music with such deceptive ease.

The core trio of Jim, William and Ben, accompanied by new drumming recruit Nick Sanderson, appeared on ITV music programme *The Beat* during the summer of 1993, where they were filmed miming to the released B-side version of 'Why'd You Want Me?' on the stage of the London Astoria.

An alternate version of the song included on the 2011 deluxe reissue of *Honey's Dead* adds a clunkily basic drum-machine backing that sits far too prominently in the mix and, unfortunately, detracts from the understated charm of the original recording. This particular take appeared on the soundtrack to *Encino Man*, a 1992 film memorably described by *Variety* upon release as 'a mindless would-be comedy aimed at the younger set'. An instrumental extract from the latter half of the alternate version of 'Why'd You Want Me?' plays for approximately 75 seconds during the 72nd minute of what unexpectedly became a considerable box office success in America.

'Sometimes' (2:52)

A rare misstep, 'Sometimes' is essentially the core structure of 'Here Comes Alice' shifted up by a key and, given the imagination that William and Jim typically brought to their B-side material, the end result feels unusually uninspired. Released as an additional track on the 12" and CD single editions of 'Far Gone And Out' and engineered once again by Dick Meaney at The Drugstore, this is about as close as the Mary Chain came during the early 1990s to producing a song by numbers. Unfortunately, it feels markedly more backwards-looking than the majority of material generated during the otherwise exceptionally productive *Honey's Dead* sessions.

In a 2015 *Guardian* interview with Mogwai frontman and longtime Mary Chain devotee Stuart Braithwaite, Jim Reid stressed how rock 'n' roll fundamentally relied upon selective borrowing from the past and reshaping the results into something new. By 1992, however, it occasionally seemed as if The Jesus and Mary Chain had perhaps come close to exhausting certain earlier influences and had instead begun drawing upon elements of their own catalogue for inspiration. Fortunately, 'Sometimes' remains very much an isolated lapse in quality control, and its apparent absence from later live performances makes it relatively easy to understand why the band seldom revisited it.

'Don't Come Down' (2:40)
Built around a simple oscillating two-note bassline and lolloping drum-machine backing, 'Don't Come Down' effectively anticipates much of the forthcoming sound of the Mary Chain's 1994 album *Stoned & Dethroned* through its combination of acoustic guitars and deeply relaxed atmosphere.

While amplified lead guitar still emerges during the outro, William's decision to largely resist the temptation of distortion, tremolo and feedback – or indeed all three simultaneously – in favour of a restrained two-note lead motif that gently drifts through the fade-out suits the mood of the track perfectly. It is difficult not to presume that songs such as this, alongside memories of the highly successful acoustic Peel Session recorded in late autumn 1985, played a major role in shaping the Mary Chain's long-discussed ambition to eventually record a predominantly acoustic album.

Sound Of Speed EP (1993)

Personnel:
Jim Reid: vocals, guitar
William Reid: guitar, vocals
Ben Lurie: guitars
Nick Sanderson: drums (tracks 1-2)
Brad Anderson: bass (track 4)
Mark Smith: drums (track 4)
Recorded at The Drugstore, South London, between 6 and 9 April 1993
Producers: William and Jim Reid
Engineer: Dick Meaney
Label: Blanco y Negro
Charts: UK: 30
Running time: 13:02

Following the rigours of the North American leg of the *Rollercoaster* tour, The Jesus and Mary Chain needed time to decompress, and it was during early spring 1993 that recording commenced at The Drugstore on a set of new tracks originally intended for release as an interim EP while the band continued to work on a follow-up to *Honey's Dead*. The studio itself was ticking over with Dick Meaney working in an engineering capacity for many of the bands who booked to work there, which, as the 1990s rolled on, included the likes of Echobelly, The High Llamas and The Divine Comedy, all making use of The Drugstore when the Mary Chain were not at home.

Out of the four tracks that constituted the new EP, which would subsequently appear in full on an identically titled second compilation album released in mid-July 1993, two were recorded as a full band in early April, featuring ex-Clock DVA, Gun Club and World of Twist drummer Nick Sanderson for the first time after a failed audition to join the Mary Chain six years previously. Sadly, despite a decent critical response in the music press upon its late June release, including receiving *NME* Single of the Week, the EP reached no higher than its initial new entry placing of number 30 in the UK charts on 10 July and, two weeks later, dropped out of the top 75 completely.

'Snakedriver' (3:39)
With impeccable rock 'n' roll swagger, 'Snakedriver' (the lead track on the EP given the early working title of 'I got syphilitic hetero friends') kicks off proceedings with Ben Lurie on bass guitar and Nick Sanderson providing a distinctive backing, the first squalls of ominous feedback beginning at the 54-second mark, cued in by the line 'But then I kissed her'. This was a clever nod to The Beach Boys' 1965 track of the same name, itself a cover of the Phil Spector-produced Crystals hit 'Then He Kissed Me', released almost exactly 30 years earlier than the Mary Chain song. With washes of distorted tremolo guitar rising and falling throughout the track in tandem with the

verses, 'Snakedriver' grinds its way towards a remarkable conclusion where Jim's heavily distorted voice, repeating some of the key lyrics from the first verses, ends the track in a duel with William's guitar.

As aggressive in its attitude as 'Reverence' had been and equally confrontational in its lyrical content, with Jim referring to 'syphilitic hetero friends' within seconds of the track beginning, 'Snakedriver' received very little support from UK radio and seemed an unlikely choice for inclusion on a highly successful film soundtrack the following year. Yet that is precisely what happened, further boosting the band's profile Stateside following their extensive touring in support of *Automatic* and, most recently at this point in time, the particularly taxing 40-date Lollapalooza involvement.

During the spring of 1993, the band were approached with an offer to contribute a track for a film adaptation of the comic superhero series created by James O'Barr, with the result being that 'Snakedriver' was licensed for use on the March 1994 release of the official soundtrack album to *The Crow*, appearing as the 12th track on the compilation approximately eight months after its inclusion on *The Sound Of Speed* LP. 'Snakedriver' was also included a year later on the Def American 1995 compilation release of *The Jesus and Mary Chain Hate Rock 'N' Roll* (US only), with the record company perhaps rather cynically capitalising on the song's prior inclusion on *The Crow* despite it not featuring onscreen during the runtime of the film itself. There was an excellent version of the track captured live in the studio for MTV's *Alternative Nation*, with Ben and William playing along to a drum machine backing track while Jim's dispassionate vocals work just as successfully as those on the recorded version. William's lead guitar contributions on this particular live take are distinctly different from those on the EP recording. Sadly, however, this performance did not feature on the deluxe reissue of *Stoned & Dethroned*, unlike the promo videos for the two EP tracks directed by Ian Owles, filmed in the sun-drenched surroundings of Almería in southern Spain from 9-12 June.

'Something I Can't Have' (3:01)

A fantastic upbeat track provisionally titled 'To my Head' and recorded at The Drugstore from the 7 to the 8 April, 'Something I Can't Have' powers through its three-minute runtime with nothing spared and is engaging from the off, not least through its killer opening lyrics delivered by Jim: 'You're in my house/you're in my face/You made me hate the human race'. William's guitar playing throughout the song is cleverly economical, only occasionally deviating from the key melody line that recurs between verses alongside a driving rhythmic backing that is alternately chiming and propulsive. It is only at the conclusion of the track, during the final ten seconds, that we hear more distinctive distorted and feedbacking guitar, almost feeling like a more fitting ending to 'Snakedriver' than the sweet pop at the heart of 'Something I Can't Have', which, above and beyond the fizzing guitar lines, cannot be more finely expressed than through the regular use of an effortless, almost throwaway 'doo doo doo' refrain that fits the song perfectly.

'Something I Can't Have' was the first of two tracks played by the band on BBC TV's *Later With Jools Holland*, broadcast on the evening of Friday 9 July, with Nick Sanderson and Brad Anderson (ex-member of American post-punk group The Wipers) slotting in on drums and bass guitar, respectively. Unfortunately, the appearance was fraught with serious technical issues concerning Jim's microphone feeding back continually, which could not be resolved and was consequently ruining every attempted take, frazzling the already on-edge nerves of Jim and William while testing the patience of everyone else present in the studio. A full version of the experience is detailed at length in the 2022-published *Later ... 30 Years Of Music, Magic And Mayhem*, written by the show's co-creator Mark Cooper, but eventually – after every other band had successfully recorded their contributions to the programme and in the aftermath of spending the intervening hours drinking and seething at a monitor engineer they had never worked with before – satisfactory live versions of 'Snakedriver' and 'Something I Can't Have' were played by the Mary Chain. Broadcast a few nights later on BBC2, the band's delivery of the two tracks is tight, tense and teetering on the brink of fury. Both are included on the bonus DVD disc of the deluxe reissue of *Stoned & Dethroned* and make for essential viewing as the Mary Chain eventually triumph in the face of adversity. There is also some guilty pleasure to be had in revisiting footage of an infuriated and inebriated Jim swinging at a roaming BBC camera after it gets in his face once too often.

'Write Record Release Blues' (2:56)

The only track on the EP to feature a drum machine accompaniment instead of live drums, this song hurries along with a fuzz bass and heavily distorted rhythm guitar backing. There is also a notable percussive synth loop used in the background, similar to that heard on some of the B-sides from the *Automatic* era, in addition to a trebly ringing guitar sound entering the mix at the 2:20 mark, achieved typically by William striking his guitar at the bridge to create a distinctive piercing effect. While blending elements of the Mary Chain's two most recent albums up to this point in their recording career, lyrically 'Write Record Release Blues' (or 'William's Blues' to refer back to its original working title) breaks new thematic ground with its pointed diatribe against the grim reality of the rock 'n' roll rigmarole, which the band were now fully part of. William would return to this subject matter just a few years later in an even more hostile attack on the institutions involved.

'Little Red Rooster' (3:26)

The final track on the EP was originally included on a 1992 compilation entitled *Ruby Trax* that celebrated the 40th anniversary of the *NME*. When approached to contribute a song, with the remit being that the Mary Chain had to choose a UK number one single from the previous 40 years to cover, the group decided to tackle the Rolling Stones' first chart-topper from 1964, itself a cover of a track popularised by Howlin' Wolf three years previously, which also carries the unique distinction of being the only blues song ever to reach number one in the UK.

With Mark 'Wiff' Smith (ex-Play Dead drummer) and Brad Anderson (ex-Wipers bassist) joining Ben Lurie on rhythm guitar alongside William and Jim, the version of 'Little Red Rooster' recorded at The Drugstore is swaggering and lurching, distorted and driving, receiving the full-on Mary Chain treatment. It is a savagely fierce rendition of the Howlin' Wolf classic, absolutely dripping with menace and noise, while Jim's vocals, deliberately overloaded in the mix, are distorted and threatening. Clearly pleased with the results of their work, the Mary Chain ensured that 'Little Red Rooster' not only closed the EP in style but also took pride of place on the full compilation album that followed. The track has since featured on both *The Power Of Negative Thinking* – closing Disc Three of the 2008 four-CD set – and the deluxe reissue of *Stoned & Dethroned*.

Stoned & Dethroned (1994)

Personnel:
Jim Reid: vocals, guitar, bass
William Reid: vocals, guitar, bass
Ben Lurie: guitar, harmonica, organ, bass
Steve Monti: drums, percussion
Recorded at The Drugstore, South London, between January and December 1993
Producers: William and Jim Reid
Engineers: Alan Moulder (tracks 1, 2, 9, 11, 14) and Dick Meaney (tracks 3 to 8, 10, 12, 13, 15 to 17)
Label: Blanco y Negro
Charts: UK: 13, Sweden: 19, Australia: 27, Canada: 43, US: 98
Running time: 47:45

From 1985 to 1989, the Mary Chain produced three consistently excellent yet sonically distinct LPs, culminating in the triumph of *Honey's Dead*, which effectively combined the strengths of each of its predecessors while embracing the ever-evolving technology of loops and sampling. The 1992-released album was a glorious amalgamation of everything that had marked The Jesus and Mary Chain out as one of Britain's most inventive rock bands, with the added distinction of achieving genuine chart crossover, albeit with disappointingly sporadic returns. However, such was the success of the Mary Chain's fusion of the elements – in terms of song structures, melodies and lyrics – that had worked so well on previous albums into *Honey's Dead*, that a stylistic shift was now necessary if the band were to avoid repeating themselves. Therefore, the mainly acoustic approach initially intended for the set of songs that would become *Stoned & Dethroned* seemed both a deliberate and logical next move.

William and Jim Reid had planned for a relatively quick turnaround of the album, and, through working alongside the trusted figures of Alan Moulder and Dick Meaney, both assisting with engineering duties, it did not seem unreasonable for the Mary Chain to expect to have a new collection of songs recorded and released within a relatively short space of time. With their music now being recorded exclusively at The Drugstore, the band were based in a familiar environment that had already produced excellent results from the majority of songs recorded there from 1991 onwards at 9A Amelia Street. Unfortunately, the idea of *Stoned & Dethroned* being recorded quickly and painlessly as a purely acoustic album never quite came to pass.

The intention for the band's new project to take the form of an all-acoustic affair was soon placed in doubt by a combination of the Mary Chain's wariness of removing so many of the elements that had previously served them so well and the fact that, for the first time since the *Psychocandy* sessions during the spring and summer of 1985, they were now willing and able to record as a full band. With Ben Lurie contributing both bass and guitar parts while Steve Monti supplied drums and percussion for all 17 songs, the involvement of these two musicians was more extensive than on any previous Mary Chain non-compilation album up to that point in their recording career.

Faced with the challenge of keeping every one of their new songs exclusively acoustic, William and Jim soon realised the limitations such an approach could entail and the knock-on effect it might have on the music being recorded. Consequently, the initial, commendably ambitious idea was adapted in order to allow the new songs to become more acoustic-sounding, if not now completely devoid of electric guitars and drums. While diverging somewhat from the original plan, the final results still became their warmest and richest record to date, all the more impressive given the background to the recording, where cracks were now beginning to appear in the previously unified front.

Stoned & Dethroned was the first Mary Chain album not to feature the customary Reid/Reid songwriting credit for each track. Instead, the extensive sleeve notes accompanying the album went further than ever before by identifying the specific songwriter for each song, whether Jim, William, or, in the singular case of 'Save Me', both brothers together. Significant changes had also taken place in their personal lives, with both William and Jim separating from the girlfriends who had been with them since the early days of the band. William would later begin a new relationship with Hope Sandoval, the singer of acclaimed US band Mazzy Star, who – alongside Shane MacGowan of The Pogues – would play an important role in the recording of *Stoned & Dethroned* by taking on a guest lead vocal slot, another first for The Jesus and Mary Chain.

Previous unhealthy habits that had, for the most part, been confined to touring now began to encroach upon the recording process itself, something the Mary Chain had largely avoided up to that point. Suddenly, the proximity of a pub situated all too conveniently across the road from The Drugstore on the corner of Amelia Street and Walworth Road – however grim both it and its regulars may have been – seemed an ideal place to adjourn while waiting for microphones to be set up and mixes to be completed. No longer watching the clock due to owning the very studio in which they were recording inevitably led to a more relaxed attitude towards sessions, something made very clear from William Reid's own frank admission in a *Melody Maker* cover feature published a month before the release of *Stoned & Dethroned*:

> ...we've got our own studio, we can mosey down and make a record whenever we feel like it.

Originally scheduled for release in April 1994, the album was delayed until August as more B-sides were recorded and further mixing took place, with the band continuing to tinker with the results of the previous year's extensive recording sessions. Upon release, *Stoned & Dethroned* reached number 98 on the US charts – their highest and only Stateside placing to date – while the album managed a disappointing number 13 in the British charts, only one position higher than *Honey's Dead* more than two years previously. This was despite the strength of lead single 'Sometimes Always', which itself stalled at a disheartening number 22, yet another indication that the Mary Chain remained out of step with the ever-transient tastes of the UK music scene.

Many in the British music press regarded *Stoned & Dethroned* as country-tinged solely on the evidence of lead single 'Sometimes Always', an assumption that did the remaining 16 songs a considerable disservice and was certainly not representative of what may lyrically be the darkest album the Mary Chain ever recorded. With a greater emphasis on songwriting and atmosphere than ever before across a set of 17 songs stripped back to their bare essentials – in stark contrast to the layered composites of *Honey's Dead* – it can be argued that *Stoned & Dethroned* is musically closer in spirit to *Darklands*, itself recorded in the wake of their painstakingly pieced-together 1985 debut. It certainly sounds like their most organic album since *Psychocandy*.

However, the music business they had entered almost a decade earlier was changing radically as the 1990s progressed, and increasingly The Jesus and Mary Chain found themselves at odds with many aspects of it, perhaps more so than ever before.

In the 2024 memoir *Never Understood*, Jim identified the position in which the band found themselves by the time *Stoned & Dethroned* was ready for release:

> ... by the time baggy and shoegaze and grunge had come and gone, and Britpop had taken over, it didn't matter how good the music we made was – and I honestly think *Stoned & Dethroned* and the next album *Munki* are as good as, if not better than, anything else we ever did.

The title of their new album itself provided more than a hint as to how William and Jim felt they had been deposed from their once-vaulted position within the music scene, usurped by all manner of lesser groups and left as an afterthought. Evidently, little respect was now being shown towards the Reids for the Mary Chain's considerable efforts, which, ironically, had helped blaze a path for a new generation of guitar bands to subsequently steal a march on them.

Stoned & Dethroned was released in August 1994 during the very same week as *Definitely Maybe*, which soon became the fastest-selling debut album in UK chart history, cementing the position of Oasis as the dominant force within the British music scene. Two bickering brothers in a guitar-heavy, uncompromising band who also happened to be signed to Creation – the irony was not lost on the Mary Chain that their own experience with Alan

McGee a decade earlier was now being viewed almost as a rehearsal run for the all-conquering success Oasis were enjoying in their first flush of fame.

Faced with the prospect of playing to the same crowds in the same venues as before, The Jesus and Mary Chain ultimately opted not to embark upon a European tour to promote their new album, although an American tour consisting of two months' worth of dates was booked for later that autumn. No British dates were played whatsoever during 1994 aside from a one-off, music press-heavy launch gig for *Stoned & Dethroned* in London. Fans were instead left alone with the new album, given time to absorb and appreciate the refreshing stylistic shift it represented.

'Dirty Water'

The opening track may initially give the impression that the Mary Chain had mellowed, but 'Dirty Water' is far from passive and would have made for a more than suitable single were it not for the gloriously barbed chorus that includes the jarring promise: 'Fuck with me and I'll fuck with you/Isn't that what we're supposed to do'. Nearly ten years into their recording career at this point, the band had certainly not eased off but instead actively diversified their sound to impressive effect. By broadening their sonic palette, the Mary Chain were able to experiment with a style that allowed them to incorporate new melodic elements into their songs, and Ben Lurie's harmonica contribution is a particularly notable feature of 'Dirty Water'.

A guide vocal demo version, with William leading proceedings from the opening count-in onwards and recorded during a two-day session devoted exclusively to the track on 15-16 February, was included as an outtake on the 2011 deluxe edition of *Stoned & Dethroned* and appears to have been recorded directly in the live room at The Drugstore. This bonus track, largely unmixed and missing Ben's harmonica part, serves mainly as a curiosity for committed fans. However, an excellent live version of the song formed part of a Black Sessions radio broadcast recorded in Paris on 6 September 1994 alongside several other tracks from the new album.

'Dirty Water' may initially have been regarded as something of a low-key album opener, but it ultimately stands as every bit as bold a first-track choice as 'Just Like Honey' in 1985, 'Darklands' in 1987 and 'Reverence' in 1992. Setting the tone for the album while immediately establishing its low-key mood, the Mary Chain – restless as ever – were once again pushing themselves in a new direction.

'Bullet Lovers' (3:37)

The longest track on *Stoned & Dethroned*, while also being the second to exclusively feature William playing all acoustic and electric guitar parts, 'Bullet Lovers', in both mood and lyrical content, conjures a doomed romantic spirit with an understated undercurrent of retribution and revenge from the song's protagonist. The track also has the distinction of being one of the earliest on which the Mary Chain worked, with recording devoted exclusively to 'Bullet Lovers' over a three-day session from 3-5 February. This followed less than a week after an intensive four-day period devoted to an early incarnation of 'Sometimes Always', which at the beginning of 1993 still retained the working title 'Sandy Song' (a similarly titled 'Sandy Shaw One' had intriguingly formed part of the day's recordings during a 19 May 1989 *Automatic* session) and represented the first piece of music recorded for the new LP.

Reportedly, the inspiration for 'Bullet Lovers' came from a news report William happened to watch during the Los Angeles leg of the Lollapalooza tour in which two drive-by serial killers were being interviewed live on television and, in a truly *Natural Born Killers*-style twist, one of the murderers' girlfriends appeared particularly aroused by her partner's exploits.

For a band who had faced regular criticism regarding their supposed debts to The Velvet Underground – as if that were ever something worthy of disdain – *Stoned & Dethroned* frequently recalls the quieter 1969-era Velvets of tracks such as 'Jesus' and 'I'm Set Free', with emphasis placed upon melancholia rather than outright violence. However, 'Bullet Lovers', with its steady tick-tick-tick backing suggesting a countdown before 'Someone's gonna get shot tonight', certainly makes the latter possibility feel distinctly plausible.

'Sometimes Always' (2:32)

The lead-off single from *Stoned & Dethroned* and the first Jesus and Mary Chain track to feature a duet with an outside vocalist, 'Sometimes Always' is a perfect pop song that deserved a far higher UK chart placing than the lowly number 22 achieved during the week of its mid-July release. It remains a beautiful moment in the band's history – a doomed lovers' song addressed both to each other and themselves – and seems almost tailor-made for delivery by a cocky Nancy Sinatra/Lee Hazlewood pairing or even a grinning Sonny & Cher partnership.

Instead, the duet was recorded at The Drugstore by Jim and Hope Sandoval, singer with Mazzy Star, who had previously supported the Mary Chain under her band's earlier incarnation as Opal during the late 1980s. Admirers of her distinctive vocal style, William and Jim had long intended to ask Hope to sing on one of their own songs, although it was not until 'Sometimes Always' that the ideal opportunity finally presented itself. Mazzy Star's autumn 1993 UK tour allowed Hope to visit The Drugstore between 30 and 31 October to record her vocals for the track.

A persistent belief that has cemented itself into Mary Chain lore in the decades since the release of *Stoned & Dethroned* is that cult 1960s artist Lee Hazlewood had originally been approached to sing the male lead part. However, the truth remains somewhat more convoluted, with Jim himself offering an explanation of sorts during a December 2010 interview with *Artrocker* magazine:

> I think the original idea was to get Lee Hazlewood to sing on that album. I can't remember if it'd actually been decided which song. I think it might have been 'Drop'. He agreed to do it, and everything was going okay. And I think maybe the plan was going to be a duet with Hope Sandoval.

Unfortunately, a misunderstanding involving over-officious security backstage at a Los Angeles Lollapalooza date – combined perhaps with Hazlewood's unfamiliarity with the practice of waiting in a VIP area beforehand – led to the legendary singer-songwriter taking offence at not being able to immediately meet William and Jim in person. His initial willingness to contribute vocals soon transformed into increasingly expensive and unreasonable demands upon the Mary Chain to accommodate him while in London. Sadly, this brought an end to what could have been a fascinating collaboration, although there would also have been something rather fitting about Hazlewood returning the favour by singing on one of the Mary Chain's shortest – and most Hazlewood-in-spirit – tracks, 'Drop', after they had covered his own similarly brief 'I'm Glad I Never' in such style.

Replacing what might have been with a delivery that at times sounds as though there are genuine emotional stakes involved, Jim's vocals on the recorded version of the song are engagingly wry while Hope's own delivery remains beautifully blank, as 'Sometimes Always', over the course of its perfectly judged two-and-a-half-minute runtime, charts the return of the prodigal boyfriend. Despite its relative brevity – and ideal timing for a pop single with chart ambitions – the song is actually a deceptively slow-burning track. Gradually building momentum as verses are traded back and forth, Hope, after chastising the 'lucky son of a gun', reaches the climax of the verses with 'You went away/But now you're ba-a-a-a-a-ack', which then cues in the second of William's gloriously fuzzed-out guitar solos that, in its joyous release, helps emphasise the happy ending for the lovers, bringing 'Sometimes Always' to a close in style, with Jim – who both opens and closes proceedings – getting the final word.

In the accompanying promo video, directed by Sophie Muller and filmed in and around Los Angeles between 1 and 5 March, elements of classic Americana are unmistakably brought to the fore, with cowboy hats and dusty desert roads among its most obvious visual motifs. During the promo, the Mary Chain trio are shown propping up a bar beside Hope Sandoval in a setting that feels entirely appropriate, as verses are exchanged while Jim and Hope deliberately avoid each other's gaze. Stills from the promotional video were used to striking effect within the artwork for *Stoned & Dethroned*, not least the image of an open highway stretching into the distance that served as the album's front cover.

'Sometimes Always' was released as a single in the United States during October 1994 and holds the distinction of being the only track by The Jesus and Mary Chain ever to enter the *Billboard* top 100, peaking at number 98.

This achievement was arguably aided by the presence of the Mazzy Star vocalist, whose own band at that point were enjoying both critical and commercial success following the deserved acclaim surrounding their remarkable earlier single 'Fade Into You'. When The Jesus and Mary Chain toured America during autumn 1994, support was provided by Mazzy Star, with 'Sometimes Always' frequently appearing as an encore. Augmented over the years by a variety of guest singers, the track remains a firm favourite within the band's catalogue and ranks among their finest moments.

'Come On' (2:12)

The first solely Jim Reid-written song to feature on *Stoned & Dethroned*, the album version of 'Come On' is a full minute shorter than the 'new version' released as a single in September 1994. Both takes nevertheless contain the key elements one would expect, with all the familiar Mary Chain components present and correct – a core three-chord structure, Jim's faultless delivery and a welcome use of fuzz bass within the mix. The integration of the latter, played by Jim himself while Ben is credited with providing the standard bassline, proves an especially interesting sonic touch. In the past, the Mary Chain may well have opted for an uncompromising layer of feedback at the same point, but with such a sweet-sounding song, an alternative approach was clearly considered necessary and is entirely justified.

The inclusion of a backwards guitar loop at the 2:14 point in the 'new version', running for approximately 20 seconds, is an intriguing concession to a more contemporary-sounding production style, reminiscent of similar moments from Loser by Beck, which, by spring 1994, had become near ubiquitous on MTV and American college radio. Featuring a neat lyrical nod to 'Viva Las Vegas' in the opening line of the second verse, the accompanying promo video for 'Come On' finds the Mary Chain appearing more comfortable with their role onstage, even if not entirely at ease with the inherent artificiality of miming to the track.

Sophie Muller, directing her second promo for *Stoned & Dethroned*, cleverly tapped into this glitzy sense of pretence by placing a variety of suitably wannabe Las Vegas acts – including a drag queen, stripper, aspiring starlet and seasoned lounge singer – centre stage, intercut with footage of the Mary Chain bathed in glowing red light against a backdrop of dry-ice smoke plumes. Both of Sophie Muller's promotional videos for the album are included on the DVD bonus disc of the deluxe edition of *Stoned & Dethroned* and capture a point in the band's career where they appeared noticeably more accepting of the format, resulting in two of the most visually striking promos they ever produced. Also included on the reissue are all four tracks from the band's BBC radio session recorded on 6 July 1994, where the shorter album version of 'Come On' is faithfully performed by the full band lineup of the period.

Unfortunately, despite Blanco y Negro once again adopting a sales-minded multi-format strategy – including two separate CD singles that at least justified their existence through the inclusion of six additional tracks across both discs – 'Come On' could only limp to number 52 in the UK charts, a dispiriting 30 places lower than the peak achieved by 'Sometimes Always' only a few months earlier.

'Between Us' (2:37)
On a 17-track album, there is always the danger that certain songs may slip through the cracks and not receive the appreciation they deserve, and 'Between Us' – an underrated gem – is a perfect example. Opening with a rhythm guitar figure that functions almost like a countdown into the main structure of the song, the initial root-note bass pattern soon evolves into a more propulsive line while William appears to address the state of an ever-changing relationship through lyrics that could equally be interpreted as reflecting the Mary Chain's own development from their earliest days and the emotional toll of the journey they had undertaken: 'We were never scared of light/but the shadows that it throws/are digging deep inside of us/and I think we're full of holes'.

The reflective atmosphere of 'Between Us', enhanced through a combination of jangling rhythm guitar, a country-tinged lead guitar break and another fuzz bass contribution from Jim, is capped by one of the Mary Chain's most familiar hallmarks – a 'doo doo doo' vocal refrain that runs through the final 40 seconds of the track, adding yet another irresistibly melodic touch to what was already a fine addition to the album.

'Hole' (2:13)
Both engineered and mixed by Dick Meaney at The Drugstore, 'Hole' is one of the tracks on *Stoned & Dethroned* that comes closest to being a solo Jim Reid recording, aside from Steve Monti's drumming and percussion contributions and William's additional acoustic guitar part. Every other instrument on the track – electric and acoustic guitars, bass and fuzz bass – is played by Jim on a song that, sonically, bears strong similarities to several of the descending barre-chord-based tracks from the 1991 *Honey's Dead* sessions, most notably 'Heat' and 'Teenage Lust'.

During his largely positive review of *Stoned & Dethroned*, *NME* writer David Quantick – notably the first journalist ever to write about The Jesus and Mary Chain after witnessing their live debut in June 1984 – commented upon 'the Mary Chain's addiction to a very small family of chords', and 'Hole' is certainly one of the tracks where the familiarity of earlier songs, not necessarily derivative but nonetheless comfortingly recognisable and almost quintessentially Mary Chain, exerts a noticeable presence.

To the band's credit, however, 'Hole' resists the temptation to lean heavily upon effects-laden guitars, instead concentrating on the gradual build-up of quiet tension, and, as one of the shortest tracks on the album, never once overstays its welcome.

'Never Saw It Coming' (3:32)

Initially recorded during a two-day session from 23-24 April and built around a simple repeating chord pattern alternating between E and A, 'Never Saw It Coming' returns to one of the recurring subjects that has surfaced throughout the Mary Chain's career – death – although seldom has the theme been treated in such a lush and melodic fashion. Reminiscent of the beautiful gospel-inflected 1965 single 'People Get Ready' by The Impressions, written and sung by Curtis Mayfield, 'Never Saw It Coming' possesses a similarly plaintive and direct emotional quality.

With a wash of organ gradually entering the mix from the 2:54 point alongside a brief two-note guitar solo shortly afterwards, the song succeeds – through its careful development of the meditative atmosphere at the heart of *Stoned & Dethroned* – in generating a sense of coming to terms with life and its inevitable disappointments. There is also a subtle complexity within the arrangement itself, which gradually becomes more sophisticated across the song's three-and-a-half-minute runtime through the careful addition of complementary instrumental parts and individual sounds. The rhythm guitar strumming, for instance, grows increasingly forceful as the song progresses before a chiming upper note eventually enters the mix. Such skilful layering of individual elements ultimately elevates 'Never Saw It Coming' far beyond what more casual listeners may initially dismiss as little more than a basic two-chord acoustic strum.

'She' (3:06)

Another Jim Reid-written track, which features William contributing rhythm guitar backing only while Ben Lurie supplies the lead guitar parts, 'She' is an impressive addition to the dream/nightmare-girl songs that the Mary Chain were able to produce with consummate ease. With lines such as 'No, I just don't get her at all/she doesn't speak at all', the song inhabits familiar emotional territory while simultaneously sounding more melodically sophisticated than many of the band's earlier efforts.

'She' invites favourable comparisons with mid-period The Beatles, particularly the *Rubber Soul* era, through its cyclical arpeggiated guitar motif, which carries the song far beyond a simple three-chord structure. The ability of the track to evoke the melodic economy and colour of 1965-66 Lennon and McCartney compositions is especially noteworthy, although one would be hard-pressed to find a Beatles song quite so brazenly celebrating a love interest who 'comes complete/with a switchblade and her speed'.

Despite this lyrical deviance, 'She' would have made for a fine single release during the promotion of *Stoned & Dethroned*, although it inevitably faced stiff competition from several other standout tracks on the album.

'Wish I Could' (2:40)

Opening the second side of the vinyl edition of *Stoned & Dethroned* – by the mid-1990s an increasingly antiquated format – 'Wish I Could' features William on lead vocals, his warm and measured delivery contributing heavily to the weary, burned-out atmosphere of the track.

Unfortunately, this remains one of the less impactful songs on the album, with the quality of the lyrics ranging from genuinely evocative imagery, such as 'sparks glowing in the dark' to the rather clumsy 'Jesus walked on the water/we walk on dampness too/yes we do/through and through'. The pedestrian pacing of the song similarly lacks the vitality present elsewhere on the record, and while there is no denying that 'Wish I Could' is carefully structured and sensitively arranged, it ultimately does not rank among the strongest compositions on *Stoned & Dethroned*.

'Save Me' (2:41)

Introduced through a lovely arpeggiated guitar figure played by Ben Lurie, which runs through most of the track and sounds almost like an extension of the drowsy beauty of Sunday Morning, 'Save Me' functions as the Mary Chain's own slightly twisted lullaby.

It is also worth remembering that, despite the frequent comparisons made to *Psychocandy*, it is actually the material on *Stoned & Dethroned* that most consistently resembles the work of the late-period The Velvet Underground. Beneath its unashamedly attractive musical exterior, 'Save Me' presents a strong undercurrent of hope amid the personal wreckage of a narrator who feels 'sick and unholy' and is 'living like dirt'.

The only track on the album to share a joint writing credit between Jim and William Reid, 'Save Me' initially appears to stand in direct opposition to the darker arrangements traditionally associated with the Mary Chain. Yet beneath the music – including a relatively simple guitar break that nevertheless conveys considerable emotional weight despite its brevity – there exists a curious paradox which William Reid himself neatly identified during a 1994 interview with *Melody Maker*, when he observed 'The songs may be musically bright, but lyrically not so'.

'Till It Shines' (3:15)

With its original working title of 'Everybody Is A Star', this particular track originated in an earlier version from the 1991 *Honey's Dead* sessions, and a three-day focus from 26-28 August certainly suggests that the Mary Chain recognised its potential, hence its being earmarked for inclusion on their next album a few years later. Another William Reid-led track featuring acoustic rhythm guitar backing from both Ben and Jim, 'Till It Shines' drifts past with an effortless sense of melody and restraint. The instrumentation may once again be stripped back, but the song possesses a quiet grace that helps sustain the reflective mood at the heart of *Stoned & Dethroned*.

If anything, 'Till It Shines' suffers only through being one of several similarly strong tracks on an album that frequently utilises the same instrumental palette and leisurely pacing. Taken in isolation, however, it remains an understated and highly effective piece of songwriting whose understated charms become increasingly apparent with repeated listening.

'God Help Me' (2:45)

The second track on *Stoned & Dethroned* to feature guest vocals, 'God Help Me' is delivered in suitably wracked fashion by Shane MacGowan, the legendary Pogues frontman who occupied a similarly maverick role within the British music scene to that of the Mary Chain themselves. William had been dissatisfied with his own original vocal attempt and subsequently suggested that the song be sent to MacGowan as a demo in the hope of securing his contribution. With the track having been developed over the course of three separate sessions at The Drugstore from the end of January into early February 1993, it would appear that it had already been earmarked as having considerable potential. It is also worth noting that the four-song Radio 1 Evening Session recorded for the BBC in early July 1994 contains a version of 'God Help Me' featuring an excellent lead vocal from William, offering a fascinating glimpse into how the track may have sounded had he not decided otherwise.

Mutual admirers of one another's work, the process of persuading MacGowan to sing on the album initially appeared straightforward enough, and so, with Jim acting as emissary, a demo tape of 'God Help Me' was duly dispatched. Yet after several months had passed – accompanied by repeated reminders and corresponding promises from Shane that he would still gladly contribute vocals – when he finally arrived at The Drugstore on 6 October, effectively shepherded there by a friend determined to ensure he kept the appointment, it transpired that MacGowan had little idea what the song he was expected to sing actually sounded like.

Coached line by line through the performance the band hoped for, Shane attempted numerous takes of steadily diminishing quality, having seemingly expected to be singing on something closer in spirit to a Pogues track. It was ultimately left to the considerable talents of Alan Moulder to skilfully assemble the usable fragments into a coherent vocal performance which, to his immense credit, does not remotely resemble the patchwork creation it reportedly became according to later recollections from both Jim and William. However, upon final playback, the assembled version of 'God Help Me' featuring Shane's initial vocals sounded too exuberant – closer in tone to an upbeat Pogues performance – as Jim later recalled in *Never Understood*:

> Shane's delivery just seemed too aggressive – it was done with too much gusto.

This alternate vocal take, which indeed sounds somewhat too energetic for the bruised confessional atmosphere the band were seeking, would later appear as one of the bonus tracks on the 2011 deluxe edition of *Stoned & Dethroned*.

To their considerable credit, both the Mary Chain and MacGowan persevered and, after a new vocal track was recorded on 15 November, the second completed version of the song ultimately became one of the standouts on the album. The self-flagellating nature of 'God Help Me', with its genuinely bleak lyrics, is elevated to an impressively desperate level through Shane's delivery, and while there can be little doubt that either Jim or William – or perhaps both together – could have performed the track to a more than satisfactory standard, it remains significant that the Mary Chain recognised this particular song, with its themes of emotional collapse and exhaustion, required something beyond the traditional confines of the band itself.

In his review of *Stoned & Dethroned* for the *NME* during August 1994, David Quantick praised MacGowan for contributing 'the best vocal on the album ... immensely moving ... both desperate and peaceful at the same time.' During an extended hiatus from The Pogues, Shane later joined the Mary Chain to perform 'God Help Me' at the launch-party show for *Stoned & Dethroned* held at the legendary Soho nightclub Madame JoJo's, where several Pogues songs were also added to the setlist for familiarity. Ironically, it was drunken mistakes from Ben and William during 'Ghost Of A Smile' that reportedly provoked the ire of a comparatively sober MacGowan. A mistake-free Mary Chain studio version of this Pogues classic later appeared as a B-side on the second CD single release of 'Come On' and remains a suitably stomping tribute.

'Girlfriend' (3:15)

With a near-identical fuzz bass and slide guitar sound to that first heard on 'Why'd You Want Me?' during the *Honey's Dead* sessions, and with an early version of the song attempted at The Drugstore on 22 August 1991, 'Girlfriend' could easily be identified as quintessential Jesus and Mary Chain, not least through Jim's delivery of lyrics centred on 'dirty little stories about needles and skin.

There is little doubt that the guest appearances from Hope Sandoval and Shane MacGowan brought additional brightness and variation to *Stoned & Dethroned*, their distinctive vocal contributions providing welcome contrast to some of the album's more introspective moments. However, 'Girlfriend' requires no such assistance. The version recorded on 15-16 April 1993 and further developed over subsequent months at The Drugstore is an energetic and expertly crafted pop song whose suitably twisted lyrics generate their own momentum and appeal.

On an album that frequently feels like a conscious reinvention for the Mary Chain, the new artistic direction is perhaps best encapsulated through one particularly telling lyric that almost functions as a mission statement for the band themselves: 'Don't wanna live in the same old place/got new ideas/and I got new taste'.

A live version of 'Girlfriend' debuted during the Black Sessions recorded on 6 September 1994 and is, perhaps understandably, performed at a noticeably faster tempo than the studio recording while featuring an especially distorted fuzz bass sound. Nevertheless, it retains the same upbeat and infectious quality. An excellent live performance of the song was also recorded at Bristol's Trinity Centre on 19 April 1995 and initially released as part of the BBC *Live In Concert* series before later being included on the deluxe edition reissue of *Stoned & Dethroned*.

'Everybody I Know' (2:12)

A delicate song rippling with quiet tension, 'Everybody I Know' comes closer than perhaps any other track on *Stoned & Dethroned* to fulfilling the Mary Chain's original vision of making an entirely acoustic album – an ambition that, in the end, was only partially realised.

Reminiscent in places of the melodic phrasing from 'Here She Comes Now' by The Velvet Underground, 'Everybody I Know' is distinguished through its intertwining acoustic guitar parts, all played by William, alongside a gently descending arpeggiated motif heard during both the introduction and, more prominently, the closing moments of the track.

The reflective mood that permeates so much of *Stoned & Dethroned* once again comes to the fore here through lyrical references to 'ghosts of people I have been' and 'ghosts of things I've said and done come to haunt me', while Steve Monti's restrained percussion provides the lightest possible rhythmic framework beneath the song.

Initially worked on by the Reids over two days from 12-13 April at The Drugstore, 'Everybody I Know' would feature over a year later as one of four tracks recorded for an early July BBC Radio 1 Evening Session, all of which were included in full on the deluxe edition of *Stoned & Dethroned*. A similarly impressive live version was also performed in studio for MTV's *120 Minutes* a month later, featuring William playing a stripped-back, effects-free acoustic guitar with the introductory arpeggio figure significantly clearer in the mix than on the studio recording itself. The complete session performance, which also includes 'Come On', can be found on the DVD bonus disc accompanying the deluxe reissue.

'You've Been A Friend' (3:34)

Stoned & Dethroned proved a far more emotional album than many listeners may initially have expected from The Jesus and Mary Chain, and with 'You've Been A Friend', the band reach one of the record's clearest moments of emotional vulnerability regarding how difficult circumstances may already have been becoming behind the scenes.

Given the group's steadily declining commercial standing following *Honey's Dead* alongside the worsening relationships at the core of the band itself, it is difficult not to view the song as quietly prescient concerning the direction in which both Jim and William's personal and professional lives now appeared to be heading. Yet even amid the mounting despair and exhaustion that must surely have accompanied the aftermath of Lollapalooza and the growing sense that the Mary Chain's momentum was beginning to falter, 'You've Been A Friend' ultimately closes on a note of genuine gratitude and perhaps even cautious hope.

Beginning with a weary, woozy lullaby-like guitar introduction, the song gradually builds towards an unexpectedly uplifting outro which subtly increases the pace and lifts 'You've Been A Friend' towards a surprisingly positive conclusion, aided greatly by a welcome – if frustratingly understated – organ contribution from Ben Lurie.

'These Days' (2:14)

Sounding uncannily like a slowed-down variation on the opening track 'Dirty Water', it is at this point – the 16th song on the album, lest it be forgotten – that the Mary Chain return to a recognisably familiar chord progression which, while not entirely derivative, is certainly more than merely reminiscent.

In retrospect, *Stoned & Dethroned* arguably stands as the group's most sonically unified album, with Ben Lurie and drummer Steve Monti filling out the Mary Chain sound more completely than ever before. It is also worth recalling that this was the first album since *Psychocandy* to feature entirely non-electronic drums and one where the songs, taken collectively, work together to sustain a singular mood with remarkable consistency and precision.

That meditative atmosphere of resignation, reflection and gradual acceptance reaches perhaps its clearest expression on 'These Days', the album's penultimate track, where William's restrained delivery of the sparse lyrics evokes a weary acknowledgement of both the wider world and his own place within it.

Played at a stately pace throughout and featuring only the bare minimum of lyrical content, 'These Days' never outstays its welcome and, at just over two minutes in duration, remains one of the shortest tracks on the album. There is also the distinct sense that, in the hands of a different band, the song would almost certainly have been expanded through an elongated outro and obligatory guitar solo. Not so with the Mary Chain of *Stoned & Dethroned*. Instead, 'These Days' reaches what might best be described as the right side of grace, ending precisely when it should and resisting any unnecessary embellishment.

'Feeling Lucky' (2:15)

As an album closer, 'Feeling Lucky' is strikingly minimal lyrically, with William delivering only four lines during the opening 25 seconds of the track. Yet what little is said, with its understated embrace of love and cautious optimism, neatly encapsulates much of the emotional core of *Stoned & Dethroned* itself – direct, unadorned and quietly affecting.

The closing section of the song, with Jim contributing percussion, is as grand as a two-minute track could reasonably hope to become and represents the only moment on the album where the Mary Chain fully surrender to the temptation to extend proceedings beyond strict concision. The final 90 seconds unfold as a gently expansive instrumental outro, which carries 'Feeling Lucky' – the 17th and final track on the band's fifth studio album – calmly towards the finishing line.

Rather than concluding *Stoned & Dethroned* with drama or noise, the Mary Chain instead choose quiet resolution. It is a surprisingly graceful ending to one of the most emotionally revealing records of their career.

Contemporary Tracks

'Till I Found You' (2:06)

Purportedly an unused track from the *Stoned & Dethroned* sessions, yet sounding more akin to a *Honey's Dead*-era offcut from 1991 or 1992, 'Till I Found You' shares the upbeat feel and brisk electro-acoustic guitar backing of 'Far Gone And Out' while also featuring some notably busy drumming from Steve Monti throughout. Included first on *The Power Of Negative Thinking* in 2008 and subsequently on the 2011 deluxe edition of *Stoned & Dethroned*, the track would later be radically revisited by William Reid in solo form as the opening piece on his second Lazycame album, *Finbegin* (2001). Retitled 'God', the deconstructed reinterpretation sounds almost entirely removed from the tightly structured Jesus and Mary Chain original, demonstrating just how far William's increasingly experimental instincts had evolved by the turn of the millennium.

'The Perfect Crime' (1:35)

Appearing as the principal B-side to 'Sometimes Always' in July 1994 and included across all formats of the single, this brisk 90-second composition written by Jim once again hints at the influence of Lee Hazlewood, perhaps functioning as the grim counterpart to the Mary Chain's stylish cover of 'I'm Glad I Never'. 'The Perfect Crime' also featured among the four songs recorded for the Radio 1 Evening Session broadcast shortly before the single's release in the UK.

The song works best as a brief vignette, sketching out the collapse of a doomed relationship with more than a hint of menace, not least through the chilling confession: 'I lost control/I got a hold of a knife/I took a hold/and then I ended your life'.

Were it not for the overt darkness of its subject matter – something distinctly at odds with the carefully sustained mood of *Stoned & Dethroned* – 'The Perfect Crime' could easily have found a place on the album itself.

Despite its brevity, the track remained a favourite within the band's live repertoire from 1994 onwards and would later resurface during Jim Reid's solo performances in the mid-2000s.

'Little Stars' (3:13)

The final B-side included on the various formats of 'Sometimes Always' before reappearing just over a year later on the Def American compilation of recent rarities, oddities and B-sides, 'Little Stars' – complete with its charmingly Hank Williams-inspired 'cookin'/good lookin'' lyric – is a curiously disjointed affair that often sounds like two separate song fragments awkwardly fused together.

Where this particular structural approach had worked to magnificent effect on 'Some Candy Talking' back in 1986, the results here are less successful despite William delivering several genuinely heartfelt lyrical moments. Unfortunately, these are somewhat undermined by a final throwaway line that earns the song an otherwise unnecessary explicit-language warning on modern streaming platforms. Nevertheless, there remains something endearing about 'Little Stars', not least because of its evident willingness to experiment beyond more conventional song structures.

'Drop' (Re-recorded) (1:53)

(See previous section on *Automatic* for fuller discussion of alternative versions of this track)

The re-recorded version of 'Drop', featuring newly recorded vocals and additional understated lead guitar contributions from William in the languid style that dominated much of *Stoned & Dethroned*, appeared as the second of three CD single B-sides accompanying the release of 'Sometimes Always'. The song was also performed live, with Hope Sandoval providing beautifully languorous vocals, during the 4 June 1994 *Undrugged* concert celebrating ten years of Creation Records at the Royal Albert Hall – a knowingly tongue-in-cheek title, given many of the participants involved that evening.

'New York City' (1:59)

The freedom afforded by working extensively within The Drugstore encouraged the Mary Chain to experiment more openly, and several of the B-sides accompanying the 'new version' releases of 'Come On' demonstrate a willingness to move beyond the established sonic framework of *Stoned & Dethroned*.

A delicate and overtly folky composition, 'New York City' reflects William's longstanding admiration for Bob Dylan, an influence he regularly acknowledged whenever musical inspirations became the subject of interviews. Delivered through a suitably surreal set of lyrics while 'trippin' out in the pouring rain', the track continues the Mary Chain's complicated love-hate relationship with America, this time in a dazed and slyly rebellious fashion – 'Hey Mr President/get down on your knees' – within a style not typically associated with the band during this period, even if its acoustic connection to *Stoned & Dethroned* remains apparent.

The melodic appeal of the song is undeniable, yet it is William's stream-of-consciousness lyricism, indebted to Dylan at his most playful and elliptical, that ultimately elevates 'New York City' beyond merely being another sweetly melodic two-minute tune.

'Taking It Away' (2:13)

Effectively a solo Ben Lurie composition, re-recorded from its home four-track origins at The Drugstore and supplemented by an additional William Reid guitar part, 'Taking It Away' emerged from material Lurie had been developing independently before being offered for consideration as a B-side. Given that 'Come On' required six supplementary tracks across its various formats, the availability of further suitable material was understandably welcomed.

Built around a steady two-chord rhythm guitar pattern complemented by organ textures and Steve Monti's characteristically tight drumming, the song also features a William lead guitar line that follows the vocal melody rather too closely, perhaps suggesting a relative lack of emotional investment in the material or – unusually for him – a decision to play things cautiously within another songwriter's framework.

'Taking It Away' remains perfectly serviceable as a B-side, yet lacks the distinctive spark and tension that so often elevated the Reid/Reid partnership above more straightforward songwriting exercises.

'I'm In With The Out Crowd' (2:38)

Gloriously noisy from beginning to end, with a high-pitched distorted jangle introducing proceedings and even the audacity to incorporate a barely disguised refrain from 'Gimme Hell', Jim's inspired B-side contribution 'I'm In With The Out Crowd' points directly towards the rougher, more abrasive sound the Mary Chain would later explore in far greater depth on *Munki*.

Its liberating sonic departure from the largely restrained atmosphere dominating the *Stoned & Dethroned* sessions proves particularly invigorating, although it is worth recalling that the *Sound Of Speed* EP tracks 'Snakedriver' and 'Something I Can't Have' had also been recorded at The Drugstore during roughly the same period in spring 1993.

Featuring the self-aware and defiantly committed lines, 'I've been trying/but I don't get far/I've got nothing/hey but I'm a star', alongside a healthy scattering of expletives, 'I'm In With The Out Crowd' captures The Jesus and Mary Chain reconnecting with the uncompromising and unapologetic spirit that had defined their earliest work and the song is all the more exciting for it.

'Ghost Of A Smile' (2:55)

Originally appearing on *Hell's Ditch* (1990), the fifth studio album by The Pogues and the final release to feature Shane MacGowan, 'Ghost Of A Smile' was a particular favourite of the Reid brothers and chosen as a fitting song to reinterpret in tribute. It is entirely possible that this was the track MacGowan mistakenly believed he had been invited to sing upon when first asked to visit The Drugstore rather than 'God Help Me', yet Jim's vocal performance here – strongly supported by Ben Lurie's backing vocals – proves every bit as compelling as the original.

Performed live alongside MacGowan at the *Stoned & Dethroned* launch show at Madame JoJo's in Soho, 'Ghost Of A Smile' also appeared during the Black Sessions recording for Radio France several weeks later, this time with Jim resuming lead vocal duties. Whether heard live or in studio form, the Mary Chain's version remains faithful to the spirit of the Pogues' original while subtly reshaping the arrangement through alternative instrumentation, including understated organ parts in place of the traditional banjo, accordion, whistle and mandolin backing.

'Alphabet Street' (2:18)

The second of two tracks engineered by Nick Addison and recorded while the band were reportedly in an advanced state of intoxication, this gloriously chaotic dismantling of Prince's 1988 single 'Alphabet Street' sees the Mary Chain returning to the extreme deconstructionist approach that had long characterised many of their cover versions.

With a thin, distant drum pattern reportedly captured through a remote microphone positioned on a stairwell at Amelia Street, where the kit had been set up, the recording is almost consumed beneath layers of sludgy overdriven guitar and Jim's heavily distorted vocals. Yet there is also a palpable sense of liberation running throughout the track – the sound of the Mary Chain experimenting recklessly within the comfort of their own studio environment. The addition of 'Sympathy For The Devil'-style backing vocals only strengthens the impression that, amidst all the sonic vandalism, the band were clearly enjoying themselves immensely.

'New Kind Of Kick' (2:49)

A live cover version of a 1981 EP track by The Cramps, this recording was powered entirely through solar energy at the University of California San Diego during the autumn 1992 leg of the Rollercoaster tour before later appearing on a Greenpeace compilation LP in 1994, following a three-day visit to Los Angeles from 8-10 February, when the track was mixed by the band. The Mary Chain had long professed admiration for The Cramps, frequently citing the psychobilly pioneers during interviews throughout their career, and this dedicated rendition of one of the group's strongest tracks demonstrates precisely why.

I Hate Rock 'N' Roll (1995)

Personnel:
Jim Reid: vocals, guitar
William Reid: guitar, vocals
Ben Lurie: bass, guitar
Nick Sanderson: drums
Recorded at The Drugstore, South London, between 13 and 29 March 1995
Producers: William and Jim Reid
Engineer: Dick Meaney
Label: Blanco y Negro
Charts: UK: 61

'I Hate Rock 'N' Roll' (3:46)
One of the most directly challenging and uncomfortably masochistic singles the band ever released, 'I Hate Rock 'N' Roll' is an anti-love song to the music industry, bristling with distaste for the machinations that nurtured it while leaving behind a trail of unloved, ignored and disenfranchised people – and bands.

By the time 'I Hate Rock 'N' Roll' was released as a single in the UK in June 1995 (it would also feature on a similarly titled compilation LP in the States later that same year), The Jesus and Mary Chain had spent over a decade in the music business and there can be little doubt that ever-diminishing returns in terms of critical acclaim and record sales had taken their toll, not least on William Reid, who delivers the song with the perfect level of resentment. By the middle of the 1990s, he had had more than enough of the whole business and the organisations that helped sustain it.

A key line from this most uncompromising – lyrically and musically – Mary Chain track, which still contains an incredibly catchy melody, is 'I hate rock 'n' roll/I hate it cause it fucks with my soul', and in a June 1995 interview with *Melody Maker*, essentially to help promote the forthcoming single, William was forthright in detailing where he firmly believed the problem lay:

> It's not really about rock 'n' roll. It's about the rock 'n' roll business. It's fucked with my soul, it's fucked with me since day one. I'm disenchanted, disillusioned, disenfranchised, disengaged, disconnected.

A combination of romanticism towards – and naivety regarding – the true machinations behind the façade of the music industry, alongside inevitable frustrations at finding his band trapped on a relentless treadmill, had taken its toll. In addition, the Mary Chain's own artistic progression was now barely being acknowledged, let alone rewarded, with the laudable *Stoned & Dethroned* criticised in many quarters for the band supposedly no longer sounding like themselves. Ultimately, this led William to pen the venomous set of lyrics for 'I Hate Rock 'N' Roll', the hostility of which is matched by the ferocious nature of the music unleashed alongside them, perfectly described in a November 1995 review by Dave Thompson in *Alternative Press* as being a case of 'the Chain don't so much bite the hand that feeds them as rip it off at the wrist, and impale it on a spike.'

Resentment, frustration and deep-rooted disappointment power 'I Hate Rock 'N' Roll', and the uncompromising nature of the track reveals itself from the off with the sounds of the Mary Chain literally plugging in, switching on and charging up prior to launching into one of their most scathing and corrosive songs. The key elements typically associated with the band – unapologetically feedback-laden guitars, singalong melodies and undeniably misanthropic lyrics – are all present, but it is their alchemical combination here that helps secure a magnificent return to the noisy form that made The Jesus and Mary Chain so incredible in the first place. Its inclusion three years later on *Munki* speaks volumes, too.

Delivered via heavily distorted buzzsaw rhythm guitars and driven by the superbly propulsive drumming of returning member Nick Sanderson, the first verse of 'I Hate Rock 'N' Roll' is seemingly at odds with the title of the track itself, as William sings of his love for rock 'n' roll and 'all the people with nowhere to go/...nothing to show'. However, it is with the second and then third verses that the guns are well and truly trained on the true targets of the song – the commercial behemoths of the BBC and MTV – whom William holds responsible for manipulating the music industry that 'fucks with my soul'. During the third verse of 'I Hate Rock 'N' Roll', the former emotion from the love/hate dynamic disappears completely, replaced with its opposite, which becomes the dominant mood for the remainder of the track.

The next 90 seconds of 'I Hate Rock 'N' Roll' are filled with unrelenting waves of gloriously escalating guitar noise, the likes of which the Mary Chain were easily capable of dispensing but had seldom opted to do so in such a caustic, concentrated manner since the *Psychocandy* days. Their 1985 debut was now becoming something of an albatross for the band, with many in the music press seemingly unable to stop themselves from making jaded references back to the group's initial impact, almost wishing they had indeed called it a day after their debut LP had been released.

Within the first minute of this extended break in the track, there is also the sound of a wah-wah guitar battling against swells of feedback and distortion that ring on and on until the 2:04 mark, where all of the guitars temporarily drop out of the mix, leaving only Ben Lurie's single-note bass pulse and Sanderson's ride cymbal maintaining the pace before 'I Hate Rock 'N' Roll' begins to build back into what the average listener would reasonably expect to be the next verse. Instead, even more unforgiving noise is added to the mix at the 2:38 point and again 11 seconds later, where a burst of teeth-drilling feedback bears more than a passing resemblance to the multiple loops carefully sampled and punched into tracks back in the days of working at Southern Studios. It is almost as if the Mary Chain are saying to their critics: if this is what you really want, then let's remind you exactly how it sounds – we could have done this at any point but never wanted merely to repeat ourselves. And as listeners reach that very same realisation, 'I Hate Rock 'N' Roll' halts for a perfectly timed pause before William re-enters the song – after close to two minutes of guitar assault – to remind us of the facts, over and over again, as the track powers to a close: 'I hate you rock 'n' roll/ rock 'n' roll hates me'.

After previously working alongside Alan Moulder and the band, Dick Meaney had continued his role with the Mary Chain on the B-sides for 'Come On' as well as selected tracks on *Stoned & Dethroned*, and he was again engaged at The Drugstore on engineering duties for 'I Hate Rock 'N' Roll' and its accompanying B-sides. Despite the decidedly anti-commercial nature of the track, its release as a single reminded fans of the very reason why they loved The Jesus and Mary Chain in the first place. Sadly, however, 'I Hate Rock 'N' Roll', utterly starved of daytime airplay, decidedly at odds with the prevailing Britpop climate and even subjected to a rather pathetic ban of sorts when a BBC Radio 1 live broadcast from Bristol's Trinity Centre on 19 April 1995 removed the track from the setlist, spent a solitary week at number 61 in the UK charts. This carries the unwelcome distinction of being the lowest return for any of the band's major-label releases in Britain.

Regardless of its lack of commercial success, 'I Hate Rock 'N' Roll' easily remains one of the greatest singles in the Mary Chain's career, and the fact that Jim, William and Ben shot and edited their own promo video – correctly predicting it would receive next to no airplay – demonstrated both their faith in the song and admirable defiance in the face of mounting adversity. The unsurprisingly rarely seen promo is included on the DVD bonus disc of the 2011 deluxe edition of *Munki* and features the band filming themselves both holding and placing spray-painted signs bearing the song's key lyrics in and around a sunny London city centre, with particular focus given to the area outside the BBC's main building.

The final word on this classic Mary Chain track belongs to an unrepentant William, both belligerent and fatalistic, who told *Rolling Stone* in late 1995:

> I think there are a lot of people in rock hating me now because they take it as a personal attack. Maybe this song will finish our career. If it does, I'll have proven my point.

'Bleed Me' (3:37)

Written and sung by Jim, this track was the main B-side to 'I Hate Rock 'N' Roll', included on the cassette single as well as the 10" and CD releases. Recycling – albeit with slight alterations – the opening lyrics to 'Don't Come Down' from the *Honey's Dead* sessions a few years earlier, 'Bleed Me' is a pleasant, largely acoustic-based tune built around a cyclical arpeggio pattern that sounds as though it originated as a *Stoned & Dethroned* offcut.

The song passes pleasantly enough until the 2:40 mark when, instead of petering out towards an expected conclusion, the track suddenly roars into life and, for the next 50 seconds or so, powers through an extended sequence of fuzzy distorted guitars and wah-wah soloing. A combination of the two distinctive styles the Mary Chain had been developing at The Drugstore during 1993 and 1994, 'Bleed Me' remains an intriguing mixture of pastoral balladry and guitar blitz, even if it never quite fully satisfies as either.

'33 1/3' (3:17)

Studiously ignoring further melodic complexity in favour of a Suicide-influenced two-note, two-chord structure, '33 1/3' is most interesting for indicating the musical direction in which the Mary Chain were heading by the mid-1990s and would ultimately perfect – albeit under the most challenging circumstances – on their next album.

Opening with a more overt use of keyboards than ever before and bringing to mind the type of extended tracks that Spacemen 3 had made their own by the close of the 1980s, '33 1/3' is almost overwhelmed by trademark Mary Chain guitar noise running intermittently throughout the remainder of the song alongside Jim's subtly distorted vocals, which allow him the opportunity to quote from the Stones' 1965 single 'Satisfaction', a huge inspiration for both Reid brothers.

'Lost Star' (2:05)

Built around a gently strummed four-chord pattern in the key of G, 'Lost Star' occupies the same mature musical vein as the majority of *Stoned & Dethroned*, alongside which – much like 'Bleed Me' – it seems naturally to belong. Another relaxed and melodic track with a relatively brief runtime, the song lyrically reaches a form of elegiac realisation through lines including 'Life ain't so bad when you're a star'.

Featuring regularly on later reissues and compilations, 'Lost Star' possesses the doomed romanticism that William's more ballad-oriented songwriting had achieved with relative ease by this point in the Mary Chain's career.

Munki (1998)

Personnel:
Jim Reid: vocals, guitar
William Reid: vocals, guitar
Ben Lurie: guitar, bass
Nick Sanderson: drums
Recorded at The Drugstore, South London, between 1995 and 1997
Producers: William and Jim Reid
Engineers: Dick Meaney (tracks 1 to 7, 9 to 12, 14, 16, 17) and Alan Moulder (tracks 8, 13, 15)
Label: Creation (UK), Sub Pop (US)
Charts: UK: 47, Sweden: 49
Running time: 69:28

The creation of the Mary Chain's 1998 album was a convoluted and stressful affair, which nevertheless resulted in one of their most impressive records: a consistently strong 17-song set produced under circumstances wholly unlike anything the band had previously experienced, with the principal songwriters recording initially together and later almost entirely apart. A subsequent lukewarm response from Warners brought a 12-year association to an end, with the completed album eventually being thrown a lifeline by the group's first manager – now enjoying considerable success – more than a decade after his dismissal.

Following the mid-1995 release of 'I Hate Rock 'N' Roll', The Jesus and Mary Chain played a series of European festivals, appearing in Portugal, Spain, Belgium, Greece and Germany over the next 12 months. Between these performances, recording sessions took place at The Drugstore, where new material was developed by the core trio of the band, supplemented by Nick Sanderson and engineered almost exclusively by Dick Meaney. The initial results were looser and rawer than those on predecessor *Stoned & Dethroned*, although the Mary Chain's melodic strengths remained as impressive as ever. At this stage, there was still the sense of a cohesive live band functioning effectively together, and by the summer of 1996, approximately ten tracks – supplemented by the 1995 single 'I Hate Rock 'N' Roll' – had been recorded and mixed. These songs were considered strong enough for inclusion on a new album, notably marking a return to the shorter track listings associated with the band's releases from *Darklands* (1987) through to *Honey's Dead* (1992).

As part of her role working alongside Geoff Travis in the running of Rough Trade management since 1987, Jeanette Lee visited The Drugstore, where, despite the album not yet being fully complete, her encouraging response to the material played to her gave the Mary Chain renewed confidence. This proved particularly important given the increasingly alienated position the band occupied within the UK music scene by the mid-1990s. Upon relaying her thoughts to Travis – described in an interview with Zoe Howe for the essential band biography *Barbed Wire Kisses* as 'Not radically different, but good' – the tracks were duly sent on to him, and not unreasonably the Mary Chain expected a similarly positive reaction. Perhaps a smooth route towards releasing the album by the end of 1996 would now follow, with their principal supporter and key link to Blanco y Negro still firmly behind them. Sadly, this was not to be the case.

A few days after receiving mixes of the tracks, Travis contacted the band and, over the course of a single phone call, brought his ten-year association with the Mary Chain to an abrupt end. As Jim later recalled in *Never Understood*:

> ... telling us that *Munki* wasn't up to our usual standard, in fact (it) was the worst record he'd ever heard. He went through the album, trashing it track by track, and then told us he didn't want to work with us anymore. We were devastated.

The damage inflicted upon the band's already precarious confidence by Geoff Travis's rejection – perhaps, with hindsight, a coldly pragmatic assessment that the Reids' time had passed – was compounded by the similarly unenthusiastic response that followed when the mixes were subsequently played to their record company. Rob Dickins suggested that the album, in its current state, required additional tracks suitable for release as singles, and while it remains unclear whether this was merely an attempt to delay an inevitable separation, the advice at least enabled Jim and William to return to The Drugstore. There they embarked upon a series of increasingly fractured recording sessions which steadily accelerated what now seemed an unavoidable march towards the collapse of The Jesus and Mary Chain by the close of the decade.

Another significant dissolution during this period was the departure of manager Chris Morrison, whom the band dismissed before failing to appoint a permanent replacement. This was despite the presence of potentially suitable candidates, including fellow Scotsman Colin Wallace, who, following his lengthy association with 4AD, briefly took charge and later reflected during a 2020 online interview:

> I loved working with the Mary Chain, but when I was managing them during that *Munki* record, that wasn't such good fun. William was in a very strange place at that time...

Whether Chris Morrison, Colin Wallace, or anyone else could realistically have intervened to repair the rapidly deteriorating relationship between William and Jim remains debatable. Matters were further exacerbated by escalating alcohol and drug consumption, much of which was now taking place in the studio, and the inevitable destructive effect this had upon both brothers' personalities. The absence of strong management became merely one additional pressure among many. By this stage, the internal dynamic that had sustained the band for so long had effectively fractured, resulting in a recording process where the earlier collaborative core of the album was supplemented by tracks recorded separately by either Reid at different times and with different personnel present, rarely together as they almost always had been previously. In a strangely prescient twist, this mirrored how both William and Jim had originally envisioned their own separate groups before ultimately joining forces as The Jesus and Mary Chain.

The band had effectively split into two camps. William recorded late at night or over weekends, accompanied by Dick Meaney at The Drugstore or sometimes entirely alone, while Jim worked on his songs alongside Ben Lurie, again with Meaney generally present. The one constant between these increasingly separate versions of the Mary Chain was Nick Sanderson, who drummed on both brothers' material. Contributions from Terry Edwards on trumpet, guest vocals from Hope Sandoval and Linda Reid ('Sister Vanilla'), and engineering and mixing work from Nick Addison and Alan Moulder were among the few exceptions to the otherwise divided recording process through which the album was completed.

Additional songs, including 'Cracking Up' and 'I Love Rock 'N' Roll' – which ironically would later emerge as singles, albeit for another label – were recorded and mixed over the following 12 months. By the summer of 1997, despite the continuing disintegration of the brothers' relationship, the completed album – now titled *Munki* at the suggestion of younger sister Linda – was presented to Warners to a distinctly lukewarm reception. Rob Dickins bluntly informed the group that Blanco y Negro would still release the record if both Jim and William insisted, but warned them that Warners would make little effort to promote it, given the near-total lack of investment in either the album or the band. The implication was unmistakable: perhaps the Mary Chain would be better seeking another outlet that genuinely believed in their music.

A separation following this meeting now appeared inevitable, and with The Jesus and Mary Chain simultaneously management-less, label-less and internally fractured, many observers may well have expected the circumstances to finish the band entirely, leaving their final album unreleased and known only to a small circle of friends, associates and industry insiders who possessed privately circulated cassette copies of *Munki*. Lesser groups would surely have collapsed under such conditions.

It was through Jim's reconnection with Alan McGee – and the resumption of a friendship abruptly terminated in autumn 1986 following McGee's dismissal as manager – that a suitable route for the album's release unexpectedly emerged. On paper, an established alternative rock band with a celebrated back catalogue should have represented a major signing coup, but by 1997, there appeared to be remarkably little industry interest in The

Jesus and Mary Chain. William addressed this state of affairs directly on 'Never Understood', one of the album's key tracks, while Jim later reflected in the *Munki* reissue notes:

> We were pretty much screwed by that time – nobody was interested in the Mary Chain then. I'm not really sure why. We had a reputation as fuck-ups that weren't worth investing in.

For McGee, meanwhile, the romanticism of the prodigal sons returning to Creation must have held considerable appeal and, with an album already largely completed, the financial risk involved in re-signing the Mary Chain was minimal. From the Reids' perspective, they were now joining a label that at least appeared genuinely invested in their music, unlike Warners, who had merely tolerated it. Creation also possessed a degree of financial stability – due largely to Sony's substantial investment after acquiring approximately half the label in 1992 – meaning the company that the Mary Chain had helped launch 14 years earlier now represented a very different proposition from the independent operation responsible for the 11 singles released before 'Upside Down'. Shortly after the official announcement of their return to Creation, the Mary Chain also secured a Stateside deal with the critically acclaimed Sub Pop label, who would release and promote the album in America.

With crucial label support now restored, final mastering sessions took place at The Town House in Shepherd's Bush during autumn 1997. The band also incorporated a series of additional audio snippets between several tracks. These sound collages, largely sourced from the answering machines of Jim, William and Ben – including an amusingly drunken message left by Nick Sanderson for Ben – combined with bursts of radio static and fragmented voices to give *Munki* a uniquely disorientating sonic identity unlike anything previously released by the Mary Chain. Against the odds, and despite the deeply difficult circumstances surrounding its creation, the result was a remarkably cohesive and powerful album of which the band were rightly proud.

Freed from the restrictions of an in-house art department, the album's visual presentation also marked a significant departure from previous Mary Chain releases. *Munki* adopted a far looser and more experimental aesthetic, from its striking cover image through to the deliberately chaotic yet colourful typography used for the track titles.

Preceded by the singles 'Cracking Up' and 'I Love Rock 'N' Roll', released in April and May respectively and briefly returning the band to the lower reaches of the UK top 40, *Munki* finally emerged on Creation Records at the beginning of June 1998 following its long and troubled gestation. Sadly, it also became the poorest-selling album of the Mary Chain's career, reaching only number 47 before disappearing from the UK top 100 after a single week. Despite several notably positive reviews from American publications including *Rolling Stone*, *Entertainment Weekly* and *SPIN* – in marked contrast to the generally indifferent response of the British music press – *Munki* failed to chart at all in the United States, representing another bitter disappointment.

Ironically, the situation Rob Dickins had warned might occur had the album remained at Warners now effectively unfolded at Creation once the initial excitement surrounding the band's return had faded. The British music scene had moved on, Creation itself was beginning to wind down and The Jesus and Mary Chain increasingly appeared unable to catch a break. Amid a series of promotional appearances, sporadic UK gigs and select European festival performances – where the curious decision to perform in suits added another unusual visual element – tensions between Jim and William continued to intensify. William, increasingly unhappy and isolated within his own band, eventually withdrew from participating in interviews altogether, leaving Jim and Ben to handle promotional duties alone.

With the Mary Chain having played live fewer than a dozen times during 1996 and 1997, the sudden demands of a punishing touring schedule throughout 1998 should perhaps have served as a warning that matters were unlikely to end well. During a 2017 interview promoting *Damage And Joy*, their first album in almost two decades, Jim reflected ruefully on how the dramatic collapse of The Jesus and Mary Chain's original incarnation might have been avoided:

> I really believe things would have been different if someone around us had had the sense to say: 'They just need to get away from each other, you go off here, you go off there, come back in six months.' Instead, somebody booked us into a big fucking world tour, so here we are, we can't stand the sight of each other, sitting on a tour bus in America somewhere…

And so it came to pass that an intensive American tour organised by Sub Pop during early autumn hastened the end of The Jesus and Mary Chain. After only two dates of a 19-show run, William walked out of the band following a truly chaotic performance at the House of Blues in Los Angeles, leaving the remainder of the group to fulfil most of the outstanding commitments and bringing the original era of the Mary Chain to a deeply unhappy close alongside a sadly neglected final album.

'I Love Rock 'N' Roll' (2:37)

On an album bookended by Jim's 'I Love Rock 'N' Roll' and William's diametrically opposed 'I Hate Rock 'N' Roll', it is worth recalling that while the 1995 track is singularly scathing about the music business at large and the corporations who wield control over it to the detriment of the majority of artists involved, the former is a joyous ode to the redemptive power of music itself, reflected in the upbeat tone of the song that opens *Munki* in suitably positive fashion.

Recorded as part of the Mary Chain's response to Rob Dickins' recommendation that the material played to Warners during the summer of 1996 be supplemented with additional tracks, 'I Love Rock 'N' Roll' was written by Jim to counter the negativity he felt William had expressed so strongly in his own take on the subject. This was evidently something that rankled the elder Reid, not least because his song incorporated several of the exact same lyrics, albeit twisted into something considerably darker. In stark contrast to the 1995 single, 'I Love Rock 'N' Roll' is an unashamedly positive affirmation of the power of music that had inspired the Mary Chain, offering both brothers an opportunity to express themselves artistically while escaping the stifling surroundings of their upbringing for a lifestyle that would otherwise have been unimaginable. Early in the 2010 feature-length documentary *Upside Down: The Creation Records Story*, Jim expressed the same sentiment when he explained on camera that 'Everything we were and everything we had, we got from rock 'n' roll. It was totally heartfelt.' Rock 'n' roll had saved both Jim and William Reid, and, clichéd though the phrase may seem, the opening track on *Munki* never once sounds insincere or forced.

Aside from Nick Sanderson's fantastic powerhouse drumming, which propels the song from beginning to end, 'I Love Rock 'N' Roll' is also notable for featuring Terry Edwards, whose contribution added another fresh texture to the Mary Chain sound, much as Ben Lurie's harmonica had done on 'Dirty Water' four years earlier. Having previously contributed to albums by artists as varied as Tindersticks, Gallon Drunk and Spiritualized, Edwards had already demonstrated his admiration for the band through the endearingly sincere 1991 instrumental EP *Terry Edwards Plays The Music Of Jim And William Reid*, where his trumpet faithfully emulated the vocal melodies and even gamely approximated the guitar playing – and feedback – of 'Never Understand', 'Everything's Alright When You're Down', 'The Hardest Walk' and 'Break Me Down'. A cassette copy of the release was passed on to the Mary Chain and reportedly impressed them so much that they ordered a boxful to distribute among friends. There was therefore only ever likely to be one name in mind when the time came to bring a horn player into the sessions at The Drugstore.

Edwards' contribution to 'I Love Rock 'N' Roll' consisted primarily of a relatively simple melodic trumpet line shadowing the song's central hook, a request that may initially have surprised such an inventive musician. Nevertheless, the use of trumpet on both this track and 'Man On The Moon' undoubtedly added another nuanced layer to the music, something clearly appreciated by both Jim and William to the extent that Edwards also joined the band for several UK live performances during 1998. He additionally appeared on a version of the song recorded for a Radio 1 Evening Session during April of that year alongside 'Moe Tucker', 'Degenerate' and a radically slowed-down rendition of 'Reverence'. All four tracks from what proved to be the Mary Chain's final BBC session appearance were later included on the 2011 deluxe reissue of *Munki*.

Also featured on the reissue – and again including Terry Edwards, though notably not Nick Sanderson due to his commitments with Earl Brutus – is the excellent promo video for 'I Love Rock 'N' Roll'. Geoff Donkin, Nick's drum technician, proved a more than capable stand-in drummer, performing with the band at several European gigs and promotional television appearances. Donkin later rejoined the Mary Chain during the September-October US tour following a serious shoulder injury suffered by Sanderson that forced him to withdraw from the remaining dates.

Shot on an empty white soundstage with a 'Punk Rock' backdrop replacing the famous 'Candy' sign, the promo for 'I Love Rock 'N' Roll', directed by Ben Unwin, deliberately echoes the iconic 'Just Like Honey' video from more than a decade earlier. The expanded six-piece lineup – including Phil King, Geoff Donkin and Terry Edwards – appear dressed in black suits and white shirts, all in varying states of dishevelment. While the band's stark monochrome appearance is reinforced by Ben Lurie's striking black-and-white Stratocaster, Unwin's frenetic direction and the painstaking scratches manually etched onto the film negative ensure that the finished promo is anything but restrained. The result is an energetic and visually arresting companion piece that comfortably matches the quality of the music itself.

Released during May 1998 as the second and final Mary Chain single following their return to Creation, and backed by three strong B-sides on the CD digipak edition, 'I Love Rock 'N' Roll' only just scraped into the UK top 40 at number 38 a week before *Munki* itself was issued to what proved to be a largely indifferent public. The principal exception appeared to be the band's increasingly diminished but still fiercely loyal hardcore fanbase. Sliding rapidly to number 81 the following week before disappearing from the charts altogether, 'I Love Rock 'N' Roll' deserved far better and, to date, remains the final Jesus and Mary Chain single to reach the UK top 40.

'Birthday' (3:57)

The first of the 'William songs' on *Munki*, 'Birthday' is a superb collaborative effort featuring both brothers sharing vocal duties over a track driven by drum machine, fuzz bass, a repeating crystalline keyboard motif and, most strikingly of all, a sample of the opening drumbeat from 'Just Like Honey'. This instantly recognisable rhythm first emerges subtly in the background at the beginning of the song's opening chorus around the 1:07 mark.

Another key moment arrives at 1:40 with the introduction of an immensely overdriven fuzz bassline, created through the band's experimentation with pushing a bass amplifier to maximum volume in order to achieve the desired crushing effect. Jim elaborated on the process during a 1998 interview with *Total Guitar* magazine:

> A lot of the fuzz bass comes from turning the Ampeg up to ten, which gives great distortion. You can't hear what you are doing, cause it's too loud, but if

you put it in a different room, you can feel it on the floor, and it just sounds great on tape.

Lyrically, 'Birthday' conveys a strong awareness of time slipping by through its repeated refrain of 'And it's Christmas time again', while the linking of Christmas and birthdays initially seems unusual until one recalls that Jim was born on 29 December. It is also worth considering that, given the song's thematic link to the passing of time, William's own birthday is 28 October, less than two months from the beginning of the festive season. The glance back to the summer of 1985 through the sampled drumbeat from 'Just Like Honey' further reinforces the song's nostalgic atmosphere, though perhaps even more revealing in the context of the band's increasingly fractured circumstances is the contrast between the lines delivered by the two brothers. Jim, balancing sneer and drawl perfectly, laments 'I'm a mean motherfucker now/but I once was cool', while William appears considerably more resigned to the loss of fame as he sings 'I couldn't care/if I'm never on TV/I'm fine and fit/I'm wasted and I'm free'.

'Birthday' became the first release on the band's new American label as part of the 1998 Sub Pop Singles Club, a monthly series of limited-edition 7" singles. Backed with 'Hide Myself' and pressed on particularly attractive blue vinyl, the Mary Chain's contribution served as the April 1998 entry in the series. Reportedly limited to only 2,000 copies for US subscribers, it quickly became one of the group's more elusive releases outside America.

An excellent song, and one of the final examples of William and Jim working together so effectively, 'Birthday' remains among the strongest tracks on *Munki*. It bears all the hallmarks of a mature band fully confident in its songwriting abilities while continuing to develop its distinctive sound, albeit with more than a hint of wistful reflection directed towards the past.

'Stardust Remedy' (2:26)

Launching with a similarly forceful drum assault while maintaining much the same energetic pace as 'I Love Rock 'N' Roll', 'Stardust Remedy' is propelled by one of Nick Sanderson's most pummelling performances on the album. Jim's opening pair of songwriting contributions to *Munki* are comparatively straightforward indie rock songs that deliberately return to the brevity of the band's earliest punk-pop material, and 'Stardust Remedy' is especially notable for its autobiographical lyrical references, including the line 'drunk on punk/and then I found my feet', alongside the explicit nod to the hugely influential 'Velvet Underground ... Sister Ray'.

A robust and immediate track, 'Stardust Remedy' became a regular fixture in the Mary Chain's 1998 live sets and featured prominently in a BBC broadcast recorded at London's Electric Ballroom on 27 April – itself a return to the venue that had hosted one of the band's most infamous early performances almost 13 years earlier. A nine-song edit drawn from the complete 16-track set was later included on the 2011 deluxe reissue of *Munki* and features an especially powerful live rendition of 'Stardust Remedy', a song that, in its studio incarnation, might well have succeeded as a single had it not faced such strong competition from elsewhere on the album.

'Fizzy' (3:39)
With its surreal stream-of-consciousness lyrics concerning Elvis, Bob Dylan and even OJ Simpson's wife, alongside almost throwaway lines about Ben Lurie's relationship with alcoholic beverages, 'Fizzy' may initially seem no more than a low-key gem on *Munki*, often overlooked in retrospectives in favour of other tracks on the album. However, upon repeated listening, its Big Star dynamics and lovely chiming guitar solo, introduced approximately 90 seconds into the song and then repeated a minute later, help elevate it beyond the initially baffling lyrical conceit. By the end of 'Fizzy', William dispenses with further bizarre wordplay and instead delivers some hard-fought wisdom in the form of 'If you don't know yourself/it's bad for your health'. On a 17-track album featuring so many different styles and reference points drawn from the Mary Chain's extensive back catalogue, 'Fizzy' seems most closely connected to the sleek, turbo-charged sound of *Automatic*, although the innovative lyrical approach on this track remains decidedly unique.

'Moe Tucker' (3:19)
Another of Jim's contributions intended to expand the album beyond the initial ten tracks played to Warners during the summer of 1996, this particular song is not actually about the legendary Velvet Underground drummer, but instead takes its title from Linda Reid's guest lead vocal, which functions as a more than suitable homage while also generating another distinctive change of mood five songs into *Munki*.

Originally, the plan had been for Linda to sing on one of the band's songs during the *Stoned & Dethroned* era, when the idea was that she would appear on a B-side carrying the less-than-subtle working title of 'Suck My Coke'. However, given the sheer number of tracks being worked on during 1993-1994, the idea was not pursued further until a few years later during a visit from Sister Vanilla to The Drugstore. By this point, the track, later described by Jim with blunt honesty as 'a song about taking cocaine', something barely disguised by lyrics including 'You know I think it's time you gave the girl a line', had evolved into 'Moe Tucker', which the band regarded highly enough to include on *Munki* rather than relegate to B-side status.

Poppy, upbeat and carried by endearingly sweet vocals, 'Moe Tucker' debuted as part of the BBC Radio 1 Evening Session in early April 1998, while Sister Vanilla also appeared at several of the band's later British gigs that year, having made her live debut with the group at the Benicàssim festival in Spain during August 1996 when she had been introduced affectionately by Jim as '...

my sister Linda Reid, she's going to sing you a little tune'. The session version omits the sound of a baby crying heard at the end of the studio recording, credited to Sean Le Bon and accompanied by a photograph superimposed onto Dick Meaney's own profile picture on the *Munki* inner sleeve. It is also missing the synth solo played by Jim on a 1983-produced monophonic OSCar synthesizer, whose alternately spluttering and oscillating tones occupy the space where a conventional guitar solo might ordinarily have appeared. This was something that later grew into a point of contention from William's perspective, as subsequently detailed at length in the band's 2024 memoir.

Both the studio and session versions of 'Moe Tucker' employ a false ending at the 2:05 mark where the song briefly falls away to little more than the hum and buzz of amplifiers before Nick Sanderson's drums cue the outro, extending the track beyond the three-minute mark through repeated refrains of 'It ain't free/so it ain't easy, yeah'.

The protracted recording sessions for Sister Vanilla's *Little Pop Rock*, eventually released by Chemikal Underground in early 2007, just months before the Mary Chain's reunion appearance at Coachella, contributed significantly to the mending of the fractured relationship between Jim and William post-*Munki*, and it was the success of 'Moe Tucker' that helped pave the way.

'Perfume' (4:39)

A common criticism across several contemporary reviews centred upon the supposedly confusing mood of the album, which some critics felt veered too sharply between contrasting styles, and 'Perfume' was frequently singled out as a track that did not justify its inclusion. This largely stemmed from how dramatically it departed not only from the other 16 songs on *Munki* but also from the firmly established expectations, fair or otherwise, surrounding what The Jesus and Mary Chain were supposed to sound like.

Yet many years on from the album's original 1998 release, 'Perfume' stands as one of the most intriguing tracks on *Munki*. Its lolloping trip-hop beats, Hope Sandoval's alternately haunting and giggling guest vocals as she effectively 'meows' her way through what might conventionally be regarded as the song's verse sections, and the short bursts of organ accompanying William's fragmented vocal contributions all combine to create something genuinely unusual. These are the most immediate elements of the song, while a muted rhythm guitar drifts in and out of the mix, maintaining the track's plodding momentum throughout.

There is a distinctly psychedelic, late-night atmosphere to 'Perfume' which moves beyond mere eccentricity into something far more otherworldly over the course of its runtime. The American publication *Entertainment Weekly*, in its largely positive review of *Munki*, singled the track out for praise, memorably describing it as 'a keyboard-spiked séance'. As the song closes with Hope commenting to William from behind the microphone that there is no more music, it genuinely feels as though the listener has been allowed access to something intensely personal and strangely unsettling.

'Virtually Unreal' (3:38)

Beginning and ending with a buzzing looped drone of rhythmic noise, 'Virtually Unreal' combines muscular riffs and tuneful pop melodies into a track that appears, almost singlehandedly, to have influenced a new wave of guitar bands emerging around the turn of the millennium, most notably California's Black Rebel Motorcycle Club. The latter endured much the same criticism early in their career regarding perceived Mary Chain influences as William and Jim Reid themselves once faced concerning The Sex Pistols, The Stooges and especially The Velvet Underground.

Beyond the persistent drone buried deep within the mix, there is also a pronounced psychedelic edge to 'Virtually Unreal'. William's fuzz-wah guitar parts remain comparatively restrained on the studio version, yet during the band's 1998 live performances, the scorched guitar sound elevated the track considerably. The excellent rendition of 'Virtually Unreal' included on the 2011 deluxe edition of *Munki*, which closes the April 1998 Electric Ballroom set, demonstrates clearly that it was arguably within the live setting where this particularly impressive song achieved its fullest impact.

'Degenerate' (5:29)

One of three tracks from *Munki* mixed by Alan Moulder and undeniably reminiscent of 'T.V. Eye' from The Stooges' 1970 masterwork *Fun House*, this William-penned track pays tribute in its own distinctive way to one of The Jesus and Mary Chain's key inspirations.

Post-Britpop, as the UK music scene thrashed around in search of the next band to hype regardless of genuine merit, there were few acts capable of producing this level of 'diseased acid-punk', as a 2017 feature on the Mary Chain in *Q* magazine so aptly described it. During the closing years of the 1990s, when flash-in-the-pan 'flavours of the month' seemed to appear almost weekly, 'Degenerate' sounded defiantly untamed and authentically dangerous.

With William building the central riff around the minor third, it is equally the tone and tempo of the performance that make the track sound so unmistakably Stooges-like, and it is none the worse for that resemblance. Once again, Nick Sanderson's drumming is phenomenal, perfectly complementing both the pace and sheer force of a song that frequently served as the opening number during the Mary Chain's 1998 live shows and also featured during the BBC radio session recorded in early April that same year.

Sanderson's ferocious playing style inadvertently created a few problems with the tempo of 'Degenerate' because the drumming noticeably accelerated as the song progressed, gradually knocking the remainder of the mix out of sync. This led to the band adjusting the varispeed control on a copy of the multitrack recording in order to lock the drums back into alignment with the rest of the track. As Ben Lurie later recalled in his contribution to the sleeve notes accompanying the deluxe reissue of *Munki*, although almost impossible for an untrained ear to detect, the unintended consequence of strictly regimenting the drum tempo was that the percussion gradually dropped in pitch as the track unfolded. A small price to pay, admittedly, and virtually undetectable without access to the original multitrack recordings, but an amusing studio anecdote nonetheless.

One of the few genuinely worthwhile new bands to emerge around the turn of the millennium, and one clearly indebted to the Mary Chain despite the inevitable criticism that followed, was Black Rebel Motorcycle Club. William himself later admitted that he sympathised with the trio, given the accusations levelled at them. Even more so than the previously discussed 'Virtually Unreal', it is arguably the sound of 'Degenerate' to which the three-piece owed the greatest debt, particularly on their 2002 track 'Whatever Happened To My Rock 'N' Roll (Punk Song)', which borrows heavily from the Mary Chain song's vocal phrasing, tempo and overall feel, with even the climactic breakdown sounding strikingly familiar, almost note for note. By this point, however, The Jesus and Mary Chain had already disbanded, and it would have seemed churlish to complain about the younger band's appropriation given that imitation remains the sincerest form of flattery. As Mikko Kapanen succinctly observed in *Psychotic Chain Reaction*, his recommended mid-noughties overview of the group:

> Borrowing isn't necessarily a bad thing if you do it with style and, like the Mary Chain themselves, only take from the best.

'Cracking Up' (4:40)

Recorded following Rob Dickins' recommendation that the band attempt additional material with greater single potential, 'Cracking Up' – rough, rugged and uncompromising – stands as one of the greatest singles The Jesus and Mary Chain ever released.

A celebration of the outsider while simultaneously skirting the edges of self-loathing, William's unrepentant 'Cracking Up' takes a defiant stance against those predicting the imminent collapse of the group while also appearing, within its murky lyrical mind-spill, to address the fractured relationships at the heart of The Jesus and Mary Chain itself. Offering commentary on personal struggles inevitably intensified by alcohol and drug abuse, the song's alienated perspective is established immediately through the defiantly non-conformist opening lines: 'Some said I was a freak/I am a freak/ They said I was weak/I am a freak/They said I was incomplete/I am a freak'.

While the track recalls the primal simplicity underpinning many of the band's earliest songs, 'Cracking Up' is notably free of feedback overload and contains remarkably little overt distortion. Musically, the song is brutally straightforward on the surface, driven by its repetitive two-note riffing, a low-register lead guitar line evoking the Duane Eddy-inspired breaks from 1988's 'Sidewalking', and a basic drumbeat periodically energised by bursts of frenetic tambourine. Yet repeated listens reveal increasingly prominent ominous piano notes woven throughout the track, especially during the closing moments where they emerge clearly within the mix, intensifying the song's crackling sense of menace.

Equally striking is the stop-start structure of 'Cracking Up', which repeatedly cues William's vocal entrances, alongside the fact that the track never truly builds towards a conventional climax. Instead, after one final repetition of the central riff – by then thoroughly lodged in the listener's mind – the song simply winds down, with guitars and vocals dropping away entirely at the 4:27 mark, leaving only the root piano notes and percussion to carry the final ten seconds.

A major live highlight during the band's 1998 performances, 'Cracking Up' was one of a small handful of Mary Chain songs, alongside 'Fizzy' and 'I Hate Rock 'N' Roll', to feature William on lead vocals onstage. Jim, meanwhile, was relegated to centre-stage tambourine duties, an undoubtedly unusual position for someone who had occupied the spotlight, however reluctantly, since the band's earliest days. As the second song performed during their spring 1998 appearance on *Later ... With Jools Holland*, fans were later able to revisit this curious moment in the group's history thanks to its inclusion on the bonus DVD accompanying the 2011 deluxe edition of *Munki*.

The single itself received reasonably positive reviews in the UK music press ahead of its April release, although one critic rather sniffily remarked that the central riff bore more than a passing resemblance to an early Devo track. 'Cracking Up' was accompanied by a remarkable promo video directed by Ben Unwin that combined grainy handheld footage shot by the band in Paris with scenes of William filmed inside the infamous Columbia Hotel in West London, as well as wandering through a particularly seedy-looking Soho, accompanied by two models alternately teasing and encouraging their increasingly intoxicated companion for the evening.

The atmosphere generated by the promo is so grimy and disorienting that it perfectly complements the song itself. As an evidently drunken William, sporting enormous bug-eyed glasses, becomes progressively more erratic in his behaviour, the footage captured is simultaneously deeply unflattering and perversely compelling. Enhanced by a barrage of scratched negatives, rapid-fire edits and spliced-in words – 'Help' appearing onscreen more than once – alongside the near constant presence of bottles of wine or beer in William's hands, the resulting film remains genuinely unsettling viewing. Preserved on the bonus DVD accompanying the deluxe reissue of *Munki*, the promo for 'Cracking Up' is not easily forgotten once seen and remains the ideal visual counterpart to one of the Mary Chain's finest singles.

Sadly, the song itself received scant commercial reward, managing only a brief appearance in the UK top 40 at number 35 on 18 April before plunging 24 places the following week and disappearing altogether shortly thereafter.

'Commercial' (7:02)

Undoubtedly the most challenging track to make the final cut for the album, uncompromising and decidedly uncommercial regardless of its presumably ironic title, 'Commercial' is either an intriguing sonic experiment that sees the Mary Chain break genuinely new ground or a droning 12-bar blues jam masquerading as an endurance test that quickly outstays its welcome. Regardless of the track's inevitable 'Marmite effect' upon listeners, several contemporary reviews of *Munki* at least acknowledged 'Commercial' as a commendably radical departure from the band's previous work, and it remains a fascinating entry within what was by this stage an extensive repertoire.

The cyber-blues of 'Commercial' had already appeared in shorter form as a B-side on the CD single release of 'Cracking Up', clocking in at 3:24, but the album version more than doubles that runtime, with a full minute and 47 seconds passing before William's vocals finally emerge. During this extended introduction, colossal drum fills dominate proceedings and continue to do so for much of the next five minutes alongside heavily effected guitar work played on one of the Mary Chain's favourite instruments, the Gibson 330. In a 1998 interview with *Total Guitar* magazine that included a discussion surrounding the recording of *Munki*, Ben acknowledged that despite experimenting with alternative instruments, William's preferred guitar had ultimately been used almost exclusively:

> I know we used others, but this guitar is almost the only one on the album. It always sounds good and is easy to play. In fact, we rented a lot of old guitars just to try something different, but the Gibson 330 just sounded better.

With its deliberately simplistic lyrics – 'fool/cool/cruel' rhymes and all – and the love-it-or-loathe-it wobbling chorus effect applied to the guitars, 'Commercial' remains a mammoth improvisation lodged at the heart of *Munki*, one whose unique qualities are every bit as contentious now as they were upon the album's original release in 1998.

'Supertramp' (3:37)

A mixture of yearning vocals and fuzz bass set against a backdrop of sizzling, blistering distortion, 'Supertramp' tears through its three-and-a-half-minute runtime, propelled by a drum pattern clearly rooted in the distinctive hypnotic triplets played by the often unfairly maligned Ringo Starr on The Beatles' 'Tomorrow Never Knows', the unforgettable closer to their 1966 masterpiece *Revolver*. Whether intentional or otherwise – and given the Reids' longstanding admiration for The Beatles, it seems unlikely to have been accidental – the rhythmic backbone of 'Supertramp' gives the track a strongly psychedelic feel.

Also notable are the high-pitched backing vocals of 'I'm a real believer', which recall the layered harmonies that characterised the golden run of T.

Rex singles during the early-to-mid 1970s. A first lead guitar break enters the mix at the 1:58 mark before giving way to a second solo 15 seconds later, after which the bass once again surges to the foreground alongside the relentlessly pummelling drums.

'Supertramp' remains one of the strongest tracks on *Munki* and, given the difficult circumstances surrounding the recording of the album, it is difficult not to read additional meaning into the neatly Bob Dylan-referencing lines delivered by Jim towards the close of the song: 'We know that we've blown the past/Maybe we could change the future/Don't think twice and don't look back/Maybe if we run then maybe we could run forever'.

'Never Understood' (4:14)

Considered in retrospect as something of a requiem for what was, at the time, still a living band, 'Never Understood' stands alone as the song on *Munki* that most closely resembles the Mary Chain's earlier work on *Stoned & Dethroned* through its sparse acoustic stylings. It also functions as the emotional centrepiece of the album, where, beginning with its title alone, there is a palpable sense of the band having come full circle. William's lyrics – and indeed the weary manner in which he delivers them – evoke a mood of exhaustion and acceptance, perhaps even a reluctant coming to terms with matters that must have weighed heavily upon him by this point.

Beginning with William alone against a minimal acoustic backdrop, 'Never Understood' takes its time in the build-up, much like the strongest moments from the band's previous album, allowing listeners to absorb the emotional depth within the reflective lyrics. This is particularly evident in lines such as 'I think I'm going out of style/I think I've known it for a while', which possess something of the confessional quality associated with Plastic Ono Band-era Lennon and, in particular, the closing track 'God' from his landmark 1970 album. The cyclical chord progression of 'Never Understood' further strengthens this comparison, although William's self-awareness never develops into the wholesale rejection of the past found within Lennon's famous litany of denouncements.

Throughout the song, there is an increasing sense of William reflecting upon his own status and, by extension, that of The Jesus and Mary Chain itself before the music briefly pauses, neatly introduced by the quietly devastating request: 'Why don't you break with me?' What follows is a beautifully understated guitar solo that unfolds for approximately 50 seconds before giving way to a deceptively gentle reprise of the song's opening passage, ultimately concluding with a final cymbal crash and one last distorted strum of rhythm guitar.

'I Can't Find The Time For Times' (4:17)

Following the *Revolver*-era drum patterns of 'Supertramp' and the Lennon-esque confessional mood of 'Never Understood', the Fab Four references become even more overt when William opens the next track on the album with the lines 'I love Beatle John/She loves Beatle Paul'.

Beyond this knowingly transparent opening couplet, however, the remainder of the lyrics rank among the most inscrutable on *Munki*, although there are still discernible references to the intoxicating allure of pop culture throughout. These include nods to glam-rock-era duality and gender ambiguity through lines such as 'I'm a boyfriend/and a girlfriend/in your eyes' as well as the rather less subtle observation that 'they do bad drugs/and on top of the pops/I could close my eyes/but the fun might stop'.

The inclusion of a psychedelic piano solo at the 2:18 mark, replacing what might conventionally have been a guitar break in much the same manner as the synthesizer part used so effectively on 'Moe Tucker', introduces a welcome shimmering texture to the track. Elsewhere, 'I Can't Find The Time For Times' is driven forward by a chugging rhythm guitar that propels the song steadily from verse to verse, while buzzing overdubbed chords strengthen the bridge sections. The same piano motif briefly returns during the song's closing moments, although there is perhaps an argument that it could have been utilised more prominently during the finale.

The in-studio experimentation heard intermittently throughout *Munki* would be explored far more fully on William's debut solo release, *Tired Of Fucking*, a four-track EP issued by Creation in early 1998 and recorded during the closing months of the previous year at The Drugstore. William would soon expand upon these sonic experiments through the increasingly challenging work released under the Lazycame name on either side of the millennium, while Jim, alongside Ben in Freeheat, would continue to favour more traditional song structures.

'Man On The Moon' (3:41)

Interspersed with disorientating bursts of coruscating wah-wah guitar, 'Man On The Moon' is a particularly curious track in that its carefully sustained quiet and reflective mood – bordering at times upon lonesome ballad territory, with Jim employing an especially hushed vocal delivery during the verses – is violently disrupted on two separate occasions, first at the 1:25 mark and again precisely one minute later. Thereafter, a simple three-note trumpet motif supplied by Terry Edwards, making his second contribution to *Munki*, carries the song towards its conclusion, where elements of the opening passage subtly re-emerge.

What might otherwise have been a relatively straightforward meditation on alienation, with Jim singing of his 'planetary prison cell' and 'walking in the godless freeze', acquires far greater depth through both the dramatic shifts in dynamics and the increasingly bleak lyrical undertones that emerge around the midway point of the track. The line 'Another perfect day/it means nothing/when you live this way' introduces a notably darker emotional register, while the earlier image of 'staring at the mirror's face' becomes increasingly ambiguous and unsettling in retrospect. The notion of living alone 'on the moon' consequently takes on a far more disquieting significance.

Given Jim's own acknowledged struggles with drug use during this turbulent period in the band's history, it does not seem unreasonable to interpret 'Man On The Moon' as, at least in part, an oblique commentary on the psychological effects such habits were beginning to exert.

'Black' (5:18)

In the now post-Britpop musical landscape, where Oasis had to a major extent, and Blur to a lesser one, acknowledged a certain level of debt to the Fab Four, it perhaps seemed high time for the influence of The Beatles to begin appearing more clearly in the music of The Jesus and Mary Chain. This certainly proved to be the case on several songs from *Munki*, but perhaps most noticeably so with 'Black', where the sophisticated songwriting style of the track, introduced initially through a C/Em/F progression before shifting onto G and D chords, recalls The Beatles of *Rubber Soul* blended with the classic power-pop of the Chilton/Bell era of Big Star.

There is no hint of self-parody in the familiarity of the component parts that make up 'Black', which are combined to such great effect. If anything, the melodic strength of the track helps confirm that The Jesus and Mary Chain were by this point more able than ever to integrate themselves seamlessly into the pantheon of classic rock 'n' roll. Particularly fitting, given that 'Black' absolutely exudes the essence of classic guitar pop, is the sense of things having finally come full circle since it was the peerless songs of The Beatles that had first awakened the Reids, as children, to the thrill of music itself. In what sounds like a looped radio-broadcast sample beginning at the 4:06 mark, during which the only clearly distinguishable word is 'Scotland', the Mary Chain even place a neat sonic detail within the track that feels almost like a lost transmission from the past or, given the American voice delivering the otherwise largely indecipherable speech, perhaps even a strange foretelling of where William would soon relocate following his departure from the band.

With the benefit of hindsight and the safe distance of many years having passed since the song was first written, certain lyrics from William's contributions to *Munki* seem to have acquired increased significance, especially following the extensive discussion surrounding the album's difficult creation and messy aftermath since the band's timely 2007 reformation. A couple of key lines from 'Black' are particularly revealing when considered against the changing dynamics within the Mary Chain during the recording process.

When William sings, 'Nothing here belongs/no one here is on my side/nothing here is mine', the lines can reasonably be interpreted as a reflection of his growing dissatisfaction with life inside The Jesus and Mary Chain. The increasingly close friendship between Jim and Ben had led to William feeling alienated within his own group, a belief worsened by the perception that both men now frequently operated as a united front in opposition to him.

As an interesting aside pertinent to the central themes of 'Black', Ben Lurie acknowledged in a 2021 online interview, while reflecting on the recording of *Munki* and relations within the band at that point, that...

> ...in hindsight, I should have been more conscious of the relationship between Jim and William. In my defence: we were all relatively young, going through uncharted waters. At the time, I agreed more with the way Jim felt about things. Possibly, William felt we were ganging up on him. Which wasn't an intentional thing.

'Dream Lover' (3:05)
Not a cover of the Big Star song from their own troubled 'final' album, *Third/Sister Lovers*, the penultimate track on *Munki* is also among its weaker moments and, while certainly not unpleasant, its power-chord strumming feels more indebted to a generic 1960s rock sound, even suggesting The Troggs at times – an unlikely reference point perhaps, but difficult to shake once heard.

'Dream Lover' explores themes of unrequited love and the inevitable frustrations accompanying such a situation, made all the more affecting when Jim admits in the telling line, 'But you don't exist'. Even when the song shifts up a key at the two-minute mark, the track struggles to match the quality of much of the surrounding material on *Munki* and may ultimately have worked better as a B-side than as part of an already densely packed album.

'Dream Lover' was, however, played regularly during the band's 1998 live shows promoting *Munki*, and it was arguably in this environment that the song truly came to life. The track also features on the live set excerpt broadcast by the BBC from The Jesus and Mary Chain's appearance at the Electric Ballroom in London, recorded on 27 April 1998 and later included on the bonus disc of the 2011 deluxe edition.

'I Hate Rock 'N' Roll' (3:42)
Unlike 'Rollercoaster', which was released between albums and subsequently appeared in an arguably weaker re-recorded form on *Honey's Dead* two years later, 'I Hate Rock 'N' Roll' was neither re-recorded nor significantly altered for inclusion on *Munki*, instead appearing in the same form as its original 1995 release. The previous chapter provides a more detailed discussion of the track's standalone single release, but within the context of *Munki*, it stands apart from several of the other William Reid compositions through its greater sense of energy and abrasion.

The song also functions perfectly as the counterpart to Jim's decidedly optimistic album opener, bringing proceedings to a close in a manner that is simultaneously nihilistic and oddly anthemic, highlighting one final contradiction at the heart of The Jesus and Mary Chain's music.

Contemporary Tracks

'Hide Myself' (3:31)

Featured as the flip side to the Sub Pop Singles Club release of 'Birthday' in April 1998, this quiet ballad sounds very much like an outtake from the *Stoned & Dethroned* sessions, although if anything, it is richer than some of the songs ultimately selected for inclusion on the 1994 album. Worthy of far more attention than it would have received tucked away as a B-side on the UK digipak release of 'Cracking Up', 'Hide Myself' remains a lovely late-period Mary Chain track – curiously uplifting despite its dark lyrical content – and another example of a quality song that deserved far better.

'Easylife, Easylove' (4:05)

With a chiming guitar sound running throughout the background of the track that may remind listeners of a similarly effective part on Buffalo Springfield's 'For What It's Worth', Jim's 'Easylife, Easylove' was selected as one of the B-sides for the release of 'I Love Rock 'N' Roll' in May 1998. There is a stoic quality to the lyrics as well as a palpable sense of impending dissolution, with the demise of the Mary Chain by this point only months away. The doomed romanticism of the rock 'n' roll lifestyle and its impact upon those caught within it is undeniably evident throughout the song, which, despite its lyrical themes, remains free-flowing, relaxed and – appropriately enough given its title – among the easiest listens associated with the *Munki* era, recalling the more mellow moments of *Stoned & Dethroned* four years earlier.

'40,000K' (2:52)

Included as a B-side on the CD digipak release of 'I Love Rock 'N' Roll' and featuring prominent use of the archetypal Mary Chain fuzz-bass sound, '40,000K' also contains an excellent burst of synth doodling at the 1:10 mark that runs for approximately 15 seconds while a fiery wah-wah guitar appears almost to solo independently around the song's two principal chords of G and C for the remainder of the track. It is particularly interesting to hear Jim deliver the telling line, 'Well I broke up with my band/and I'm doin' the best I can', which inevitably acquires additional significance given what awaited The Jesus and Mary Chain barely four months after the single's release.

'45 RPM' (1:51)

Essentially a faster, re-recorded version of the 1995 B-side '33 1/3', this track sounds like an even earlier *Stoned & Dethroned* demo and may indeed have originated from that period before its radical reinvention a couple of years later, with the feedback removed and the chorus line altered to 'I got the world putting me down'. The song appeared on the various-artists compilation *104.9 – An XFM Compilation Album*, released in 1995 to support the station's application for a new London broadcasting licence after XFM had previously lost out to rival bidders on several occasions.

'Nineteen666' (3:30)

Indicative of the late-night solo experiments William had begun immersing himself in at The Drugstore, 'Nineteen666' is less a carefully structured Mary Chain song in the traditional sense than a baffling studio experiment committed to tape with the assistance of Dick Meaney. Despite its undeniably confusing mood, however, the track rewards repeated listening as individual elements gradually emerge more clearly. These include random snippets of vocal ad-libs in the recording booth, heavily percussive keyboard sounds and crashing cymbals, while especially notable is the limited use of electric guitar, with what little appears mixed conspicuously low in the final recording.

Ending abruptly following a simulated stuck-groove effect and despite its challenging nature, 'Nineteen666' was still thought of highly enough by the Mary Chain to be included as a B-side on the digipak release of 'I Love Rock 'N' Roll'. The track was later featured on both the deluxe reissue of *Munki* and *The Power Of Negative Thinking* box set, while also serving as the band's intro tape during both their British and American tour dates.

'Rocket' (3:01)

Originally included as a B-side to 'Cracking Up' and later featured on both *The Power Of Negative Thinking* and the deluxe reissue of *Munki*, 'Rocket' was written and recorded during the earliest incarnation of the album prior to the band presenting material to Warners during the summer of 1996. The song is essentially a solo Ben Lurie composition – and a very strong one at that – with Ben and Nick Sanderson responsible for the instrumentation while Jim supplied the vocals.

There was ultimately little room within The Jesus and Mary Chain for a third regular songwriter, especially by this stage in the band's increasingly fractured existence, but 'Rocket', beyond its own melodic strengths, offers a useful glimpse into the type of music Jim and Ben would soon begin working on together during late-1997 sessions at The Drugstore. Initially discussed in the music press as a side project operating under the loose working title of TV69, these recordings would, in hindsight, prove a precursor to the post-split four-piece group Freeheat.

Damage And Joy (2017)

Personnel:
Jim Reid: vocals, guitar, production (tracks 8, 12)
William Reid: vocals, guitar, production (tracks 8, 12)
Brian Young: drums
Recorded in England (Wandsworth), Spain (Andalusia), Ireland and the US
Producer: Youth (tracks 1 to 7, 9 to 11, 13, 14)
Engineers: Michael Rendall and Josiah Mazzaschi (tracks 8, 12)
Additional engineering: Jamie Grashion, Conor Brady
Additional mix engineering: Tommaso Colliva, Marcus Locock
Label: Artificial Plastic
Charts: UK: 16, Austria: 32, Germany: 34, Ireland: 22, Italy: 70, New Zealand: 1, Portugal: 24, Spain: 31, Switzerland: 43, US (*Billboard* Top Rock Albums): 38, US (*Billboard* Top Alternative Albums): 22, US (*Billboard* Independent Albums): 9
Running time: 53:05

Released almost a full decade after the band's return as a touring entity, and 19 years on from their previous album *Munki*, the arrival of *Damage And Joy* in late March 2017 was eagerly anticipated. Behind the scenes, however, the prolonged build-up to recording what became the Reids' seventh full album was understandably complex, given how events had unfolded at the tail end of the 1990s.

Following a much-anticipated reunion at Coachella on Friday 27 April 2007, where the version of the group performing beyond the brothers was essentially comprised of Jim's backing band – by then used for increasingly sporadic solo gigs – talk inevitably turned to the possibility of new Jesus and Mary Chain music. With that came renewed pressure. The first tangible result of the reformed partnership, beyond the band's return as a touring force, was a track entitled 'All Things Must Pass', which William had initially developed as a demo before presenting it to his brother shortly after the reunion. Those close to the band viewed it as an early attempt to re-establish the core songwriting relationship.

The track was subsequently licensed for the NBC television series *Heroes*, which ran from September 2006 to February 2010, and appeared on the March 2008 official soundtrack album credited to William Reid. The reformed band also performed 'All Things Must Pass' live on *The Letterman Show* during spring 2007, between a series of US tour dates that confirmed to Stateside audiences that the Mary Chain were well and truly back. The song would later reappear a decade on as a standout track on *Damage And Joy*, though at this stage the album itself remained a distant prospect, and the idea of working closely in a studio setting for an extended period was not something Jim readily embraced.

Concerns about a breakdown in the brothers' relationship resurfacing under sustained studio conditions clearly influenced Jim's reluctance to commit to a new record. This was despite his later acknowledgement, in 2018, of the need to record material already in circulation:

> ...we still had all these songs coming out of us, and we've got new songs now. And when you know you're sitting on songs that you think are worth having a lifespan of their own, I think it's a waste if you don't actually record them. It seems a shame.

Early attempts to begin work on a new album included sessions in Los Angeles in late summer 2008, with William by then an American resident making only occasional visits back to Scotland alongside the band's touring schedule. However, Jim's abstinence from substances contrasted sharply with his brother's willingness to record under the influence, and tensions inevitably resurfaced. The situation was further complicated by the cost of studio time at a point when advances in home recording technology made far cheaper alternatives viable.

Following the Coachella reunion and subsequent US touring, there had been hopes that both Jim and William might also pursue solo projects. The band's then-manager, Kevin Oberlin, was tasked with balancing the interests of both brothers while gently encouraging a return to joint work once they had both expressed an interest in recording a new album. In 2009, Oberlin compiled a rough selection of around a dozen demo tracks drawn from post-1998 solo material. The strength of these recordings – including 'All Things Must Pass' – served as a reminder that a substantial body of 'new' Mary Chain-related music already existed, albeit scattered across independent releases by Sister Vanilla, Freeheat, Lazycame and Jim's solo work.

In the interim, touring continued alongside archival releases, including the 4CD set *The Power Of Negative Thinking* (2008), and the double-disc compilation *Upside Down – The Best Of The Jesus and Mary Chain* (2010). A five-disc Warner-era reissue series followed in 2009 as part of the label's *Original Albums Series*, offering a low-cost entry point for new listeners. This was followed in 2011 by a comprehensive deluxe reissue programme via Edsel/Rhino, covering the band's full catalogue, including *Munki*, with bonus discs of rarities, live recordings, mixes, videos and interviews.

Alan McGee's return to management duties in 2014 coincided with plans for a 30th anniversary tour in which *Psychocandy* was performed in full. The tour introduced the band to a new generation of audiences, many encountering them for the first time. The experience, along with McGee's advice regarding potential studio collaborators, helped set the conditions for a return to recording.

Jim later reflected in 2018 that the timing had simply felt right:

> We still want to make music. That it's not just about the 1980s and 1990s. That's all we were trying to do. We just wanted to get back to what the Mary Chain used to do. The Mary Chain used to make records.

With both brothers finally committed to a new album, the decision to bring in Martin 'Youth' Glover as producer alongside William and Jim Reid proved significant. His experience, coupled with his ability to operate in volatile studio environments, made him a practical choice. As a former member of Killing Joke – long associated with their own brand of internal tension – he was no stranger to difficult dynamics.

Given the band's longstanding preference for self-production, the decision to work with an external producer was as much about containment as experimentation. Jim later explained in a 2017 interview:

> We were quite nervous about how it was going to be in the studio, which is one of the reasons why we decided to get a producer – the other being that we've never done that before. And it was nice to have the glue to keep it together if things got silly between my brother and me.

Alongside production duties, Youth also contributed bass guitar parts, while engineer Michael Rendall played a key role in shaping the sessions, working closely with the band to translate material into a cohesive sonic framework.

Across studios in Wandsworth and Andalusia, Youth encouraged the band to revisit material from their post-split solo and side projects. This approach proved effective, reinforcing the strength of existing songs while reducing the risk of conflict during writing. It also helped refocus attention on the material already in circulation, allowing the sessions to develop with fewer distractions.

Jim later reflected on the process:

> We actually bonded in a weird way during the recording of that album, and we got along much better than we had for many, many years. I think that album, the recording of it, repaired a lot of an abandoned relationship.

This sense of repair is central to understanding the sessions. It allowed the brothers to re-establish a functioning creative relationship and move forward with renewed confidence.

A further factor in the success of the recording process was the shift in studio technology. Compared with earlier eras, the tools now available significantly altered both workflow and efficiency.

Jim addressed this in a 2019 interview with *Atwood Magazine*:

> It's quicker because technology's moved on quite a bit since we last made a record ... It was the first time we had used a producer, but there was also a guy who worked all the computers and stuff, Michael Rendall, and he was amazing. He'd sort of come up with an idea that, back in the old days, you'd spend maybe the entire day trying.

The result was a 14-track album with distinctive artwork and a title that neatly referenced the fraught relationship at its core. While not radically different from earlier work, it presented a more polished and radio-friendly sound, shaped in part by Youth's production and the renewed clarity of the vocal performances.

Musically, *Damage And Joy* revisits the broad palette of styles explored since the mid-1980s, ranging from slow-burning ballads to more urgent, rhythm-driven tracks. It also draws from material developed independently by both brothers in the intervening years, much of it re-recorded for the album.

For long-time fans, many of the songs were already familiar in earlier forms, and online discussions often mapped their origins in detail. However, the decision to re-record them as a unified body of work gave the material a coherence it had previously lacked. In doing so, *Damage And Joy* offered renewed visibility to overlooked material and marked a stabilising point in the band's later career, both creatively and personally.

'Amputation' (3:24)

Announcing the group's return after a very long hiatus, the opening track on *Damage And Joy* had its first release as a solo Jim Reid single – his second on the Transistor indie label – back in 2006, produced by Jim with Phil King and recorded by future Mary Chain bass player Mark Crozer. Essentially a reworking of one of Jim's earliest solo songs called 'Dead End Kids', when retitled and produced to a higher standard than that of a decade before, 'Amputation' serves as an ideal opener to the album.

The track successfully channels the mood it was written in at a time when Jim felt as if his previous band and, indeed, himself as a still active and recording musician had been almost entirely expunged from the music industry. In a 2017 interview with *Louder Than War* on the eve of the release of *Damage And Joy*, Jim expanded upon the song's inspiration:

> That particular song could be about the end of a relationship, but the relationship is actually our relationship with the music business … It was me feeling at the time like I had been expelled from this exclusive club that I'd sort of gatecrashed decades before, and I was now a life in exile – that's what it felt like. That's what it means – 'I'm a rock 'n' roll amputation', like I'd been chopped off from this thing called the music business and no longer allowed to take part. That's the way it felt at the time.

Introduced through 13 seconds of rising white noise, whistling and distortion evidently generated from a monophonic synthesizer, the backing to 'Amputation' is provided by a robotic and decidedly tinny, muted-sounding drum machine track. A close listen reveals what could be the addition of live tambourine towards the close of the track, but it is similarly thin and compressed in sound. While complementing the drum machine pattern in perfect sync, given the advances in studio technology since the Mary Chain last recorded in earnest, there is every possibility that this additional percussion element was also synthetic in origin.

While the pace of 'Amputation' has been increased on the newer version of the track, the initial backing vocal harmonies from the previous version remain in place, ending with the introduction of a near-acoustic rhythm guitar part from 0:39 that accompanies the first verse onwards. The fickle nature of either the music industry (or perhaps an ex-partner) is introduced in the opening lines through 'trying to win your interest back/but you ain't having none of that'. Subsequent instrumental breaks and chord progressions in the song are smooth and restrained, which allows for some bold lyrics about 'fucked-up girls like drugged-up guys/that won't keep them warm at night' to receive more of the spotlight. The mantra of 'I'm a rock and roll amputation' also works effectively as a chorus hook, and it is notable that the vocals are mixed higher than any other element in the song.

Released online in early December 2016 as an initial advance track ahead of its parent album the following spring, 'Amputation' may have been quickly recognised by hardcore fans as Jim's previously recorded 'Dead End Kids', but the sound quality on the new version is significantly improved and clearly demonstrates the benefits that a more sophisticated recording environment can bring to the material. The success of revisiting an older track as the opening to *Damage And Joy* sets the standard for the other previously released (or at least demoed) tracks that feature on the album, and given its low-key origins from a decade previously, 'Amputation' undeniably works well as an opener.

'War On Peace' (4:34)

Reminiscent of the slow-burn nature of classic *Darklands*-era tracks such as 'Nine Million Rainy Days', as well as a few of the more downbeat songs from *Honey's Dead*, the length of 'War On Peace' at over four and a half minutes is also a link back to the more melancholic side of The Jesus and Mary Chain's output throughout their recording career.

Omitting an opening guitar riff from an earlier demo take that was close enough to that of the Stones' evergreen 'Satisfaction' to be a distraction, 'War On Peace' is both slow in tempo and darkly subdued in mood for most of its runtime before coming to life and accelerating in pace for the track's finale.

Weary and resigned in tone, the mood of the track is largely generated through its Mary Chain-filtered psychedelia (the swirling assemblage of guitars in the background rises and falls at key points) and, towards the end of the track, aggressive motorik powered by Brian Young's drumming contribution, which explodes into life. Young, a highly experienced and extremely skilled musician in his own right, was a founding member of US power-pop band Fountains of Wayne before taking on the role of touring drummer for The Jesus and Mary Chain from 2012 to the close of 2021, and his faultless playing features almost exclusively throughout *Damage And Joy*.

'War On Peace' is further distinguished by William's harmony vocal contributions alongside his brother's own singing, which stand out in the mix. The relatively rare instance of the Reids' vocal tracks being blended is arguably as notable in the song as William's signature descending chord patterns, which have a distinctly languorous feel, interspersed with percussion marked by echoes of tambourine and ride cymbal crashes. Additionally, a rich lead guitar part appears at the 1:26 point, similar in feel and approach to the solos that featured on the more stately tracks on *Darklands* three decades earlier.

On a song that generates an inarguable state of ennui for most of its duration, lyrics including 'Love don't live here anymore/don't come knockin' on my door/I just can't get peace of mind/there's a peace there I can't find' create a sense of frustration and hopelessness. This is further strengthened with a powerful chorus hook of 'So what if I run/Where would I run to?' prior to the 3:30 mark, when the track abruptly quickens in pace with a boost in percussion that sounds decidedly motorik, redolent of the metronomic beat heard most strongly in Krautrock bands of the 1970s, especially groups such as Neu! (*Hallogallo*) and Can (*Mother Sky*). Jim's 'Ahh-ahh' counterpoint harmonies make one more pass through during this powerful coda alongside distorted chugging rhythm guitar before 'War On Peace', after close to a minute of fast-paced riffing and robotic drumming, slows down firstly to its original tempo and then to a complete stop, bringing the second song on *Damage And Joy* to a close.

'All Things Pass' (4:34)

Prior to the album teaser release of 'Amputation' at the end of 2016, 'All Things Must Pass' (in its original incarnation) had been the band's only previous new piece of music shared with fans for the best part of 20 years, and on *Damage And Joy*, it receives a sturdy reworking in re-recorded form while sporting a new, slightly tweaked title. The third track on the comeback album, it is arguably through the strength of 'All Things Pass' that listeners feel reassured that, despite the intervening years, the Mary Chain had secured something of a triumphant return.

Any fears that the percussion track might be relegated to thin drum machine pulses akin to those that featured on the album opener are quickly put to rest when the full band charge in and the song really lifts off. The quickened pace, combined with Brian's powerful drumming, gives 'All Things Pass' a particular boost, with the thumping breakdown at 3:17 being especially impressive in its force and precision. William's contributions – from the distinctive backdrop of shuddering feedback that introduces the track to a cyclical lead guitar riff that is played intermittently – stand out upon initial listen due not only to their relative simplicity but also in how well they complement the song as a whole.

With a somewhat grudging acknowledgement of the need to let go of previous bad habits (sex, drugs and rock 'n' roll, although not necessarily in that order) for their health, the song's stance on a reforming of character is ultimately celebrated in the sing-along chorus: 'Hey/Look out here it comes/All things must pass/but not too fast'. Offering up an engaging mix of alternately anxious and self-deprecating lyrics, moving from concerns that 'Each day I wake It's gonna be my last' to the wry irony contained within 'I have taken a vow/to prove myself/to find me/I'm regrettin' it now/'cause I found me!', in its definitive album form 'All Things Pass' is an extremely catchy track that had already been well received by audiences as part of Mary Chain live sets several years prior to its eventual reworked appearance on *Damage And Joy*.

'Always Sad' (2:52)
A return to the melodic highlights of *Stoned & Dethroned* (with the most immediate comparison being with 'Sometimes Always') and featuring William's then partner (now wife), Bernadette Denning, singing with Jim, 'Always Sad' was the second track to be given an advanced release prior to *Damage And Joy* being issued and was accompanied by a promo video that contained a series of rare images (including shots of both brothers in the early 1980s pre-Mary Chain) compiled by William. The first of the album's four duets, Bernadette's lovely vocals provide a bittersweet counterpoint on the song and continue the established Mary Chain pattern of utilising guest female vocalists with aplomb.

Originally written in the late 1990s by William and considered for inclusion on the Sister Vanilla album with a duet mooted that would feature either Stephen Pastel or Bobby Gillespie, 'Always Sad' was subsequently demoed in 2014 during an off-day while on tour in South America. The resulting recording of the track, taped in an Argentinian studio that had been booked exclusively for the band to work in, saw Bernadette take the vocal and, despite a few other singers being considered, when the time came to record the song for inclusion on *Damage And Joy*, William's partner once again reprised the role. Alternative options had been considered for the duet, among them asking Linda Reid to provide the vocals, but the notion of her singing a love song with one of her siblings was soon dismissed as being too weird. Isobel Campbell may also have been considered, but having already appeared on three tracks from the album, a further contribution on 'Always Sad' may well have tipped the balance towards what some might have considered a full-on collaboration album. Ultimately, it is the shy and self-confessed non-singer who provided the final recorded vocals on the track when it was completed in Dublin, and despite her lack of experience in the role, the endearing contribution captured is one of the album's high points.

After an opening single note is pounded out for eight seconds in a manner similar to that heard all the way back on 'Some Candy Talking', the song then drops down into a mid-tempo track that effortlessly fuses classic three-chord rock 'n' roll with Spector pop. Further complemented by some single-note guitar riffs employed judiciously throughout, and with the unmistakable 'Be My Baby' opening drumbeat making a welcome return in the chorus, 'Always Sad' is a superb reminder of prime Jesus and Mary Chain with a modern twist, while the sound of Jim and Bernadette harmonising so beautifully together is easily one of the highlights of the entire album.

A distinctive boy/girl dynamic runs throughout the track, tweaking the lyrics accordingly with the initial 'You ain't like those other girls', sung by Jim, replaced with 'guys' when it's Bernadette's turn in the second verse. The two then combine on the chorus, sharing vocals on the rather poignant 'think I'm always sad/think I'm always gonna be sad'. In addition, the lines heard on the bridge, 'A million miles between us now/why can't we just work things out?', take on extra significance when one considers the serious fracture in the relationship between William and Jim post-*Munki* fallout, although both have since acknowledged that the rot had set in well before then.

'Song For A Secret' (3:21)

First debuted in 2005 on a split single shared with Sister Vanilla, 'Song For A Secret' was Jim's first release on the Transistor indie label. The track featured his then partner Julie Barber sharing vocal duties in addition to Mary Chain stalwart Phil King providing guitar and bass contributions, while the presence of a glockenspiel part played in the studio by producer Marc Shearer adds another sweet element to what was a sadly unappreciated song that barely received any attention at the time of its limited release. Given its quality, it comes as no surprise that 'Song For A Secret' was identified as being ideal for revisiting when Jim and William collated previously recorded music worthy of inclusion on their comeback album.

Sharing some of its vocal melody with 'Sometimes Always', the second duet on *Damage And Joy* features the vocal talents of Scottish singer-songwriter Isobel Campbell, who, after starting her career in Belle and Sebastian during the mid-1990s, has released a series of impressive solo albums as well as notable collaborations with Bill Wells and the late Screaming Trees frontman Mark Lanegan. Fans of her voice, the Mary Chain were keen to have Campbell lend her talents to 'Song For A Secret', and her contribution enhances the song considerably, working wonderfully alongside Jim's vocals.

The band did not actually meet Campbell in person during the recording of the track, with the latter's vocals instead submitted remotely. Jim commented on this process, made easier through modern technology, during a 2018 interview with *Atwood Magazine*:

> These days it's easier. You just email your track to someone in LA. Isobel Campbell sang on the record and I'd never met her. Still haven't met her. I was just a fan of her voice and her music. We were just looking for people to ask and we heard she was keen.

With its cascading harmonies, jangling riffs and even the use of bell-like chimes, what had originally sounded faintly similar to 'For What It's Worth' by Buffalo Springfield back in its original 2005 release is taken to an impressive new level in its incarnation on *Damage And Joy*, with a superbly crafted soundscape generated that moves the song comfortably into near dream-pop territory.

'Song For A Secret' is a captivating and mellifluous track where the familiar Mary Chain theme of finding salvation in the love of another is revisited in style. Jim begins the first verse with the lines 'too old to crucify but too young for suicide', but any troubling hints of darkness are swiftly dispelled by the following hook of 'Oh I'm glad I found you/I'll wrap myself around you', where the overlapping vocals of both Reids mesh wonderfully. At this early point in the song, William's playing and an accompanying ride cymbal-dominated backdrop help propel things forward, while a lead guitar line that cleverly utilises an inverted melody is also notable.

More dominant drumming becomes prominent in the mix from the second verse onwards, at which point guest vocalist Isobel Campbell delivers her vocals unaccompanied: 'After all the shit that you've been through/all I've got is time for you/oh yeah I'm just glad you found me/just wrap yourself around me'. The instrumental section that then follows is quintessential Mary Chain, with the main chords in the track alongside punctuating guitar lines further strengthened by a see-sawing two-note melody.

Following a momentary halt at the 1:55 minute mark, 'Song For A Secret' then resumes with Jim singing 'kiss the feet/of the reason my heart beats /if a kiss could kill maybe this one will/but a kiss can't kill but maybe this one will', before Isobel returns once again to share a lushly produced harmony vocal. Following a further verse that features Isobel solo once again, the track's outro then offers a beautiful overlay of both voices that is even more remarkable when one recalls that Campbell wasn't present in the studio at any point during the song's recording.

'The Two Of Us' (4:12)

The second appearance from Isobel Campbell, following directly after 'Song For A Secret' on the original running order for the 2017 album, this track first appeared in its earliest form a mere two years after the release of *Munki* on an EP entitled *Don't Worry Be Happy*, featuring four Freeheat songs. 'The Two Of Us' would later feature as the final track on *Little Pop Rock* (2005/2007), the Sister Vanilla debut album written by Jim and William, along with contributions from Linda. Closing the album, the duet was shared with Stephen Pastel, while Nick Sanderson played drums once more on the song.

Originally, the vocals during the Freeheat days had been shared between Jim and bass player Romi Mori, but for the *Damage And Joy* sessions, there were two vocal takes recorded featuring Isobel Campbell and Sky Ferreira, with the latter version included on the 2022 deluxe edition of the album released on Fuzz Club, which included a different running order in addition to three bonus tracks. Also of interest is the live version played on *The Late Show With Stephen Colbert* from May 2017, which featured a nervous-looking Ferreira on vocals being encouraged rather sweetly by Jim, mouthing some of the lyrics to her during the performance, with both then exchanging smiles (of relief) at the end.

'The Two Of Us' opens with a short burst of introductory guitar feedback before the same two-note organ riff from the Modern Lovers' evergreen 'Roadrunner' kicks things off properly, and we very quickly hear that this take is a substantial improvement on the old tune. This definitive Jesus and Mary Chain version has keyboards added to the mix as well as a far more stripped-down musical accompaniment on the verses than before. There is also an added emphasis now placed upon Jim's vocal track, which creates a richer texture that had not been the case on the 2000-2002 EP recordings.

With a set of alternately sturdy and jangling riffs playing throughout alongside more bassy drones and even some industrial clangs heard in the mix, there is a firm musical bedrock to 'The Two Of Us' while the heartfelt lyrics convey the significance of a key relationship in helping someone to better manage their own life and retain hope for the future: 'You're the reason I'm alive ... the two of us are getting high/We don't need drugs cause we know how to fly'.

Youth's production is especially evident in the more defined shift in this version of 'The Two Of Us', which begins at the 2:31 mark with Jim singing 'Well I was born the day that I met you' and Isobel countering 'I couldn't leave you if I tried'. The call-and-response vocal exchange builds to a close with the repeated line 'you're the reason I'm alive', before Jim delivers the chorus hook first in duet with Isobel and then alone on the second line, enhanced by a distinctive echo effect. A brief pause follows, after which the Mary Chain re-enter and the track resumes for a further 50 seconds, ending on the same organ note that opened the song almost exactly four minutes earlier.

'Los Feliz (Blues And Greens)' (4:54)

A slow burner of a song, 'Los Feliz' first appeared as a William Reid demo uploaded to his MySpace account in 2008 under the original title of 'And Greens'. Its inclusion on *Damage And Joy* ensured that one of the most impressive and emotionally satisfying post-split tracks written by either brother was finally given the production, time and care that it warranted.

This definitive version, now titled 'Los Feliz (Blues And Greens)', retains the same descending chord progression as the original but dispenses with the previous static-note guitar count pattern that ran intermittently throughout the track, instead adding strings to the arrangement. Jim takes over lead vocal duties, although William provides backing vocals as well as distorted guitar, just on the edge of feeding back, during both the build-up and the chorus itself.

The basic structure is supported by percussive-sounding piano chords, while keyboard strings help strengthen the overall wall of sound. The steady pace of 'Los Feliz (Blues And Greens)' is maintained throughout by Brian Young's measured drumming, and his relaxed playing on the track, never intrusive but always perfectly on point, helps explain why he retained his place as a key part of the Mary Chain's rhythm section for the best part of a decade.

The delivery of the lines 'God Bless America ... God lives in America/in the land of the free/wishing they were dead' tells the listener everything they need to know about the theme of the track. While 'Los Feliz' makes clear the love-hate relationship the brothers have always had with the US, the song takes on an extra layer of complexity when one recalls that William left the UK for good to settle in California during the early 2000s. The lyrics 'God Bless America/God Bless the USA/God lives in America/In the land of the free' take up the bulk of the chorus, but the twist that follows leaves open the same perpetual Mary Chain doubts with the line 'Wishing they were dead/ wishing you were dead/instead'.

The reference made during the song to 'the Sunset Strip train' is a nod to Carney's Restaurant, an actual train carriage converted into a hot dog and burger restaurant situated on Sunset Boulevard, while Los Feliz is also a genuine location, described online as an affluent hillside neighbourhood in the central region of Los Angeles, adjacent to Hollywood and encompassing part of the Santa Monica Mountains. A ballad of undeniable quality marking the halfway point on the album, 'Los Feliz (Blues And Greens)' contains all the suspicion and wariness the Reid brothers have ever felt towards America, and especially Los Angeles, their misanthropic attitude towards the US already long established.

'Mood Rider' (4:04)

One of only two songs on the album not produced by Youth, 'Mood Rider' is instead credited to The Jesus and Mary Chain with assistance from two separate engineers alongside a pre-production credit given in the sleeve notes to Dave Trumfio. Along with his brother, both ex-Pulsars, Trumfio had worked with William on a planned solo album that was ultimately abandoned in favour of recording *Damage And Joy*. This track, alongside 'Simian Split', had already been completed for inclusion on a more pop-oriented William Reid album in stark contrast to the music featured on his more challenging and decidedly experimental Lazycame output prior to the group's reunion.

Given its origins, it is perhaps understandable that 'Mood Rider' possesses a rougher-edged sound than most of the tracks included on *Damage And Joy*, although certainly not to its detriment. A driving full-band rock song, the drumming is also noticeably different from that heard elsewhere, with Chris Phillips' playing from an earlier recording retained in the studio while Jim's lead vocals replace those of his brother, who once again provides backing instead.

With choice lyrics delivering a further commentary on mortality, including the killer lines 'I think I'm turning to dust/Love is turning to lust/I think I'm turning to dust/only as I must', there is a definite undercurrent of fatalistic darkness running throughout the song. However, an economical lead guitar part working alongside a set of wordless harmony vocals from the 3:02 mark through to the conclusion combines effectively to bring some light into 'Mood Rider' at its close.

An accompanying promo video was shot for 'Mood Rider', which is suitably hallucinatory, featuring shuddering camera work and an overwhelming white light shone directly at Jim, who is filmed against a bare wall. With lyric extracts overlaid onscreen alongside brief glimpses of keyboard and guitar, despite its unusual visual aesthetic and the notable absence of William in the video, the 2017 promo suits the track very well.

'Presidici (Et Chapaquiditch)' (3:36)

Familiar to fans under its previous title of 'The Kennedy Song', and featuring several nods to elements heard in Mary Chain songs from earlier in their career – JFK and America most clearly, although nostalgic references to a few 1970s musical obsessions should not be overlooked either – 'Presidici (Et Chapaquiditch)' is an upbeat and catchy pop number with roots firmly planted in the glam and glitter era that some of the song's lyrics directly reference.

The track is another drawn from William's early 2000s songbook and, aside from its obvious musical appeal, the central guitar riff is engagingly basic while instantly memorable; it is packed full of clever lyrics that are alternately amusing, enigmatic and, at times, rather sentimental as the song delivers a particularly perky form of nostalgic catharsis.

Emerging out of a cloud of feedback, the song's key guitar hook soon begins and Jim delivers the opening lyrics with a definite presidential theme: 'If anyone can/a Kennedy can/If any clan can/a Kennedy can'.

Loath to discuss Mary Chain lyrics at any great length, and understandably so, both Jim and William Reid have left 'Presidici' open to fan interpretation. However, if any clan could effectively get away with something as career-destroying as the notorious Chappaquiddick incident, which involved Senator Ted Kennedy, the youngest member of the family, abandoning the scene of a serious crime, then it would indeed be the Kennedys. A subtle tweaking of the Massachusetts location amusingly echoes a pop-culture phenomenon of the early 2000s, *Harry Potter*, just as much as it references another infamous example of the supposed Kennedy curse.

The lyrics that follow throughout the remainder of the song vary in coherence but contain several further pop-culture references within their jumbled logic that never quite connect into a true narrative and at times seem plainly bizarre. One possibility is that lines such as 'a gold-capped tooth is always misunderstood/Christopher Walken's in a terrible mood' were originally used only as placeholders, intended to be replaced further down the line, but ultimately retained by the time 'Presidici (Et Chapaquiditch)' was recorded for inclusion on *Damage And Joy*. Whatever their origins, they are certainly memorable.

The next verse contains a lovely nod to the Reid brothers' family when Jim sings how 'I was made in deep space and I was raised on the moon/fell to earth/and I was born in June'. With William born in October 1958 and Jim in December 1961, reference to their mother's first name was a motif returned to seven years later on *Glasgow Eyes* in the form of the beautiful 'Second Of June'. A further autobiographical reference takes the listener all the way back to the Reids' love of early-1970s pop culture, when the Fab Four post-break-up cast a long shadow over the British musical climate, with the line 'and we grew up with the Spiders/and the Beatles from Mars/tiger feet and the T-Rex cars'.

Even more engaging than the song's nostalgia-infused lyrics is the neatly layered bridge section where both William and Jim sing together, 'behind black eyes/my mind is fine' before Jim returns to solo delivery with the hard-earned wisdom of 'If you can't love yourself/it's bad for your health', which closes out the track.

'Get On Home' (3:31)

'Get On Home' sounds like the Mary Chain letting loose and relaxing a little in each other's company, which, given the worries both brothers harboured regarding a resumption of working together in the studio, probably felt like a minor miracle at the time.

A brief burst of guitar hum introduces what was previously released as a Freeheat song on the 2016 compilation *Back On The Water*, issued in the US on Planting Seeds Records, and while the recording here inevitably sounds more polished, the guitars employed on the track feel weaker than before. The drum machine accompaniment is also thin and compressed, a pale choice of backing on this occasion rather than the live drums that would arguably have given the song more power.

There are a couple of distinctive guitar breaks where a noisy squall enters the mix, and there is also a brief hint of the descending chord pattern from 'I Wanna Be Your Dog' previously heard on the ironically titled Radio Mix of 'Reverence'. In addition to some choppy and jagged-sounding rhythm guitar playing that first appears at the 1:45 mark, there is a further, even more concentrated guitar blast towards the end of the song, which reinforces the synth-rock amalgamation at the heart of 'Get On Home'. Listen closely and it is even possible to discern a whistling synth sound rising and falling in pitch in the background of the track.

The lyrics, delivered by Jim, are arguably the most limited on *Damage And Joy,* but, with their roots stretching back to the early 2000s when the song was first written and played live, it is perhaps unfair to judge them too harshly. Given the memorable, not to mention amusing, inclusion of lines such as 'I spent the night with a blow-up girl/and some LSD/Well the girl didn't blow up/but she made it on the MTV', it would appear the Mary Chain were definitely in on the joke.

'Facing Up To The Facts' (3:05)

Previously released by Freeheat on both their US and UK EPs, 'Facing Up To The Facts' in its 2017 form is an effective rewrite with many of the original verse lyrics replaced and a new groove taking the place of the rather lumpen percussion heard before. Gone, too, are the intro lyrics from the previous version where Jim rattled off a staccato set of complaints, although the original chorus remains intact, now strengthened by the expected improvements in sound quality, with Youth's production once again impressive.

The Mary Chain were never shy when it came to repurposing a good idea, and their own back catalogue is cherry-picked once again to benefit 'Facing Up To The Facts', with the low-slung grinding bassline of 1988's 'Sidewalking' lifted and bolted into place on a new track almost three decades later. Through the use of this old-new bassline, and with Brian Young's inspired drumming locked tightly into William's rhythm playing, the deliberately primitive stomp of 'Facing Up To The Facts' in its original incarnation is replaced with a groove similar to the revered single that helped The Jesus and Mary Chain successfully transition from their *Darklands* era into the early 1990s.

Similar to a number of other tracks on the album, most notably 'Amputation' and 'All Things Pass', there is a distinctly reflective element to 'Facing Up To The Facts' where the Mary Chain appear to have acquired a degree of hard-earned maturity through looking back at their former selves and past conflicts, reaching the realisation that 'You know there's no safety net/you know this is all we get'. Lines such as these seem to reflect the restored creative communication between William and Jim while simultaneously acknowledging the unavoidable familial antipathy forever at the heart of the band.

Along with the original's 'Don't worry be happy' coda, retained for the new version of the track, 'Facing Up To The Facts' perhaps most memorably echoes a line from the 1987 B-side 'Kill Surf City' through its admission that 'I hate my brother/and he hates me/and that's the way it's supposed to be'. Simultaneously reflecting on the past while coming to terms with the present, seldom, if ever, has the creative relationship at the core of The Jesus and Mary Chain been addressed so honestly. While there does appear to be an element of tongue-in-cheek in the fact that the line here has been tweaked from the flip side of their most successful hit single, and therefore functions as a nod towards former glories, the fact that fans of the group would readily agree with the sentiment expressed speaks volumes.

'Simian Split' (4:14)

One of only two completely new songs to feature on the album, 'Simian Split' commences with an assemblage of jumbled audio clips that help reaffirm the Mary Chain as, at heart, a boldly experimental group. The influence of producer Youth on the track is especially notable, with the collage of dub-jazz riffs, random samples, off-kilter drum rolls and woozy synth sounds creating a decidedly avant-garde backdrop most closely related to William's more eccentric solo output as Lazycame or perhaps even the sonically radical *Munki*-era songs such as 'Nineteen 666', 'Perfume' and 'Commercial'.

The title of the track is a reference to palmistry beliefs that a single crease line running between the palm of the hand, formed through the fusion of the normal head and heart lines, is a sign of an intensely focused personality due to its blending of emotional and intellectual traits. Not merely an interesting song title, a simian split functions as an identifier of several personality characteristics frequently associated with musicians, which, given the lyrical focus of this particular Mary Chain song, is even more fitting.

Providing a rather warped take on the Nirvana frontman's suicide with the unapologetically contentious opening lyrics 'I killed Kurt Cobain/I put the shot right through his brain', the track, similar again to some of the more challenging material from *Munki*, sees the group boldly stepping into new musical terrain, although the jolting effect of the opening lines seems to have focused most attention from casual listeners.

In a 2017 interview prior to the release of *Damage And Joy*, Jim attempted to explain that anyone reading too much into the provocative lyrics to 'Simian Split' was wasting their time:

> It may sound silly, but it's playful ... It's fiction. It's total fiction. It's not meant to be taken too seriously. It's just a work of fiction, and people shouldn't get too het up about it.

Following its Cobain conspiracy fan-baiting opening, 'Simian Split' broadens its lyrical scope to provide stark commentary on the boredom of rock stardom despite its luxury trappings, with the closing lines 'Set sail can't get any land/Pet jail is life in a band' being especially memorable. With additional discordant saxophone sounds mixed alongside Arabic-scaled synth parts, this track is arguably the most adventurous piece of music to feature on *Damage And Joy,* and such is its unusual nature that it may well have puzzled some fans upon first listen. It is to the Mary Chain's credit that they ensured their comeback album included as many examples of their unfettered creative progress as possible, and 'Simian Split', with its fearless soundscape and striking set of lyrics, is certainly a prime example.

'Black And Blues' (3:23)
One of the more recent Jim Reid solo demos at the time of recording the album, 'Black And Blues' is transformed from its sparse, two-and-a-half-minute home demo origins into a track that evokes the richer, acoustic-oriented sound of *Stoned & Dethroned*, complete with a guest vocalist delivering an appealing performance in another memorable duet.

Early in the planning stages for *Damage And Joy*, it became clear that several songs would work best as duets, prompting the Mary Chain to seek recommendations for suitable female vocalists. Sky Ferreira, who had recently appeared on Primal Scream's 2016 track 'Where The Light Gets In', was suggested by Bobby Gillespie. A second version of 'Black And Blues' featuring Isobel Campbell was also completed during the sessions, and while the Ferreira take was ultimately chosen for the penultimate position on *Damage And Joy*, the 2022 deluxe edition includes both versions, identical musically aside from the alternate vocals.

A fan of the Mary Chain to the extent that she had attended several of their American shows a few years prior to recording with the band, Sky Ferreira's contribution works particularly well. Her voice first enters alongside Jim at around 24 seconds, before her first solo passage shortly after, with 'You know we're livin' in shit/Guess that love is where you find it'. Beautifully melancholic and tightly balanced in the mix, the duet form allows Jim's vocal to stand at its strongest on the album, while Sky provides an effective contrast with her softer, more lyrical delivery.

By the time the pair sing 'we could leave this world behind/and die/die in the morning', the emotional tone is fully established, and even the most cynical listener is likely to respond to the beauty of the vocal blend despite the darkness of the sentiment. At this point in the track, around 1:35, the arrangement shifts as crunching and buzzing textures enter alongside a low, reverberating guitar figure and a double-time rhythmic lift.

The archetypal doomed-lovers scenario is played out to full effect in 'Black And Blues', with Jim and Sky exchanging unguarded romantic lines shaped by an underlying sadness – this is The Jesus and Mary Chain after all. The distinctly American imagery of a wide-open highway, introduced early in the song, returns towards the end as the couple drift off into the sunset under a wash of echoed 'Bah bah bahs', with William's backing vocals particularly clear in the mix. Sky Ferreira's presence helps draw out both melody and melancholy in equal measure, and 'Black And Blues' stands as one of the strongest tracks on *Damage And Joy*.

'Can't Stop The Rock' (3:21)
A duet with Sister Vanilla, the closing track on the album is a reworked version of a song originally included on the 2005 Japanese CD edition and the 2007 Chemikal Underground release of *Little Pop Rock*. Jim had previously issued an earlier version of the song on a split CD/7" single alongside 'Song

For A Secret' in 2005. In its final form here, 'Can't Stop The Rock' provides a more upbeat conclusion than the one that closed *Munki*, leaning instead into a celebratory sense of guitar-driven optimism.

The song unfolds with an easy, unforced momentum over its three-minute runtime, with Jim and Linda sharing vocals on lyrics that affirm the enduring appeal of rock 'n' roll: 'Share your imagination/and your deep dark inspiration/Wrap the whole thing up in wonder'.

The guitar work remains relatively understated throughout, although a circular motif introduced at around 2:23 locks neatly into the song's steady groove. William's backing vocals gradually build before Jim joins him in harmony, accompanied by a brief chiming guitar line. Jim's spoken 'Stop!' – a familiar cue from the band's live history – brings the track to a close as it draws *Damage And Joy* to its conclusion.

Contemporary Tracks

'Ono Yoko' (4:04)

Included on the 2022 reissue of *Damage And Joy* as one of three bonus tracks and issued on vinyl for the first time at that point, 'Ono Yoko' originally appeared only on the Japanese CD edition in 2017 before later being released digitally as a single ahead of the reissue.

Drawn from the same pool of early 2000s material as several of William's other demos, the track is built around a single barre-chord riff that runs almost continuously throughout, with William delivering loose, stuttering vocal fragments and playing with the pronunciation of Yoko Ono's name. The result feels closer to a studio sketch than a fully developed composition.

It is possible to hear the sense of the band experimenting and unwinding in the studio, even if that alone does not substantially alter the track's limited scope or appeal. On first listen, 'Ono Yoko' sounds unlike anything The Jesus and Mary Chain had previously released, and its appearance as a standalone single – even in digital form – remains unexpected, except perhaps as a way of making the track accessible to completist listeners who missed the original Japanese release of *Damage And Joy*.

Glasgow Eyes (2024)

Personnel:
Jim Reid: vocals, instruments, production
William Reid: vocals, instruments, production
Tony Doogan: piano, programming, mixing, engineering
Recorded in Scotland (Castle Of Doom Studios, Glasgow), England (Rapunzel Studios, Devon and Sound Gallery Studios, Exeter) and the US (Casa Roja, Tucson)
Producers: William and Jim Reid
Additional engineering: George Arnold, Duncan Chave
Additional mixing assistance: Dan Doherty
Label: Fuzz Club
Charts: Scottish Albums: 1, Austria: 12, Croatia: 33, Germany: 36, Ireland: 12, Spain: 60, Sweden: 5, Switzerland: 33, UK: 7, UK Independent Albums: 1, US Top Current Album Sales (*Billboard*): 47, US Indie Store Album Sales (*Billboard*): 9, US (*Billboard* Independent Albums): 9
Running time: 48:55

The eighth Mary Chain album began to take shape in the six months prior to the grim pandemic of 2020, with close to half a dozen tracks in a state of partial completion before the COVID lockdown, which also put paid to the band's scheduled European tour of their *Darklands* album. When concert restrictions were finally lifted and venues rebooked, the much-anticipated live dates were fulfilled from mid-November to December 2021.

The Jesus and Mary Chain returned to studio work in Scotland during the autumn of 2021, where a number of backing tracks and early versions had been recorded over the course of several months in between live commitments across Europe and the States. However, upon resuming recording with the intention of completing the previously assembled tracks, the band were met with the wholly unexpected news that the music they had so diligently recorded was missing, with no back-ups having been kept. This meant that approximately half of a potential new album had been lost, and the impact upon the band was understandably devastating. After the initial shock had lessened, Jim focused on recording his own songs once again and was able to work in studios close to home and family in the Devon area. It took longer for William to recover from the shattering experience of having the music the band had worked on so meticulously disappear with no hope of recovery, to the extent that he later admitted to being tempted to give up recording altogether in the aftermath.

Things slowly got back on track following the decision to base themselves in Glasgow from February to mid-May 2023, working out of Mogwai's recording studio, Castle of Doom, located in the Finnieston district of the city. David McBride, manager of The Jesus and Mary Chain, had previously worked with Mogwai for several years and was therefore able to recommend the location to the brothers. Stuart Braithwaite, frontman of Mogwai, should also be credited with encouraging the Reids to record their new album in Glasgow after learning directly from them of the earlier crushing disappointment. While working at their new recording base, William and Jim were assisted by Tony Doogan, who ran the impressively furnished and well-equipped studio (built on the premises of a former Victorian bank) and was ideally placed to help the pair transform song sketches and preliminary ideas into cohesive, fully realised tracks that were worthy of inclusion on what would ultimately become *Glasgow Eyes*.

While not directly involved in producing the album's tracks, unlike Youth's previous work with the Mary Chain on *Damage And Joy*, Doogan nevertheless played an important role, with contributions ranging from engineering and mixing duties to programming electronics and even some piano playing. The Glasgow sessions coincided with the 40th anniversary (or thereabouts) of the formation of The Jesus and Mary Chain, and although William did not necessarily consider the location to be of particular significance – perhaps recalling how the band had been shunned in their earliest days when trying to secure local gigs – his brother, in interviews promoting *Glasgow Eyes*, spoke of drawing inspiration from spending time back in their home city:

> I'd walk around Glasgow for a couple of hours, getting in the right state of mind for the sessions, reconnecting with a place that I used to know so well.

The album's title was directly inspired by a batch of digital artwork that William had produced while designing potential sleeve images for the new release. Upon revealing his latest creations, serendipity struck when Jim reportedly remarked that the faces all had distinctive 'Glasgow eyes'. Given the location of the recording sessions alongside the Scots dialect pun of 'aye/eye', the title could hardly have been more fitting.

A notable benefit of re-recording many of the lost elements, alongside further developing earlier song ideas and sketches that had not been so carefully stored, was that the tracks were then able to evolve in unexpected directions. Whether through employing more experimental structures and chord progressions or – as was the case with a number of songs on *Glasgow Eyes* – a more prominent use of synths and drum machines than ever before, the process ultimately opened up some new creative possibilities.

Enabled by the range of equipment at their disposal within Castle of Doom, alongside ongoing developments in studio technology and production techniques, the band were able to skilfully update their guitar-driven sound with a greater incorporation of electronic elements. Far from a reinvention, this was simply another step in the evolution of The Jesus and Mary Chain. Influences that had always existed within the band's musical orbit – whether genre-defining acts such as Kraftwerk and Can, or more esoteric artists like Cabaret Voltaire and Suicide – now seemed more prominent than ever.

As a result, *Glasgow Eyes* arguably sounds more contemporary and fresh than many may have expected, with an experimental and innovative feel across a number of its tracks that is both invigorating and rather admirable for a band moving into their fourth decade of producing music.

Guitars were still present and correct, of course, but the music itself was now less reliant on them than ever before, with synths frequently utilised in place of distortion. The Jesus and Mary Chain were evolving once more, and the sound of *Glasgow Eyes* marked a distinctive progression from what had come before. In that respect, it exists as the perfect Mary Chain album – noise pop with experimental electronic elements to the fore.

In keeping with the band's long-established and admirable tradition of forging ahead in the exploration of new sounds while maintaining a high standard of both songwriting and musicianship – something many of their contemporaries had over the years been unwilling or unable to do – it should come as little surprise to fans that previously neglected, or perhaps more fairly 'underappreciated', genres were now providing inspiration.

This was something that Jim himself addressed while promoting *Glasgow Eyes*, as he acknowledged both the prominent use of synths on the album and the distinctive guitar elements present on several tracks:

> There's a lot of electronics on it. I mean, some of William's guitar playing, I think, veers into jazz almost. It's the Mary Chain gone experimental, I suppose.

Another distinctive development in the music featured on *Glasgow Eyes* is the reflective nature of several of its tracks. While it may, once again, appear somewhat fortuitous that basic geography – in this case, recording in Glasgow – had inspired the Mary Chain to adopt a more nostalgic tone, there is a clear sense of introspection running throughout the album. This lends the record a genuine emotional depth, and although songs focused on relationships and personal redemption will be familiar to anyone with even a passing acquaintance with the band, rarely have these themes been explored with such a sense of shared introspection and maturity.

The passage of time enriches the emotional depth of the tracks, not least on the album standouts 'Second Of June', where the lyrical content is especially vulnerable and moving, and 'Chemical Animal', where the confessional nature of the song is especially bold in its stark recounting of truly dark times and the lasting legacy of an addiction. There is also the self-referential 'JAMCOD', featuring lyrical fragments originally composed by Jim in the immediate aftermath of the notorious House of Blues gig in 1998 that had led to the band's splintering. Its inclusion serves as a clear indication, if one were needed, that the relationship between the Reid brothers had healed to the extent that it was now possible to revisit the painful episode that had effectively fractured their bond for the best part of a decade.

Vocal duties are evenly shared on *Glasgow Eyes*, with six songs each, and William makes a welcome return to the microphone after being noticeably absent from 2017's *Damage And Joy*, where the bulk of the record was delivered by Jim. A key feature of the album's lyrical delivery is this sense of shared introspection, and William's vocal-led tracks are no less thoughtful, nostalgic, or powerful. 'Pure Poor' and 'Silver Strings' provide a fitting homage to his – and the Mary Chain's – roots, while other recordings, notably 'The Eagles And The Beatles', as well as a track that did not make the final cut but was later released as a standalone single, 'Pop Seeds', pay tribute to the influences that shaped both brothers so significantly.

Glasgow Eyes was announced at the end of November 2023, alongside the release of the lead single 'JAMCOD'. Upon the album's release on 22 March (two weeks later than initially scheduled due to vinyl production delays), it entered the UK Albums Chart at number seven, marking the Mary Chain's first top ten LP since *Barbed Wire Kisses* in 1988. It is interesting to note that, despite being released in an era dominated by streaming services, the album still generated sufficient demand to warrant a strong physical release. As a result, *Glasgow Eyes* reached number two on both the UK Official Physical Albums Chart and the Official Vinyl Albums Chart, while also securing the number one position on both the Independent Albums Chart and the Scottish Albums Chart.

Additional high chart placings for the album were secured throughout Europe and in the States, where the Mary Chain have remained extremely popular with fans since their 2007 reformation.

In a year increasingly framed as the 40th anniversary of The Jesus and Mary Chain – one that would later include the long-awaited release of the Reids' autobiography – the band embarked on a major European tour during March and April 2024 alongside the release of their new album. Receiving some of the most favourable reviews of their music since *Psychocandy*, from across the music press – both in the printed media and, increasingly, online – *Glasgow Eyes* marked a period in which the Mary Chain were able to realign their creative approach while enjoying richly deserved acclaim.

Meanwhile, William Reid's exacting standards for the group have ensured that his long-held promise to bring things to an end if those high benchmarks could no longer be maintained remains unfulfilled. William Reid in *Uncut*, April 2024:

> There's a higher responsibility. There's a history of the whole band. It's something I take more seriously than anything in the whole world. The last thing I wanna do is put out a shitty Jesus and Mary Chain record. If that ever happened, that'll be time to finish.

'Venal Joy' (3:27)

The album opens with a track alive with electronics – whirring, buzzing and defiantly upfront in the mix – confirming that early promotional statements from Jim mentioning the likes of Suicide and Kraftwerk as direct influences on *Glasgow Eyes* were spot on. 'Venal Joy' provides a litmus test for listeners, and particularly the more dyed-in-the-wool Mary Chain fans, which Jim directly addressed in an interview with *Uncut* magazine in early 2024 at the time of the album's release:

> There's everything in that song that you should expect on the rest of the album … If you get past it, you're on board. We generally don't plan how a record's going to sound, but this time we knew we were going to get the synths out and make it more electronic.

The track is quick-paced, with synth pulses and unrelenting sequenced rhythms bringing to mind the Portastudio demos from the earliest days of the band, where the limitations imposed upon The Jesus and Mary Chain from a recording perspective actually helped to enhance the power and melody of the songs captured on their four-track TASCAM machine. That same primitive urgency is also present in 'Venal Joy' four decades later, with the focus on song structure, hooks and melody as strong as ever, all set against a backdrop of squalling electronica.

Following an opening verse that features a set of uncompromising lyrics and a wry piece of lyrical wordplay – is Jim really singing 'I was kicking the 'caine cause the cane wasn't able'? – the track moves straight into the first of several clipped power-chord interludes, which add pent-up ferocity to the already bubbling-over atmosphere. A strong harmony vocal provided by Fay Fife (from Scottish pop-punk legends The Rezillos) adds force to subsequent lines, including the defiant declaration: 'I'd piss bleach to meet you/Crawl through broken glass to meet you/But I won't just fucking die/No, I won't give up and die'.

'Venal Joy' ends with a mantra of positivity (or as close to it as repetition of 'I'm alright, I'm okay' can sound) as the track begins its gradual descent, slowing in pace from 3:00 before reaching its conclusion 20 seconds later, and as an opening to a Jesus and Mary Chain album, 'Venal Joy' sits comfortably with its compatriots from the previous seven records.

'American Born' (3:04)

Introduced with a sweet tinkling music-box melody and some lovely harmony vocals, 'American Born' slows the pace after the rip-roaring start to *Glasgow Eyes*. However, the lyrical message in this second track on the album is far from chilled-out, as it delivers an acerbic critique of the all-encompassing homogenisation of all things American.

A successor of sorts to 'Los Feliz (Blues And Greens)' from *Damage And Joy,* which ably set out the Mary Chain's love/hate relationship with the States, 'American Born' goes a step further by detailing all manner of activities with (and like) Americans – trained, live, look, talk. The lines in the first verse are punctuated by rich synth washes and chunky, overdriven rhythm guitar parts, which, on their own, sound as though they belong straight out of American MOR rock, but, placed in the context that we find them in here, actually underscore the cultural assimilation at the heart of the song.

William may be a naturalised American resident of many years, and the father of American children, but he still retains a good degree of his clear-eyed Scottish cynicism and has lost none of his native accent either. It is therefore interesting to hear the subversive lyric, 'I'm praying for the other side', hidden away amongst the deliberately overwhelming repetition of the key line, 'I'm American born'. Contrary to this, and with an unconscious echo of the ultimate outsider Roky Erickson's 'I Walked With A Zombie' running through the track, 'American Born' is not quite the US-loving number that its title and lyrical content would perhaps initially suggest.

'Mediterranean X Film' (4:24)

One of the tracks where the recordings had been lost, requiring the Mary Chain to revisit its origins and effectively begin again at Castle of Doom, 'Mediterranean X Film', alongside its companion piece 'Silver Strings', delves into near-cinematic territory in its use of evocative imagery. The instrumental backing is less regimented than elsewhere on the album, with the rhythms more aligned to light, loose jazz percussion and quick tempo shifts occurring between the song's verses.

William's impressionistic lyrical portrayal of political and post-punk connectivity is first ushered in through an unknown American voice intoning words laden with significance and a fair degree of intrigue – 'Television/light/transmission/revolution' – alongside pulsing synth sounds, more prominently mixed guitar and the aforementioned shuffling rhythms. He then delivers his own idiosyncratic selection involving 'Churchill and De Gaulle/Berlin and the Wall/The Bunny Boys and The Fall/I think I loved them all', which creates an air of nostalgic fondness on the track in a somewhat nebulous manner, alongside a further reference to 'June Cash, she loved everyone/It looks like we love everybody', prior to a notable gear change in the second half of the intriguingly titled song. Similar namechecking is found elsewhere on *Glasgow Eyes*, but the subtle instrumentation and odd atmosphere generated on 'Mediterranean X Film' are distinctly different from those heard later on the album when we reach 'The Eagles And The Beatles'.

Cued by what appears to be the same female voice that introduced proceedings (albeit with the sample now stretched to elongate the vocal delivery), a somnambulistic, slow and slurred incantation of 'destroy yourself' at the 2:43 point in the song signals the coda to 'Mediterranean X Film', where hazy ambient washes accompany the repetition of a whispered 'dark is dead', drawing this unique track to a close in a curiously moving manner.

'JAMCOD' (3:59)

The album's lead single served as an excellent introduction to the forthcoming eighth Mary Chain record, and while it does certainly nod in the direction of their late 1980s and early 1990s sound, it was not necessarily representative of the album as a whole, but instead allowed listeners an early insight into the enhanced experimentation with electronic textures that would feature throughout *Glasgow Eyes*. The first of two tracks to cite the band by name in self-referential fashion, 'JAMCOD' (as in JAMC overdose, and not 'jam cod', as the presenter teeing up a debut play of the single on BBC Radio 6 Music had it) describes in unflinching detail the September 1998 onstage break-up at the House of Blues Sunset Strip in Los Angeles, where William effectively left the building, leading to a nine-year hiatus in Mary Chain activity.

As befits the painful subject matter, the lyrics are far from an exercise in nostalgia, and the song's genesis instead appears to lie in the necessity to draw a line under events by addressing the matter in as forthright a manner as possible, which Jim himself explained when quizzed upon the single's release during late November 2023:

> So many people ask about the night that the shit hit the fan and it all blew up, that I just thought, 'Let's put it in a song and maybe they'll stop asking.'

After an extended introduction of reverberating electronic percussion fed through a flanger effect, an ominous low-note synth sound appears in the mix that oscillates in the background for the majority of the track, rising and falling in pitch alongside a pulsing bassline. There is a propulsive electronic feel to 'JAMCOD' with the blasts of intermittent guitar chords elevating the track above and beyond its synthetic components. Therein lies the strength of this and several other tracks from *Glasgow Eyes* – listeners don't necessarily get what they may have been expecting, but when they do – the explosions of guitar are especially monstrous at high volume here – the combination of melody and dissonance is all the more impressive.

Jim's vocals are mixed front and centre, with no holds barred in the nature of the lyrics delivered, some of which have their origins from the night in question, where certain lines were written down on scraps of paper, including 'House of Blues blues' and 'Cocaine and disabled', before being returned to many years later. Amongst the scattered self-analysis in 'JAMCOD', there can be found some fascinating glimpses into the levels of dysfunction that were afflicting The Jesus and Mary Chain by the late 1990s, and especially during their ill-fated US tour of 1998. The acerbic opening line of 'the monkey's organ grinder isn't grinding anymore' is arresting enough, but it is then followed by equally intriguing lyrics that border on the confessional in style, not least 'tears are what you want/tears are what you've got' – while perhaps most telling of all is the instruction to 'notify the other brother there's no place to go'.

The conflation of 'I'm recently deceased' with 'diseased' is also noteworthy, before the repetition of the track title, spelled out in a surely deliberate deconstructed manner ('J-A-M-C-O-D!'), leads the song into its coda, where once again the background synth sound – alternately whining and whooshing – returns to the front of the mix, and the outro of a now heavily phased and flanged drum pattern plays out, bringing 'JAMCOD' full circle.

The single was accompanied by a suitably blistering visual assault of a promo video directed by Ben Unwin that carried its own viewer-discretion warning due to the intensity of the imagery and flashing lights featured during its runtime. The promo combined live footage of the Reids onstage during the *Damage And Joy* tour alongside film of Jim at home, while glitching effects and overlays related to key lyrics appear and disappear throughout the track. Instantly memorable and the perfect accompaniment to the song itself, it is also worthy of mention that the iconic star logo associated with The Jesus and Mary Chain since the days of *Automatic* makes a welcome return at the beginning and end of the 'JAMCOD' video, cleverly sequenced in sync with the intro/outro drum-machine pattern of the track itself.

'Discotheque' (4:13)

One of the strongest – and strangest – moments on *Glasgow Eyes*, this is a song that sounds so uniquely interesting that there is a strong possibility it would be difficult, upon first listening, to discern that this was even a track by The Jesus and Mary Chain when removed from the context of the album itself. Continuing in the same atmospheric soundscape style as 'Mediterranean X Film', the main descending chord pattern employed here as the bedrock of the track is very similar to that used on the equally repetitive 'I Am Damo Suzuki' by The Fall, while the driving bass and incessant synthetic beat are reminiscent of the motorik rhythms of Neu!.

Deftly positioned around the primary descending guitar lines on 'Discotheque', there is a range of single-note electronic sounds varying in pitch and sounding rather eerie, while William weaves in brief overdriven lead parts, first appearing at the 2:19 point in the track before returning to the mix twice more during the final minute.

The carefully constructed musical backing and lyrics evoke a foggy, disorientating atmosphere in which William details an imaginary music venue complete with 'drinks, pills and thrills'. However, the rather outdated title of this nightclub as a 'discotheque', alongside references to 'absent record decks', the repetition of '19 six-five' and the clothing of choice being the decidedly dated 'satin, silk or corduroy', gives the setting an otherworldly, ethereal vibe.

'Pure Poor' (5:18)

Sequenced at the midpoint of *Glasgow Eyes*, this is a more serious and decidedly slower-paced track than anything else on the album, with its distorted guitars and grinding pace having the same impact that tracks such as 'Perfume' and 'Commercial' had on *Munki*, as well as receiving the same familiar criticisms from listeners regarding its appeal. It certainly appears to have been one of the less immediately popular songs on the album and was identified as such in reviews, as well as in a number of fan comments, upon the album's initial release. The live incarnation of the track saw 'Pure Poor' transformed into an intense, near-monstrous song of real power, which transcends the admittedly challenging nature of its recorded version.

Lyrically, this is no rose-tinted nostalgic visit to happier times, but instead a clear-eyed reflection on William and Jim's earliest years, where poverty was ever-present; less a celebration of working-class background than an unblemished reality check of their roots. The accompanying guitar tracks on 'Pure Poor' are multi-layered and, while no main parts truly stand out upon listening, they certainly fulfil a role in helping to generate a swirling atmosphere around telling lines such as, 'For millions of years/and oceans of tears – baby I was pure'.

'The Eagles And The Beatles' (3:11)

Cued in with a gloriously simplistic stomping beat combined with high-pitched white-noise sounds that cleverly emulate teenybopper screams, this track immediately sets out its playful and light-hearted approach, which is strengthened further with a clear debt to the melody and tempo of 'I Love Rock 'N' Roll', the glam-rocking Arrows hit from 1975 that was turned into a rock standard just over six years later by Joan Jett.

An ode to the Mary Chain's musical world of influences from their early years, an extensive list is issued in which some key acts are namechecked: Dylan, Beatles (curiously mentioned only once, although an earlier version of the track saw more references to the Fab Four), Sex Pistols, Crystals, Beach Boys and the Small Faces. The Velvets, Stooges and Ramones evidently didn't make the final cut, but those that are mentioned indicate the truly eclectic music tastes of the Reids while being undeniably major musical successes rather than cult acts – a dividing line that The Jesus and Mary Chain themselves have stepped over at key points during their own career.

The title of the track is somewhat curious in that lyrical references to The Eagles are entirely absent, while The Beatles are reduced to a singular mention in the final version included on *Glasgow Eyes*. William later clarified that an earlier take had featured a verse including the former 1970s soft-rock giants, but the title was retained as it sounded so good. It is instead Mary Chain favourites The Rolling Stones – at least the 1960s incarnation of those 'rock and roll disgraces' – that feature most prominently throughout the song, with a central chorus hook of 'I've been rolling with the stones/Mick and Keith and Brian Jones/Bill and Charlie have gone home'.

Upon first listen to 'The Eagles And The Beatles', it is clear that this is a song meant to be fun rather than taken especially seriously, and it instead works best as a celebratory mood-lightener. The involvement of Mary Chain cousins on handclaps, alongside some nicely timed piano contributions from Tony Doogan, helps to strengthen the notion of the band enjoying themselves at the Castle of Doom during the recording.

'Silver Strings' (3:29)

One of the most impressive aspects of the ambition and scope of the tracks on *Glasgow Eyes* is that several of the songs sound markedly different from the Mary Chain that many, rightly or wrongly, had come to expect. 'Silver Strings' is a strong example of this, particularly in its utilisation of sparkling synths alongside a regimented drum machine and synchronised bass pulse. The guitars that do feature add colour to the track but function mainly to help secure the rhythm, with William only then beginning to contribute jazz-styled solo parts as the song progresses.

While the musical backdrop is distortion-free and features some interesting timings, William's lyrics are essentially focused on the instrument that, ironically enough, is muted in favour of glistening synths and ambient swirling sections, with the latter element first appearing at the 1:29 mark. Detailing a list of objects, both desirable and dangerous, including 'dirty magazines/rockets and nuclear submarines' amongst 'one billion shiny things', a marked contrast is then established with what William has to work with in order to secure his own path ahead and a different form of riches and rewards – 'I've got six dirty silver strings'.

There is also a curious secondary lyric – 'you get in the way/in the way/in the way' – delivered alongside an eerie whisper during the runtime of 'Silver Strings', which remains enigmatic in meaning. Ultimately, the song works as an ode to the magical properties of the electric guitar when aligned with sheer imagination, an alchemical combination that The Jesus and Mary Chain have mined to considerable success throughout their long career.

A promo video was made for 'Silver Strings', which is decidedly avant-garde, featuring some memorable desert-filmed imagery directed by Ambar Navarro, interspersed with stark blue-lit footage of William and Jim together, with the former miming to the lyrics while his brother stands still and emotionless.

'Chemical Animal' (4:33)

A powerful reflection on addiction, and one of Jim's most honest and self-reflective songs ever to feature on a Mary Chain album, 'Chemical Animal' is a definite highlight on *Glasgow Eyes*. A haunting analysis of addiction, the song repurposes the beat from 'Just Like Honey' once again in order to provide its backing, but it is with the more introspective and brooding tracks from *Darklands* that 'Chemical Animal' is most closely aligned.

A swirling, meditative drone, driven by sequencers rather than the perhaps expected dominant guitars, further highlights the record's shift toward electronic and psychedelic influences. The theme of escapism – while masking deeper-rooted issues through embracing a lifestyle that eventually becomes less of a choice and more a painful compulsion – is addressed through no-holds-barred lines as transparent and unflinching in their honesty as: 'There is something you should know/There is something I don't show/I fill myself with chemicals/To hide the dark shit I don't show'.

Jim's coolly delivered lines are darkly numb (all the more appropriate given the subject matter of the track) and aptly matched by some understated tonal guitar parts that mournfully complement the mood of the song. Released as the second single from *Glasgow Eyes* during mid-January 2024 and accompanied by an excellent promo video (the second to be directed by Sasha Conti), 'Chemical Animal' – despite its despondent lyrical content – presents a superb marker of the depths to which The Jesus and Mary Chain were willing to dive in their unwavering, at times even sinister, evocation of a struggle against overwhelming inner darkness.

This was addressed in a contemporary interview with *Mojo* magazine, where Jim recalled the inspiration for the track in a typically frank manner:

> …thinking back to the times where it was like, you get up in the morning and the day was successful if I hooked up with someone who was going to sell me drugs – you were basically acting totally on instinct, and it was all about getting drugs. The humanity got sucked out for a while, I suppose – the idea of drugs and glamour is totally a myth.

'Second Of June' (3:56)

The tenth track on *Glasgow Eyes* presents a more upbeat version of Jim, especially noticeable in the immediate aftermath of 'Chemical Animal'. It also feels significant that this song of positivity and hope follows so directly after the bleakness of the preceding track. One of the most upbeat-sounding songs on the album, 'Second Of June' shares something of 'Sometimes Always' in its opening and verse structures, but is more nuanced in sound than anything heard on *Stoned & Dethroned*, while its ticking motorik backing is closer to that heard at various points on 2018's *Damage And Joy*.

This is a lovely ode to the Reids' family, as well as the bond shared within the Mary Chain, with the band name itself even appearing at the two-minute point of the song in a self-referential manner, which may sound a little cringe-inducing in print but is actually rather moving, especially following so soon after Jim's lyrics addressing firstly his mother (the June of the title) and then his brother in consecutive verses. The dramatic imagery in lines such as 'there's a storm behind my shoulder/there's a blood moon on the rise' is countered by the sadness of 'I don't feel this anymore/I don't need this anymore/I can't be this anymore/No more'.

There's a genuine sense of fragility in this track, and William's understated, single-note descending guitar interludes help maintain a beautiful melancholy that permeates 'Second Of June'. From the 2:15 point in the song, a shimmering Indian string sound can also be heard rising and falling in the background, providing another lovely textural element to the overall sonic appeal of what is undoubtedly one of the strongest tracks on *Glasgow Eyes,* and whose title also peculiarly matches the original 1998 release date of *Munki*.

'Girl 71' (3:08)

The third pre-release single, unveiled just a few weeks prior to the release of *Glasgow Eyes*, is notably upbeat and sits comfortably within the power-pop genre. It carries clear echoes of both the Velvets' 'Sweet Jane' (albeit at a higher tempo) and, more curiously, 'Living After Midnight' by Judas Priest. The latter's identifiable chord progression actually appeared earlier than the Rob Halford-led outfit's track; however, there are also more distinct echoes here of Lou Reed's 'Vicious'.

Despite these sonic similarities – and it would not be the first time that the Mary Chain have faced such nitpicking from critics and fans alike – 'Girl 71', with its unabashed genre stylings, is an excellent, if relatively straightforward, track, none the worse for its catchy simplicity. With an undertow of bubbling synth alongside chopping keyboard rhythms and more dominant guitars, this love song has an additional distinguishing feature: the subject of the track (the 'Girl 71' herself), Rachel Conti, Jim's long-term partner, provides vocals as the song develops into a duet over the course of its three-minute runtime.

Lyrically straightforward, the theme remains direct throughout, with no extraneous complications to distract from the track's melodic appeal. There is also something sweetly engaging in hearing the following sentiment expressed in a Mary Chain love song: 'Hey, we got something/I got you/We've got something/You got me – we got love'.

Accompanied, upon its late February 2024 release, by an official video directed by Sasha Conti with additional editing work from Ben Unwin, 'Girl 71' is further enhanced by a range of striking imagery. Multiple film panels feature throughout the promo, including an array of colourful visuals interspersed with flashes of Japanese text onscreen, while Jim and Rachel appear in regular close-ups; William is notably absent from this particular video.

'Hey Lou Reid' (6:15)

If any track on the album suggests that the Mary Chain remained unconcerned with expanding their fanbase (a stance worthy of respect), then surely it is this one, with perhaps second place awarded to the equally bold 'Pure Poor'.

The final track on *Glasgow Eyes* – with its altered surname spelling duly noted – is another Mary Chain composition that effectively merges two songs into one. The second half begins a few seconds shy of the two-minute mark, as the track shifts from a 'Sister Ray'/'I Can't Stand It' Velvet Underground pastiche (hence the Reed-referencing title) into a bluesy, near-ambient soundscape. This latter section is characterised by whispered, barely discernible vocals and a plodding beat that gradually slows to a standstill before the song fades out amid a twinkling celestial synth backdrop.

The opening portion of 'Hey Lou Reid' works as a direct VU homage, with a rumbling fuzz bassline and particularly strong rhythm guitar. However, William's muffled vocals render many of the lyrics almost incomprehensible, while a synthesiser backing provides a constant buzzing and whistling accompaniment. The track begins to decrease in tempo around the 1:36 mark, its repeated single-note bass pulse serving as a kind of countdown before the second half commences. This latter section functions almost as a hidden track rather than a seamless continuation of what precedes it, such is the contrast.

Arguably, 'Hey Lou Reid', and particularly its protracted second half, which helps make it the longest track on the album, would not fit anywhere else in the track listing. Nevertheless, it works well as a closer and is a worthwhile addition to the Mary Chain's extensive back catalogue.

Contemporary Tracks

'Pop Seeds' (3:36)

In addition to the dozen songs recorded, mixed and ultimately selected for inclusion on *Glasgow Eyes*, several other tracks were completed during the sessions at Castle of Doom but not finalised. The one exception was 'Pop Seeds', which had been both recorded and mixed and was therefore already at an advanced stage of readiness. It was subsequently released as a standalone single in early September 2024.

The song marks a departure from the darker electronic feel that permeates much of the album, instead aligning more closely with nostalgic Mary Chain pop. Its title evokes an optimistic sense of possibility from the band's earliest days, with lyrics recalling a cherished era of 'punk rock magazines' and 'plastic tambourines'. The single was issued to coincide with the publication of *Never Understood*, which itself offers a fascinating focus on the band's early years; 'Pop Seeds' (with its knowing nod to one of the pre-Mary Chain band names under which some demo tapes were circulated) mirrors the reflection and sentimentality captured in the memoir.

Propelled by sturdy rhythm guitar, live drumming supplied by Jamie Holmes (of East Kilbride band The Lapelles) and set against a whirring, ever-present synth drone, the melodic appeal of 'Pop Seeds' is undeniable, made all the more effective by the brightness of its lyrics. Jim sings about the elements that helped secure the Mary Chain's future, including a 'cool guitar ... drum machines, amphetamines', while the opening reference to 'midget submarines' nods towards cult favourites Swell Maps, whose song of the same name appears on their 1979 debut album, *A Trip To Marineville*.

Compilations, Live And Solo Projects

While the extensive 2011 Edsel/Demon Records deluxe reissue campaign for the first six albums comprehensively gathered together virtually all the significant B-sides, session tracks, rarities, outtakes and selected demo recordings from each era of the band, any overview of The Jesus and Mary Chain would still remain incomplete without some consideration of the compilations and live albums released from the late 1980s onwards.

Following the chart success of *Darklands* (1987) and its accompanying singles, less than a year later, the first band-curated retrospective compilation of B-sides, outtakes and alternative versions effectively gathered together much of the Mary Chain's non-album material in one affordable package, with the notable exception of several early 1985 B-sides that the group themselves considered below par. Issued as a 16-track vinyl album and expanded to 20 tracks across both CD and cassette formats (including a live cover version of Can's 1971 track 'Mushroom' recorded in Nuremberg 1986), *Barbed Wire Kisses* (1988) very nearly failed to appear at all after the Reid brothers insisted to Warners that it should be released at a budget price rather than full retail cost. The eventual compromise saw the compilation issued in April 1988 with a prominent sticker proclaiming: 'Special Low Price – Expect to pay as little as possible', thereby helping ensure that fans were not overcharged for material, much of which had previously been available elsewhere.

A rather generously titled *7 Years On The Leading Edge/10 Smash Hits 1985-1992*, featuring eight singles alongside two non-album tracks ('Gimme Hell' and 'Nine Million Rainy Days'), was issued Stateside for promotional purposes by Def American Recordings in association with Warner Bros. Records shortly after the release of *Honey's Dead* (1992). A compact collection of tracks that had, to that point, largely remained unavailable on compilation (with the notable exception of 'Sidewalking'), this promotional release, issued in a cardboard cover sleeve, served particularly well as a primer for the uninitiated.

First issued in Japan during 1992 as a 17-track release, *The Sound Of Speed* (1993) received a worldwide release a year later with an alternative cover photograph and an expanded 20-track running order across both cassette and CD formats, including all four tracks from the *Sound Of Speed* EP. Also sharing a July 1993 release date, the European vinyl version of this impressively comprehensive post-*Barbed Wire Kisses* (1988) collection omitted four tracks – including the extended version of 'Sidewalking' – due to space limitations and the desire to retain the release as a single LP. The 2013 vinyl reissue followed suit.

A mid-1990s American Recordings compilation entitled *The Jesus and Mary Chain Hate Rock 'N' Roll* (1995) collated 13 tracks in a somewhat scattergun fashion, opening with the title track from the similarly named EP before moving through two principal cuts from the 1993 *Sound Of Speed* EP, several further *Hate Rock 'N' Roll*-era recordings, an *Automatic* (1989) B-side

('Penetration') and finally concluding – four tracks later – with the risible Desdemoana Mix of 'Teenage Lust'. Some genuinely fine songs are included within the running order, but something clearly went awry during the sequencing and selection process of this now largely forgotten release.

At the start of the millennium, the BBC's Strange Fruit label issued *The Complete John Peel Sessions* (2000), a 21-track compilation comprising five individual sessions recorded for the legendary DJ, ranging from the band's debut appearance in October 1984, a full year before *Psychocandy* (1985), through to a late-1989 session when the Mary Chain were already beginning to move towards the sound and style later associated with *Honey's Dead* (1992). Given both the recording environment and the inevitable time limitations imposed upon such sessions, there are occasional weaknesses across the material, but the CD release was nevertheless extremely welcome after years during which many listeners had only been able to revisit the broadcasts via bootleg recordings.

Presented in chronological order and effectively charting the band's trajectory (and eventual commercial decline) from 1984 to 1998, *21 Singles* (2002) is an excellent compilation that neatly demonstrated the calibre of the Mary Chain's work throughout their most prolific years, spanning their journey from Creation to Warners (and back again). The two *Darklands* (1987) singles appear in shorter form than the versions featured on the album itself, while the take on 'Come On' included here extends beyond the length of its counterpart on *Stoned & Dethroned* (1994). In addition, the group elected to use the original version of 'Rollercoaster' from the 1990 EP rather than the later re-recorded attempt that jarred somewhat when it was included on *Honey's Dead* (1992). Beyond the quality and range of the music itself, *21 Singles* (2002) also featured an extensive inlay booklet containing several superb images of the band, including a candid backstage photograph of the Mary Chain and their entourage backstage prior to playing one of their earliest (and arguably most legendary) performances at Night Moves in Sauchiehall Street, Glasgow, on Tuesday 19 June 1984. Tucked away inside the booklet is a very telling reflection on the reality behind the Reid/Reid songwriting credits that populated the majority of the Warners-era Mary Chain albums, with William credited as sole songwriter on 18 of the 21 singles and only one further track listed as a co-write with Jim. Perhaps just as revealingly, the booklet also contains a short personal note attributed to both brothers, which, at the time of release, carried a genuine sense of finality regarding any future reconciliation between the pair, concluding simply: 'We killed the jamc were (sic) glad were (sic) not sad'.

Following the successful reunion of the Mary Chain at Coachella on 27 April 2007, interest in the group grew exponentially and the following year *The Power Of Negative Thinking* (2008) was issued, an expansive four-CD retrospective comprising 81 tracks that traced the band's history from the dawn of the Mary Chain in the form of the impressive 1983 William Reid demo 'Up Too High' (which bears notable similarities to the equally strong Portastudio recording of 'On The Wall' issued as a B-side some years later) through to the final days of their second stint on Creation Records some 15 years later. Released by Rhino Records, this substantial collection gathered together singles, demos, outtakes, cover versions and alternate recordings from across the group's career. Close to two decades on from its release, this lovingly compiled box set now commands high prices on the second-hand collectors' market. Featuring glossy hardback book-style packaging, an 80-page accompanying booklet and even a folded poster containing both a detailed Mary Chain family tree and a gallery of 7" record sleeves, it was an essential purchase for fans of the band and, despite the majority of the material later reappearing across the deluxe-edition album reissues, remains indispensable.

In 2009, The Jesus and Mary Chain's five Warners albums were issued together in cardboard sleeves, and without any bonus-track frills, as part of an *Original Album Series* collection released by Rhino Records in conjunction with Warner Bros. A cheap way to purchase the key albums together in one fell swoop, purists may have taken issue with the absence of *Munki* (1998) and even the somewhat incongruous presence of 'Some Candy Talking' on the *Psychocandy* (1985) disc, but there is little here that truly warrants complaint and one imagines that, post-reunion, many older fans were more than happy to snap up the set at the agreeably low retail price.

A year later, Demon Music Group, in association with Rhino, issued a 44-track double-CD career retrospective entitled *Upside Down – The Best Of The Jesus and Mary Chain* (2010). The Music Club Deluxe imprint under which the collection appeared proved a fitting banner given the breadth and scope of material spread across the two discs, including the alternative soundtrack version of 'The Hardest Walk' in place of the *Psychocandy* (1985) recording. Complemented by a booklet containing well-written sleeve notes alongside appropriately selected sleeve and promotional-video imagery, *Upside Down* (2010) remains a recommended purchase for die-hard followers and more casual fans alike.

The completist focus of the 2011 reissue campaign surrounding the first six Jesus and Mary Chain albums allowed many rarities and demo recordings from across the band's history to be placed in their proper context and even enabled the dreadful 'Jesus Fuck' (2:29) to finally be laid to rest as a tuneless studio experiment from the *Psychocandy* (1985) era, which only ever truly functioned as a frenetic live set closer during the group's earliest days. The fact that it was tucked away as the final track on the second bonus disc of the reissue speaks volumes regarding its respective merits.

Two years later, a limited-edition deluxe boxed set entitled *The Vinyl Collection* (2013) allowed fans to purchase new vinyl pressings of the first six albums alongside *The Complete BBC Radio Sessions* and *BBC Live In Concert* (featuring recordings from 1992 and 1995 respectively), both appearing on vinyl for the first time. The set also included a 30th-anniversary compilation of B-sides and rarities, with the final track listing determined via fan polling. In total, this highly desirable release (limited to 1500 copies worldwide) contained nine individual albums comprising the six studio LPs alongside three exclusive compilations available only within the box itself. The 12 vinyl records were accompanied by a large glossy soft-cover booklet containing lengthy extracts from the deluxe reissue sleeve notes in addition to a poster and four individual postcards.

The Mary Chain's first Record Store Day compilation release arrived in 2015 with a limited-edition blood-red vinyl reissue of *Barbed Wire Kisses* as part of the annual Black Friday event. A decade later, a 13-track UK-only compilation marking a 40th anniversary of sorts and comprising singles and B-sides from 1984 to 1985 (spanning both the Creation and Blanco y Negro eras) was issued as a Record Store Day exclusive under the title of *> 45s > 84 > 85 <*. Limited to 2,000 copies and appearing on fetching red-and-black splatter-effect vinyl, the release was unfortunately marred by a lapse in quality control whereby the alternative version of 'Never Understand', first issued on *The Power Of Negative Thinking* (2008), was included in place of the original February 1985 single recording.

Widely bootlegged almost from the very beginning of their career – and a cursory glance at the unofficial releases section on Discogs confirms the bewildering variety of albums and CDs that appeared from the mid-1980s onwards – the first official live Mary Chain album was the unimaginatively titled *Live In Concert* (2003), released on the Strange Fruit label. Featuring BBC-recorded sets from March 1992 at Sheffield Arena during the band's *Rollercoaster* tour (a seven-song blitz) alongside a 12-song appearance from Bristol's Trinity Centre recorded during mid-April three years later, these professionally captured performances effectively showcased the band's formidable strengths as a live entity during this period and were subsequently included on the corresponding deluxe-edition albums.

The band's sold-out performances marking 40 years (or near enough) of *Psychocandy* (1985) found a rejuvenated Mary Chain reconnecting with their iconic debut album in full and, three shows into the November 2014 tour, a recording was made capturing their appearance across two nights at Glasgow Barrowlands – a homecoming of sorts. Released less than six months later via Demon Records, both the CD and Record Store Day-exclusive LP editions of *Barrowlands Live* (2015) contained the principal 14-song set. However, the purchase of the deluxe edition allowed fans to enjoy both the main course and a fine starter in the form of a powerful seven-song prelude performance that concluded with a blistering rendition of 'Upside Down'. Unavailable in any other format for the next seven years, a CD reissue through Fuzz Club during 2022 ensured that those who had been unable to secure the original deluxe version – comprising a 10" single, LP, CD and beautifully photographed 40-page hardback book – did not miss out on either performance.

In stark contrast to their years on Warners, The Jesus and Mary Chain have enjoyed their ongoing relationship with Fuzz Club, the London-based independent label that issued the highly recommended live album *Sunset 666* (2023) a year prior to the group's eagerly anticipated return with *Glasgow Eyes* (2024). Recorded at the Hollywood Palladium in Los Angeles during a July 2018 support tour with long-term admirers Nine Inch Nails, the release captures performances drawn from two nights of a six-show residency at the venue, with Bernadette Reid née Denning and Isobel Campbell contributing backing and duet vocals early in the set. Both an essential purchase and an excellent document of the band at the peak of their later-period powers, *Sunset 666* remains, to date, their most relevant official live recording.

Sister Vanilla's sole album, *Little Pop Rock* (2007), was produced by her brothers alongside Ben Lurie and, in its definitive Chemikal Underground version (having appeared two years earlier on the Japanese label P-Vine with one fewer track), features 12 songs. Perhaps lazily described in some quarters as a Jesus and Mary Chain record with their sister on vocals, the reality is that only 'JAMCOLAS' emerged as a full Reid/Reid/Reid collaboration in songwriting terms. Elsewhere on *Little Pop Rock* (2007), four songs are credited jointly to William and Linda, one to Ben Lurie, while William and Jim each contribute three compositions, including the album closer 'The Two Of Us', which had previously appeared across two Freeheat EP releases. It is also notable that both William and Jim share lead vocal duties on 'JAMCOLAS' alongside Linda, while William performs 'Delicat' solo, a track absent from the earlier Japanese issue of the album. Definitely worthy of investigation and, sadly, to date the only full-length Sister Vanilla release, *Little Pop Rock* (2007) would already have fulfilled a crucial purpose had it merely served to recalibrate the relationship between the Reid brothers, but the fact that it also emerged as a genuinely strong record makes it all the more rewarding.

Formed in the immediate aftermath of the 1998 Mary Chain split, Freeheat consisted of Jim and Ben sharing guitar and vocal duties alongside Nick Sanderson and Romi Mori on drums and bass, respectively. The group recorded several tracks amid sporadic touring during the first years of the new millennium, and the debut release from Jim and Ben's new venture arrived in 2000 with the four-track EP *Don't Worry Be Happy*, issued on the Californian label Hall Of Records. A further EP followed two years later on UK indie label Outafocus Recordings, the 'Retox' set retaining the four-song running order of the group's earlier release while adding another track, 'The Long Goodbye', reminiscent of *Stoned & Dethroned* (1994) at its best, while closing number 'Nobody's Gonna Trip My Wire' featured Nick Sanderson on lead vocals, bringing to mind his time as frontman of the maverick Earl Brutus. Sadly, music press reaction to the band remained largely muted, and by 2003, time had been called on Freeheat by its own members. Despite this, a mid-2006 album of sorts entitled *Back On The Water* was issued by Planting Seeds Records, comprising studio recordings from The Drugstore at the tail end of the 1990s alongside ten live tracks taken from a Dutch radio-broadcast performance at Amsterdam's Paradiso. Despite the merits of the material – and anyone fortunate enough to witness Freeheat live during their brief lifespan will attest to their abilities as a powerful and tune-heavy outfit, with Mori providing outstanding backing vocals – there nevertheless remained an undeniable X-factor missing from proceedings, and that, inevitably, was William Reid.

The principal songwriter within The Jesus and Mary Chain and fully deserving of his reputation as a maverick genius, William Reid's solo output commenced at the tail end of the 1990s with the 1998 EP *Tired Of Fucking*, released through Creation and comprising four tracks recorded alone at The Drugstore during the previous autumn. Further recordings followed in the wake of the messy Mary Chain split, with the sessions seemingly conducted in a state of disarray, given the nature of the material itself, and it is difficult not to view their fractured sound as at least partially reflective of William's own state of mind as a new decade and an entirely new chapter in his life approached. The six-song sampler entitled 'Taster' appeared, on its release in 1999, to suggest that William would be working under a succession of aliases, namely CNYK, Ravenscraeg, William and Lazycame. However, it was the final moniker that he ultimately settled upon for his two solo albums, *Finbegin* (1999) and *Saturday The Fourteenth* (2000), in addition to the extended EP *Yawn!*, a release distinguished by the inclusion of 13 hidden bonus tracks amounting to a staggering near 40-minute runtime on their own.

Musically, perhaps the kindest description of the Lazycame output would be as a further progression into the sonic experimentation that William had already embraced on *Munki* (1998), albeit with a more acoustic-based approach and with songs frequently stripped of bass and drum backing, reducing many recordings to little more than bare skeletal forms with clear echoes of both Syd Barrett and Skip Spence's solo work. Regardless of their sonic bravery, the results proved even more divisive amongst Mary Chain followers than the material that had previously split opinion on the final Creation album, with cynical listeners even questioning whether William was deliberately attempting to sabotage his own legacy through such unhinged and deeply challenging work. A telling excerpt from the disorientating jumble of imagery and phrases that constituted the accompanying CD booklet for the US Hall Of Records release of *Finbegin* reads: 'r u a career masochist', while the back cover of the UK edition of the same album details that the songs contained within were 'recorded out of love and in pain', and it could be argued that somewhere between those two statements lies the rationale behind the Lazycame recordings.

The cathartic nature of the music cannot be denied but, for every disjointed, improvised and seemingly out-of-sequence track where it appeared that William had little interest in adhering even to the basics of established song structure – something that must have been a challenge for Dick Meaney to contend with while recording him at The Drugstore – there nevertheless remained beautiful moments hidden away, not least on tracks such as the lovely 'blue june' and 'mcintoshlost', which closed *Finbegin* on a strikingly personal note. Reportedly, William was so unhappy with *Saturday The Fourteenth* (2000) after listening back to it with the clarity of sobriety that he very nearly chose not to release it at all. Ultimately, however, it is to his credit that the second solo album did indeed see the light of day, even if it met with a similarly puzzled response from listeners who continued to view the recordings as further evidence of ongoing aberration. Yet William stayed the course and emerged from the other side of the Lazycame years artistically and emotionally enriched.

It would then take another five years as a US resident and new father before he resumed his rightful place in The Jesus and Mary Chain alongside his brother Jim, and this most distinctive and singular of groups returned older, wiser and with their fractured chemistry somehow not merely intact, but enduring.

Bibliography

Cavanagh, D., *My Magpie Eyes Are Hungry For The Prize* (Virgin Books, 2000)
Cooper, M., *Later... With Jools Holland: 30 Years of Music, Magic and Mayhem* (William Collins, 2022)
Gillespie, B., *Tenement Kid* (White Rabbit, 2021)
Houghton, M., *Fried and Justified* (Faber & Faber, 2019)
Howe, Z., *Barbed Wire Kisses – The Jesus and Mary Chain Story* (Polygon, 2014)
Kapanen, M., *Psychotic Chain Reaction* (POP Magazine, 2005)
McGee, A., *Creation Stories* (Sidgwick & Jackson, 2013)
Reid, W. and Reid, J., *Never Understood – The Jesus and Mary Chain* (White Rabbit, 2024)
Taylor, N., *C86 & All That: The Creation Of Indie In Difficult Times* (Inkmonkey Editions, 2020)